The Year's Best Sports Writing 2022

Edited and with an
introduction by
J.A. Adande

TRIUMPH
BOOKS

No part of this publication may be reproduced, stored in a retrieval system, or transmitted in any form by any means, electronic, mechanical, photocopying, or otherwise, without the prior written permission of the publisher, Triumph Books LLC, 814 North Franklin Street, Chicago, Illinois 60610.

Library of Congress Cataloging-in-Publication Data available upon request

This book is available in quantity at special discounts for your group or organization. For further information, contact:

Triumph Books LLC
814 North Franklin Street
Chicago, Illinois 60610
(312) 337-0747
www.triumphbooks.com

Printed in U.S.A.

ISBN: 978-1-63727-090-5

Design by Sue Knopf
Page Production by Patricia Frey

Contents

Introduction

You're about to discover why this collection of stories you're holding that celebrates the art of sports writing is so different from "The Art of Sportswriting."

"The Art of Sportswriting" (one word, more on that distinction later) was the cover story in the May/June 1987 edition of the *Columbia Journalism Review*, which sat on my nightstand throughout my last year of high school. I read and re-read the article countless times while I was a student, seeking inspiration for the career I already knew I wanted to pursue. In September of 2021, during one of my periodic purging and condensing of the old newspapers, magazines, and game programs in my garage, I came across the "The Art of Sportswriting" issue again. When I read it once more, three and a half decades later, I realized the article had led me astray all along.

"The best part of sportswriting is still a reporter at the game telling us what happened," was its key line, the one that was put in boldface in a pull quote, the one that proved so, so wrong. For one thing, it violated the three-word maxim pounded into journalism students' brains by professors everywhere: Show, don't tell. And journalists should not tell what happened, they should *explain* what happened. Explain why it matters and why we should care.

That's what Marcus Thompson II did after Stephen Curry launched into suborbital flight in April of 2021. Curry averaged 37 points for the month, with four games with at least 10 three-pointers and five games with at least 40 points, but Thompson didn't fall into the trap of engaging in a Most Valuable

Player debate. He recognized that this was something far beyond that, the type of play that might not be officially commemorated but will be historically referenced, cited by those in the know.

Thompson's story was the first that popped into my head after I was asked to edit the 2022 edition of *The Year's Best Sports Writing*. His story, entitled "Stephen Curry Is Not the MVP— He's Something Much More," is sports writing in its classical form. The rest of the selections that fill out the book represent what sports writing has become: a peek into the psyche of high achievers, a celebration of accomplishments and an examination of failures, a study of how people interact, and a discussion of societal progress and lingering inequities. In other words, all of the things "The Art of Sportswriting" story feared would happen to the profession. Yes, feared. It called the proliferation of feature stories a "danger." And the next-to-last paragraph contained this admonition: "Sportswriters seem to forget that the game is more important than the people who play it."

When I read that as a teenager I didn't dare challenge it. Now, after 15 years of working at major newspapers and a decade at ESPN, I feel confident enough to reset the order: People, then the games.

If you've read any of the previous incarnations of series editor Glenn Stout's annual best sports writing collections, you've seen very few game recaps. And that's not the only rebuke of the main premise of "The Art of Sportswriting." You'll notice the books spell sports writing with two words, not one.

"That was the first decision made when the series was created," Stout explained in an email. "Sports writing … writing about sports—is a less narrow definition than 'sportswriting' per se, which most readers think of as what you find on the sports page. It allowed the book to consider and include a wider variety of writing."

Amazing how much liberty can be gained simply by inserting a space into a word. Ironically, the main way I employed the freedom and wide range of options that were given to me when

I was presented the opportunity to edit this year's book...was to find ways to shrink the eligibility parameters. That was the only way to cut the vast array of quality articles to a manageable number.

I received hundreds of submissions from writers and their colleagues after I announced my guest editing role on Twitter. I also sought suggestions from Stout and a panel that consisted of: Paola Boivin, director of the Cronkite News Phoenix Sports Bureau at Arizona State University; Richard Deitsch, media reporter at The Athletic; Greg Lee, senior assistant managing editor at the *Boston Globe*; and Iliana Limón Romero, deputy sports editor of the *Los Angeles Times*. I'm grateful to them for bringing attention to stories I might otherwise have missed and for making clear which stories I had to include, by consensus.

Each of their lists looked vastly different. That was the point of including them in the process. It also reinforced the difficulty and subjectivity of this assignment. It meant I had to arrive at my own definition of the best part of sports writing.

My first step was to separate sports writing from sports journalism. As impressive and important as, say the reporting by The Athletic on sexual misconduct in the NWSL or by *The Washington Post* on the toxic workplace environment for the local NFL team, it wasn't the writing that made them stand out. They were significant because they uncovered secrets and brought some leveling to the power imbalance. They weren't examples of great sports journalism, they were examples of great journalism. Period. But they weren't what I was looking for.

I was looking for stories that felt important specifically because of their writing, writing that grabbed your attention right away and never relinquished it, writing that took you on a journey.

I decided this collection would consist of stories that were focused on sports in a way specifically related to 2021, not merely stories that had a connection to sports that were written in 2021. That meant stories about current athletes, not former athletes.

Stories about the central figures, not people on the periphery, such as fans or media members. (If that makes you question the inclusion of Bill Plaschke's column on Felipe Ruiz, Tommy Lasorda's trusted assistant in the last years of Lasorda's life, the Los Angeles native in me has a counter-argument: You won't find a greater feat of endurance in the entire book than the day Ruiz drove Lasorda from his home in Fullerton to his office at Dodger Stadium to a lunch appearance in Manhattan Beach to dinner in Ontario and finally back to Fullerton at 2:30 a.m.).

And why did a story about the ex-wife of an assistant football coach fit my definition? Because the mounting evidence that Urban Meyer was unfit to be the head coach of the Jacksonville Jaguars became one of the biggest sports stories of 2021, and Exhibit A should have been Courtney Smith's claims that Meyer failed to properly act on her allegations that her husband, an assistant on Meyer's staff at Ohio State, had abused her. Just because the images of Meyer with a woman at a restaurant that spread on social media seemed to have a bigger impact on Meyer's downfall doesn't mean we should not recognize the importance of "Courtney's Story" by Diana Moscovitz—and the way Moscovitz's word usage made the story so memorable.

Some of these stories made it because they struck a personal chord. I doubt Bruce Jenkins' tale of a 51-year-old big-wave surfer would have resonated with me as much had I not turned 51 myself in 2021. And Tove K. Danovich's "The Resurgent Appeal of Guinness World Records" took me back to a 1977 cross-country drive with my parents, when a paperback copy of *The Guinness Book of World Records* was my sole means of entertainment. Also, Danovich's story featured my favorite sports figure of 2021: Zaila Avant-garde, the delightful teenager who won the 2021 Scripps National Spelling Bee, set a record for bounce-juggling four basketballs 255 times in a minute, and scored bucket after bucket in YouTube footage of her high school basketball games.

There's one more flaw in the "The Art of Sportswriting" that needed updating and correcting: every sports writer mentioned in that article, both canonical and contemporary, was a white man. Every. Single. One. It's as if pioneering Black writers such as Sam Lacy, Wendell Smith, Larry Whiteside, and Ralph Wiley, or barrier-breaking women such as Melissa Ludtke, Lesley Visser, Helene Elliott, Christine Brennan, and Claire Smith, did not exist.

I sought diversity in race, gender, sexual identity, and faith among the writers and their subjects for the 2022 edition of *The Year's Best Sports Writing*. That's one reason for the higher-than-usual number of stories this year; sometimes inclusion requires expansion.

The only two subjects that felt mandatory were Simone Biles and Naomi Osaka, two athletes who in recent years have epitomized competitive greatness, the way we discuss mental health, and the way we analyze sports in the hyper-intense social media era. I chose two examples that told their stories in very different ways. Camonghne Felix got Biles to open up in what amounted to a debriefing of her drama-filled 2021, from the stress-induced pullout from the Olympics gymnastics competition in Tokyo to her Capitol Hill testimony about the ways the sports and law enforcement institutions failed to properly respond to the sexual abuse of Larry Nassar. Meanwhile, Kevin Van Valkenburg took the opposite approach to Osaka: he interpreted her actions, not her words.

When Osaka announced her desire to avoid post-match news conferences because they exacerbated her depression, it triggered an existential crisis among sports journalists who were already reeling from the access restrictions instituted in the COVID-19 pandemic. *What will we do if we can't talk to them?* Van Valkenburg's story suggests the answer is to pay more attention when we watch them. He searched for the meaning and significance in everything from the way she shifts her weight to the way she blows on her fingers.

It just hit me that, perhaps subconsciously, I wanted this book to showcase not only what was written but how it was written. I want it to celebrate and educate. Guess it's only fitting—right?—given my current role as the director of sports journalism at Northwestern's Medill School of Journalism, Media, and Integrated Marketing Communication. This book should provide teaching material.

It's a snapshot of sports writing in the past year, but it's also a continuum of the great sports writing that has existed for decades.

In "Miracle at Coogan's Bluff," famed sports writer Red Smith's account of The Shot Heard Round the World that decided the 1951 National League pennant, Smith never explicitly describes the most historical events of the day. Smith wrote about a drunken fan running onto the field amid the jubilation after the game. Smith wrote the dialog he imagined took place when Bobby Thomson and teammate Whitey Lockman found themselves both standing on second base earlier in the game. He noted that the losing pitcher, Ralph Branca, wore No. 13.

But nowhere in the story does Smith say that Bobby Thomson hit a home run to left field in the bottom of the ninth inning and the Giants beat the Dodgers, 5–4. In one of the most famous stories by one of the genre's most revered figures, the reporter at the game did not tell us what happened—specifically, the one thing that supposedly mattered the most.

Sports writing is not the first rough draft of history. It's something much more.

J.A. Adande
Chicago
Fall 2022

The Year's Best Sports Writing 2022

The Kentucky Derby of My Childhood Was a Fantasy. Now It Feels Raw, and Real

JERRY BREWER

FROM *The Washington Post* • MAY 1, 2021

Nostalgia puts me back at my grandparents' house in Louisville. It is about 1990, the first Saturday in May, and we are visiting for another Kentucky Derby party. I am 12 and wonder-struck, as usual.

It smells like barbecue and sounds like church folk letting loose, playful and loud and skirting the line of inappropriate speech. It looks polychromatic and fancy, so fancy for a house soiree, an assortment of bright clothing that seems exotic but comfortable, stylish but not too formal. It feels right, unless I'm remembering it wrong.

The Derby, still my darling sporting event, doesn't conjure the same emotions right now. Both of my grandparents died in November. Because of the pandemic, I haven't been back to Louisville since February 2020, and I have no concrete plans to visit soon. Because my parents moved, I haven't seen my hometown of Paducah, which is about 220 miles southwest of Louisville, in almost a decade. And in the aftermath of the Breonna Taylor killing, home is full of disappointment, conflict and shame.

Yet on Saturday, my mind will go where my displaced body cannot: to Churchill Downs for the 147th Run for the Roses. I might get misty-eyed when the bugler plays "My Old Kentucky Home," and I might whisper a few of the lyrics, even though Stephen Foster's song is more honest if interpreted as a wrenching tale of enslavement and not a wistful state song.

In grief and anger, some of my oldest memories have been altered. It's a crazy mental phenomenon, the fluidity of remembering, how feelings attach themselves to facts and perceptions of experiences differ, not just from person to person but within us at various stages of life. The Derby is still a love, but it's not an active romance. Kentucky is still home, still worthy of pride and vehement defense when warranted. But it is not the place for me as an adult, not now and probably not ever again.

For the first time, the annual event is about far more than romanticizing my childhood. The Derby is not the fantasy I once imagined. In a single year—the longest year—it has evolved into a magnet for tension, something that my grief and anger can manipulate with unexpected ease. And then there's this peculiar addendum: Somehow, those competing, unresolved emotions feel like a pathway to a richer and more worthwhile experience.

In *Light in August*, William Faulkner wrote: "Memory believes before knowing remembers." The words make sense now. They are personal now. As Kentuckians, we are grandfathered into loving the Derby. We may not even like horse racing, and the event is so grand that it can feel suffocating, but we enjoy being showcased, dressed up, important. We like hosting and leaning into a kindness that belies some of the state's toxic history. The Derby is not ours, but it is ours. We treat it like family and connect the warmest memories to it.

However, upon sincere reassessment, it's messy, complicated and tinged with racism. It unifies, and it agitates. To see that clearly, it took the pandemic shifting last year's race to September and hordes of people protesting the commonwealth's cavalier pursuit of police accountability and justice after Taylor's death.

In this light, there are new memories to balance the past canonization, and there is history to know—or remember—coldly. It doesn't make everything seem so beautiful, but memories don't have to be one-dimensional. In fact, once you process the meaning of it all, they are better in full.

My grandparents didn't host a Derby party every year, but it was a big deal because they made the celebration accessible to their friends, predominantly Black, who otherwise wouldn't have absorbed the truest spirit of what the Derby has become. There's really no obvious reason for Black folk to care about the Derby or horse racing in general. It's a sport that, in 1904, banned Black jockeys from several prominent racetracks in the United States, including Churchill Downs. Attend the Derby, look past how vast and opulent it can be, and in a typical year you're inclined to start counting the people of color in an audience of more than 150,000. The sport snuffed out any chance at diversity long ago.

Clearly, the Derby is not for everybody. But what it most inspires—a sense of mattering, for a city and a state—should not be an exclusive feeling. My grandparents understood that. Their Derby party emphasized that we could enjoy this, too—our way. They weren't interested in going to Churchill Downs, spending all that money for parking and walking a long distance just to stand around and bet for a long time. There were too many people, and most of them would have made them feel uncomfortable. So they held a function focused on making people comfortable.

My brother and I didn't learn to bet horses during those parties. We were taught to work a room, however. Our parents were incredibly private, but when we went to Louisville, we saw the value of bringing people together. Both sportswriters now, we received our first doses of the power of the crazy games we cover: The event around the sport means the most, and there are so many angles from which to view it.

Louisville loves itself and its eccentricities so much. Every spring, it takes pride in being descended upon, even though it means the Derby loses intimacy. The largest city in Kentucky doesn't get to sparkle often. People embrace the chance to glow and place a giant, beautiful hat atop a messy reality. It's a very Southern, very Kentucky way to act.

There is nothing wrong with raw and real, though. To truly love anything, you can't only love it when it's right. You must love it when it's wrong, too.

The scars of Kentucky and the Derby—now, in the past and the inevitable wounds to come—take the youth out of me and force a reconsideration of everything nostalgia disguises as innocence. What's left, however dirty, is authentic emotional freedom.

The Kentucky Derby isn't ours. We make it ours. The heartbreaking baggage of city and state isn't a stationary burden to ignore or denounce. It can be moved if people are willing to do the hard work. It can be shifted, like memories. If time revises the good ones in complex ways, it also has the ability to make better use of the bad ones.

On this Derby day, my first without two beloved bedrocks of family, still in a period of American crisis, the sadness speaks for itself. I control the rest. I will remember, again.

Jerry Brewer is a sports columnist at *The Washington Post*. A graduate of Western Kentucky University, during his career he also has worked at *The Courier-Journal* in Louisville, Kentucky, the *Orlando Sentinel*, and the *Philadelphia Inquirer*. He lives with his wife and two sons in Arlington.

Stephen Curry Is Not the MVP— He's Something Much More

MARCUS THOMPSON II

FROM The Athletic • APRIL 20, 2021

Stephen Curry should not be MVP.

His numbers are ridiculous, for sure—a league-leading 31.4 points per game at age 33. And he has now outdueled two MVP favorites in the last eight days—hitting Joel Embiid's 76ers for 49 points in Monday's 107–96 win in Philadelphia, and Nikola Jokic's Nuggets for 53 on April 12. And the Warriors are 28–22 when Curry plays, a win percentage good enough to be in the mix for the No. 5 seed. And you could make a strong case no one is playing better, especially with what he has around him and the defenses he's seeing.

Still, this isn't an MVP season. What Curry is doing is bigger than that. A trophy can't begin to encapsulate what we're witnessing.

The Warriors are four games back of Portland for the No. 6 seed with 14 games remaining. If Andrew Wiggins didn't foul Bradley Beal for a game-winning four-point play in the final seconds against Washington on April 9, and if Kent Bazemore makes his free throws against Boston (or Draymond Green makes that layup) on Saturday, the Warriors could be riding an eight-game win streak and breathing on Portland's neck for the

No. 6 seed. If somehow Curry leads the Warriors from a 53-point stick-a-fork-in-them loss to Toronto on April 2 all the way to the sixth seed, voters may be swayed.

But this isn't about a third such award for Curry. That wouldn't do him justice. How he is performing, at this age, doesn't belong in the realm of the quantifiable. He's pulling off feats not seen since Wilt Chamberlain, since Kareem Abdul-Jabbar, since Michael Jordan, since Kobe Bryant.

"I don't know what else to say," head coach Steve Kerr said. "It's the same thing after every game. It's just utter amazement at this guy's skill level, heart, mind, focus. It's just amazing to watch."

There are MVP levels, and then there are basketball history levels. Curry's essentially one-upping himself, pushing his transcendence to a new pinnacle, and coronating himself as a basketball revolutionary.

MVPs are rational, explainable. What Curry's doing is not.

MVPs are fodder for comparisons. Rankings are centered on production and data. Curry's play this season, especially right now, transcends discourse and banter.

Making this about where he ranks and his legacy misses the point. Making this about awards is too typical of how we've come to regard greatness.

Curry is provoking a different kind of awe, the kind that reminds you why sports are dope and why basketball is among the coolest. He scored 20 points in five minutes, 37.8 seconds on Monday. He was serenaded with MVP chants on the road, in a city known for throwing snowballs at Santa and booing young Kobe. He hit 10 3-pointers for the fourth time in five games, a few of them over his own brother.

What we should be thinking is *what a time to be alive*.

"I don't know if I've ever seen anything like the run that he's been on," said Philadelphia coach Doc Rivers, who's been on the receiving end of Curry's greatness for years. "There are guys I guess that have scored the points in the stretch that he has. But I guarantee you there is no one that has scored them the way he has. It's been an art watching him play as of late. It's just been a beautiful thing to watch."

Art is to be appreciated.

This season, this version of Curry, belongs in mythical tales. In the memories of those who watched it, who felt it. This is one of those you-had to-be-there-to-understand seasons. Like Michael Jordan in 1996–1997. Like Kobe Bryant in 2005–06. Like LeBron James in 2007–08, or last year.

Years from now, basketball fans should be able to look up this year and see Jokic or somebody as MVP, see the Warriors' record as mediocre, and have the context of what happened completely lost in the data. But those who are here for this will remember the spectacle being experienced, a level of brilliance that makes adjectives shy. The greatness of this Curry season should be the privilege of those present.

And we reserve the right to embellish this as we re-tell it to a new generation of basketball fans.

"The things he can do on the court is special," Wiggins said. "He's one of a kind. When I was on a different team, you could see it from afar, you see what he's doing, you see all the creative things he's doing. But being on his team, it's totally different. Totally different. Watching it in person, every day, every game. Just the dominance of his presence on and off the ball. It's crazy."

You can know Curry made 72 3-pointers in 10 games, but that's not the same as watching it happen, of expecting his bombs to go in yet still getting a jolt when they do.

You can be told he is the greatest shooter of all time. But that's not the same as seeing how a 6-foot-3 guard warped the game, demoralized defenses and sparked social media frenzies when he got in a groove.

"I've seen Kobe Bryant, early in his career had a stretch where he went nuts," Kerr said. "And, obviously, Michael Jordan had some stretches where he just scored like crazy. But, obviously, nobody's ever shot the ball like this in the history of the game.

And even by Steph's own lofty standards, this is so above and beyond."

Stephen Curry's Incredible April

Date	Opponent	Points	FGM-FGA	3PM-3PA
April 1	at Heat	36	9-19	5-11
April 4	at Hawks	37	12-23	3-12
April 6	vs. Bucks	41	14-21	5-10
April 9	vs. Wizards	32	11-25	5-12
April 10	vs. Rockets	38	13-21	8-15
April 12	vs. Nuggets	53	14-24	10-18
April 14	at Thunder	42	14-20	11-16
April 15	at Cavaliers	33	12-25	4-13
April 17	at Celtics	47	15-27	11-19
April 19	at 76ers	49	14-28	10-17
Per game	10 games	40.8	12.8-23.3 (54.9%)	72-143 (50.3%)

Some Warriors fans have been testy most of the season, extra critical of Kerr and Bob Myers' front office. What is happening right now is part of the reason why.

This is what they wanted to see, one of the greatest attractions in sports history. One of the all-time players who makes it clear every game, every shot, you're watching something that won't come around again. It's beyond fantastical to expect Curry to play like this for an entire season. But the Warriors' development process, Kerr's system of ball movement, the roster around Curry, felt at times like someone with a big head blocking your view of the comet.

Sports doesn't offer much better than Curry going off. He's been doing just that in April—40.8 points, 54.9 percent shooting, including 50.3 percent from three, 6.2 rebounds, 4.4 assists—and for most of the season.

It was 18 months between the 2019 NBA Finals and the start of this season. He played just five games between, enough of an absence to forget how incredible he was. Enough time elapsed to conclude he'd never be that good again. Kevin Durant was gone. So were Andre Iguodala and Shaun Livingston. Klay Thompson has now been injured for two seasons. It was easy to presume Curry's magic was over. Many did.

That's why all you can do really is shake your head at what Curry is doing. It mocks reason.

Curry is still dazzling. He's in his physical prime with a dynastic basketball IQ and nothing to lose but haters. The NBA is still in possession of an all-time treasure, one many presumed was gone. He is again provoking his particular brand of euphoria with his particularly unreal skills, his dominance another reminder to cherish the greats while you've got them.

That doesn't make him MVP. It makes him something more.

Marcus Thompson II is a lead columnist at The Athletic and a leading voice in Bay Area sports after more than two decades of covering sports in the region. He was named the 2021 California Sports Writer of the Year by the National Sports Media Association. Thompson is the author of three books: the best-seller *Golden: The Miraculous Rise of Steph Curry*; *KD: Kevin Durant's Relentless Pursuit to Be the Greatest*; and *Dynasties: The 10 G.O.A.T. Teams That Changed the NBA Forever*. The Clark Atlanta University graduate is a native of Oakland, California.

Badwater Ultramarathon: What I Lost and Found During 135 Miles of the World's Most Impossible Run

KELAINE CONOCHAN

FROM ESPN • NOVEMBER 26, 2021

"No wimpy women in *this* house."

A catchphrase, a vibe, a lifestyle that my mom bestowed upon my sister and me while growing up. She'd say it, flexing her biceps after accomplishing some feat of strength that ordinary moms wouldn't dare, like dragging thousands of pounds of wet carpet up the basement steps and onto the front lawn to dry after an unfortunate storm. My mom was not waiting around for anyone's assistance. In fact, she probably found your offer patronizing. She'll do it herself.

Her two daughters? We absorbed and became that motto and bravado. Toughness, you see, is a family value.

You want an origin story? Because this is where it all begins.

Fast-forward to July 19, 2021. I'm 38 years old, feeling plucky and primed, and in the best shape of my life. It's 113 degrees outside as I wait for the 8 p.m. start of the notorious Badwater 135. Known as the toughest footrace in the world, Badwater is a

135-mile ultramarathon across Death Valley, California—home
of the hottest temperature ever recorded on Earth.

To successfully complete this race, I'll have to endure both
face-melting heat and merciless climbing. The race starts at
Badwater Basin, the lowest point in North America (282 feet
below sea level) and ends at the portal of Mount Whitney (8,374
feet above sea level), the tallest mountain in the Lower 48. All in,
Badwater includes three sections of mountain climbs, accounting
for nearly 20,000 feet of elevation gain and loss.

Yeah, it's intense. But that's kind of the point. And that's kind
of my whole thing. As an athlete, a tomboy, a chippy kid from
Jersey, I guess you could say I've been groomed since birth to
value toughness as currency. And I want to know how much is
in my account.

STARTING AT NIGHT is the first true mindf--- of the Badwater
experience. But before we even hear the word "Go!" we're about
to get clobbered with the next one: a low-lying, hazy brown cloud
making its way toward the start line. I've never seen anything
like it.

A haboob, you say? What even *is* a haboob?

A violent, oppressive dust storm? Heading right for us?

Cool. Cool-cool-cool. Supercool. Perfect, even. Running
headfirst into a natural disaster, just like we drew it up!

I had trained for the heat and the hills, but how can you
train for weather you've never even heard of?! Too bad, sucker,
because you're in it now.

With fresh legs, no mountains to climb, and all that pent-up
excitement, the start is supposed to be one of the easiest sections
of the race, the part where you remind yourself to slow down—
take it easy!—because this is an ultramarathon, not a marathon,
and definitely not a sprint. But this haboob and its headwinds
throw my pacing chart out the window from my very first step.
It feels like being pulled backward by a set of invisible resistance
bands, and these "easy, slow miles" are slow but not so easy. My

work rate is higher than I want it to be, but what else am I going to do? Stand still?

I just have to power through it one step at a time and hope the fatigue doesn't catch up with me too soon.

THE FIRST WAVE OF GROGGINESS falls over me at about 12:30 a.m. I haven't been running for even five hours yet, so I know I have to fight it. To nap now would mean less time running while the sun, and all its fury, is still tucked away. To nap now, with 115 miles—plus three mountain sections and two sunrises—still to go, would be soft.

And I didn't train for two years to be soft.

"Find it," I tell myself. It's dark, but I'm not talking about finding the next checkpoint, the road ahead of me, or even the hand connected to my arm. It's an accidental mantra that I've wandered into during this race. Find the energy to stay awake. Find the pace that feels right. Find whatever it is inside you that will keep you upright and moving.

I don't even know why I suddenly feel so tired. I was doing great at the Furnace Creek checkpoint, and that was less than 2 miles ago. Maybe that haboob really worked me. Maybe it's that I've been awake for 17 hours already. Maybe I just need to suck it up.

I look behind me, hoping another runner might catch up to keep me company, but it's just me and the white line on the side of the road. All I see are the faint, shadowy outlines of mountains in the distance. The same mountains that trap the hot air down here and make it feel like you're standing under a hair dryer.

I guess deserts are, by definition, deserted, but I'm stricken by just how eerily quiet it is right now. The only things I can hear are the whistling wind and the shuffling of my own footsteps. I sneaky love this feeling. It feels illicit, like I'm breaking curfew. My very mediocre headlamp projects a small cone of light in front of me, just enough to prevent me from turning an ankle

or meandering off-road. Anything beyond this glowing orb is a
mystery I won't solve until I run through it.

PEOPLE ALWAYS ASK ME why I run ultramarathons, and why
Badwater in particular. Why would I choose something so gru-
eling and difficult? Why do I want to suffer this much? Why am
I not satisfied with 30 minutes of moderate exercise four to five
days a week? A marathon? A 50-miler? A 100K? A 100-miler?
Where does the madness end?

I never know how to answer those questions. They seem
more rhetorical than curious, as if the person grilling me has
run out of ways to express their incredulity, awe or disapproval.

Part of it is that I learned pretty early on that to be special, I'd
have to really work at it. I wasn't blessed with height or cover-girl
beauty, those physical gifts that require only routine maintenance.
And after I hit puberty—or more accurately, after puberty hit
me—my body was no longer the fastest or the strongest. But I
knew one thing: I could out-effort everybody.

Effort might not get you everywhere—let's admit that
Division I scholarships require some mix of nature, nurture and
divine intervention—but it'll get you pretty damn far. Hopefully
effort will get me somewhere in the neighborhood of 135 miles.

I press on.

I CLICK OFF MY HEADLAMP to see just how dark it is out here.
I look up to the night sky, so full of stars, it looks like someone
shook glitter onto black construction paper. I remind myself to
drink it all in because this is why I signed up for this race. To
experience every feeling, every view, every moment, even the low
points. Especially the low points.

Luckily, I'm not in this fight alone. Like every runner at
Badwater, I've got a support crew to help me across this forsaken,
wind-ravaged desert. Up ahead, I see the emergency flasher lights
of our van, a roving pit stop that leapfrogs me every 2 miles along

this journey. And in that van are four fairy godrunners whose job is to make sure I don't die, disintegrate or drop from the race.

My crew. My people. My lifeline.

You can't just grab four runners off the street and expect things to go smoothly for 135 miles. Even if you trust them with your darkest secrets, you can't pick your four best friends because one of those dodos will inevitably wind up excommunicated. You've got to find the right mix of people who can handle long miles, sleep deprivation and extreme heat. You need people who will challenge you and hold you accountable, but who also understand that everybody has limits and that they'll be tested out here. You need people who can both follow the plan and thrive in chaos.

Enter Ricky Haro, my crew chief and the brains of this operation. Ricky was my first pick, no hesitation. He and I already have Badwater history, working together to crew our friend Mosi Smith in 2018, when he dropped at Mile 95, and again in 2019, when Mosi made it up that damn mountain for his personal best time.

As crew chief, Ricky is the big wheel who keeps the rest of us turning. He is my coach, my meteorologist, my digestive whisperer, my therapist, my emotional support animal. Ricky is my everything at this race. Without him, I'm toast.

Ricky is also the sneakiest badass you'll ever meet. He keeps a cool head and a low profile, but among some other life-time-achievement-level accomplishments, this dude has done two crossings of Death Valley, including once self-supported. "What does 'self-supported' mean here?" you ask. A fantastic question, gumshoe. It means Ricky pushed all his own supplies across Death Valley—in a glorified shopping cart with brakes—to the summit of Mount Whitney in the dog days of August. No crew, no van for naps or lugging around ice. Just pushing his own water, food and extra sneakers up and down mountains by his damn self for three days. Dude is a *beast*. Your crew chief would never.

In that second slot, I went with my long-lost little brother, Jimmie Wilbourn. Jimmie and I have been cosmically united since we met in 2013 at Hood to Coast, a 200-mile team relay race in Oregon. We are practically the same person, but Jimmie grew up in Texas and I grew up in New Jersey. He never curses, and I can't f---ing help myself. He's a guy, and I'm not. Otherwise, twins.

Jimmie and I were instant rivals at Hood to Coast, running the same sections of the course on opposite teams and talking trash the whole time. When Jimmie's teammates learned that I ran a faster first leg than he did, their entire van of Air Force dudes started clowning Jimmie about it. Of course, Jimmie got fired up and beat me on the next two, cementing our rivalry—and an unbreakable friendship. Since then, Jimmie joined *my* relay team, and the rest is history. I'm convinced he's my patronus. I need his fire, jokes and brotherly love to get across Death Valley.

Odd as it sounds, I had never met Kalie Demerjian or Brenna Bray before choosing them to crew me at Badwater. It's important to me to have more women in sports and striving toward the toughest races in ultrarunning, so I put feelers out into the universe, had a phone call with each of them to get a sense of their vibe and experience, and voilà. Teammates. That might seem like a really high-stakes way to make friends, but here we are.

With her wind-tangled brown hair and different-colored eyes, Kalie is your mellow pixie dream girl. At first blush, you might think she's too small, too demure, too passive for Badwater. But maaan, you'd be the wrongest of the wrong. Kalie is a quiet storm. A pint-sized powerhouse. An ultrarunning *stud*, who, at just 24, ran her first 100-miler fast enough to qualify for national championships. Bonus: Kalie is introverted, a massively underrated characteristic for anyone with whom you're going to spend three days in a van. Because sometimes, everyone just needs to shut up and run.

Last but not least, meet Brenna, whose boundless energy could have settled the Wild West. She is the ultimate teammate: Minnesota nice and bubbling over with excitement about even the most mundane aspects of this Badwater adventure. Need water? Watermelon? Candy watermelon? Just say the word and Brenna will come a-running. She is ready for whatever the desert throws at her: more heat, more miles, more climbing. Just stuff it in her backpack and she'll carry whatever you need.

As I approach my support van sometime around 1 a.m. and somewhere around Mile 22, I am dragging ass. I down some Coca-Cola and a pile of candy in hopes that eating like I'm at a movie theater concession stand will perk me up. In my real life, when I'm not running an ultra, I quite literally never drink soda. And the last time I cared about candy was when I retired from trick-or-treating in the sixth grade. But during an ultramarathon, it's all about high-calorie foods that are easy to digest. Give me your white sugars, your carbs, your packaged Pop Tarts yearning to be eaten. It's like Buddy the Elf is your nutritionist.

But the sugar high hasn't hit yet. As a last-ditch effort, I ask Ricky and Jimmie to hand me my headphones.

Boom. We're right back in this.

It's like the ghost of Whitney Houston has entered my body. I wanna dance with somebody. I wanna run to you. I'm the queen of the night. I sing into the desert winds, belting out the high notes and paying no regard to any lizards or jackrabbits that might have been sleeping. Though I can't see another runner for miles, it's an all-out party right now.

Fighting off that wave of grogginess gives me a rush of confidence that carries me for miles and hours. "You got this, KC." I address myself in the second and third person, as if my mind and body are separate entities.

TO RUN AN ULTRAMARATHON, you have to listen to your body and troubleshoot the issues it brings to your attention. On the fly and under duress, you need to be able to solve problems big and small: aches, pains, fatigue, digestive issues, chafing, blisters, overheating.

Chances are, I'm going to face every single one of those challenges during this race. But this is what we trained for.

Back in February, I began ramping up my mileage. I've run a few 100-milers in my time, but we're talking about 35% more miles under significantly harder conditions. I had to start building my body and mind toward the challenge. By midspring, I was regularly running 85 to 100 miles per week. Six days a week, I woke up early and ran as far as I could—based on how my body felt and how much time I had available before starting work, because despite the time and effort, I make zero dollars from this bizarre hobby. Marketing puts food on the table, and your girl's gotta eat.

To keep up with my metabolism, I ate everything that wasn't nailed down. I slept hard just about every night, so tired from exertion, my muscles in desperate need of restful recovery.

To be clear, I *love* training that hard. The feeling of breaking down and building back up. Of emptying the tank. People might tell you that less is more, but not me. I'm a "more is more" person. I want extra miles, extra soreness, extra spice.

Besides, lacing up my sneakers and popping out the door is freedom. To think or not to think. To go where I want to go. To listen to podcasts or playlists or nothing at all. It's my time.

During those months of training, I had slow days when my legs felt heavy and tight. And cold days when the wind ripped at my face and nearly froze my lungs. But no bad days. Because I was building toward something that gave me a sense of purpose. Something I'd already worked for, something that had denied me once. I didn't want this race to get any more of me without a gnarly, knock-down, drag-out fight.

That's right, team. Because though this was the first time I had made it to the start line, it wasn't my first time training for Badwater.

In 2020, I applied and was one of the 100 runners selected to run Badwater. I trained the full cycle, and then, 10 days before the race was scheduled and just three days before I was set to leave, the race director sent the email we had all been dreading and night-sweating for months.

Fri, Jun 26, 2020, 10:39 PM
Subject: 2020 Badwater 135: CANCELED
What *didn't* COVID ruin in 2020? All those hours of heat training, sitting in the car with my windows up wearing six layers of sweats. All those days waking up while it was still dark out. All those miles and worn-out sneakers. All those squats and deadlifts. And for what?

We didn't even get a refund. Not even a credit for the next year. It was just one big, fat L.

I was pissed. I was a living, breathing version of the Michael Jordan "and I took that personally" meme. I wanted revenge. I did not want to let this race defeat me, so I used my vendetta as motivation for an entire calendar year.

Being mad at the circumstances around the 2020 race cancellation should not be confused for the actual madness of heat training, which is both ridiculous and necessary.

For a race like Badwater, it's not just about the miles on your legs. It's getting your body acclimated to extreme heat so it won't shut down or, you know, die. It's learning to recognize the difference between "Wow, this is miserable" and "I might be experiencing organ failure." Typical, totally normal stuff, right?

In June, I did every run in layers—piling on sweatshirts and long pants while running through the streets of hot and humid Washington, D.C. I looked deranged and unstable, like the kind of person who doesn't know what season it is and might wear a tinfoil hat to prevent brain goblins. I made sure to give the Secret Service agents standing near the White House a thumbs-up—*All good here, guys!*—but they nevertheless stared at me with suspicion and confusion.

As race day got closer, I spent an hour each morning in a 200-degree sauna at the gym, hydrating and sweating through every pore to train my body to process water more quickly. I sat

in the soft light reading paperback books until their bindings
melted and pages curled. My heart rate elevated as if I were doing
interval training, but I was just sitting still, roasting like a turkey.
Though it wasn't my goal, I outlasted every single other person
who stepped into that cedar box. *This is my house now.*

Speaking of my house, sorry to my supportive partner, Josh,
but I turned off the air conditioning. The good news is our electric
bill was almost nothing; the bad news is that it never got much
cooler than 84 degrees. And yet, I still put on a hoodie, long pants,
wool socks and slippers, closed the door to my home office, and
blasted a space heater. Three times a day, I had to put my laptop
in the refrigerator to cool it off so it wouldn't crap out. Me? I was
a constant sweat-ball but otherwise functioning just fine. The
things we do for love, right?

WHEN I REACH THE STOVEPIPE WELLS checkpoint at Mile
42.2, it's 4:30 a.m. on Tuesday. As the sun rises, the desert glows
with pinks and purples and ambers, like melted rainbow sherbet.

For having already run for 8.5 hours, I'm feeling strong, efficient and ready to smoke this next section, a 17-mile climb to
Towne Pass. The temperature is steadily climbing, and so am I.

"Why is this so hard?" I ask Brenna, who has been pacing
me for the past 7 miles.

"You're crushing it," she says. "Look how much you've
covered already."

I turn around for the first time in hours, and everything
behind me is downhill. What a relief to know that it isn't just
fatigue slowing me down and forcing me to feel the effort. This
terrain is no joke.

At Mile 52, Kalie jumps in to pace me for the rest of the
climb, and it's like a lightning strike. Straight energy. When she's
nudging me on, I can feel her giddy-up, almost like I'm boxing
her in. She wants to move. You can just sense it. I keep pressing
on, and soon enough, we've power hiked to the top of Towne

Pass, the first of three mountain sections between me and the finish line.

Mile 58.7 and still feeling great. Almost 5,000 feet of elevation, earned step by step from below sea level, most of which is about to evaporate as I bomb down the hills. I lean into the downward slope and careen through the steep switchbacks, focusing on my leg turnover. I don't need the road signs to announce every 1,000 feet of descent; I can feel it as my knees grind like a molcajete. No sense fighting gravity. It's better to use that free speed, even if it hurts.

When I get toward the bottom of the mountain, Ricky hops in for a strategy jog.

"Jimmie's going to mule you across Panamint. We're not going to do any crew stops because I want you to get across the kill zone as fast as possible," he says. "It's going to be hard, but you got this."

Compared to the mountains ahead and the mountains behind, the next 7-mile section of straight road looks flat and easy.

But girrrrrl, don't kid yourself. You're headed right into the heart of the beast.

Jimmie and I begin pushing through Panamint Valley, and I am instantly sweating like a dad at the YMCA. "It's freaking Hurricane Harbor in here all day," Jimmie says, spraying me down with cold water every few paces.

This is fun. This could be fun. Then, out of nowhere, this is *not* fun.

Panamint Valley is where dreams go to die. The air temperature is 114 degrees, but it's way hotter than that on the road, freshly paved black. And there is no cross-breeze in hell.

I feel like straight-up garbage. Like I want to stop—not quit— but stop running, sweating, slowly melting into glass.

Poor Jimmie keeps dousing me with water and nudging me along. He's in long sleeves and long pants for sun protection, and I'm wondering how he hasn't dried into jerky—a literal Slim Jim.

What a good friend. Without Jimmie, I'd be dead and picked over by some wayward coyotes by now.

I can see our next checkpoint at Panamint Springs Resort, and my eyes tell me it's about a mile until I get there. But then I see a road sign that practically ruins my life.

PANAMINT SPRINGS RESORT—3 MILES
I lose my mind. *How?* How am I only halfway through this? Am I on a conveyor belt going backward?

I'm furious at everything and everyone, because how is this taking so long? I want answers, but there are none in Panamint Valley. It's the closest thing to Azkaban prison I've ever experienced.

I curse the sky, screaming up at the sun like I'm the lead in a Shakespearean tragedy. *I defy you, stars!*

Jimmie had just crossed the road to restock on water and ice, leaving me alone with my angst for just a few minutes. So now I'm looking at the van—at four generous, kind people trying to keep my spirits up—and I just know that one of them is going to say something nice.

Look, I'm not proud of it, but I've had the humbling displeasure of striking out in a slow-pitch softball game. When that happens, I don't want anyone to pat me on the back and tell me it's OK. It's not OK. It's disgraceful and humiliating. I grew up in New Jersey, where our state motto might as well be "cut the bulls----." So when people patronize me or tell me lies in the interest of being nice, it offends me on a deep, molecular level.

I can endure the heat and chafing and sleep deprivation and toe blisters. But what I cannot endure is my crew lying to me and trying to protect me from the fact that this sucks right now and it's going to suck until I get from here to there using my own two feet.

I can't handle the untruth. So I preempt them, yelling across the road into the van before they have a chance.

"No one better tell me I'm doing a great job right now!"
They look at me, stunned and silent as I march past.

Fueled by my rage, I finally make it across the sandy stretch of Hades and immediately go down for a nap in the van. My thighs are tagged with red swirls, not from sunburn but from flash heating. I just want to take my shorts off. The chafing beneath the back of my sports bra feels like someone ripped off an angel's wings, which feels appropriate for having traipsed through hell.

I stretch out in the passenger seat, cover my face to block the sun and close my eyes.

IF I RECALL CORRECTLY, the boys' attitudes changed in about fourth grade. Until then, they had only ever thought of me as one of them: an athlete, a competitor, a teammate. At our elementary school field day—Applegate School's de facto Super Bowl—I was the anchor in the sprint relay. In gym class, I was always one of the first picks. I loved sports as much as or more than those boys, and I torched most of them in the mile run during the national physical fitness test.

I was still the same kid, so I didn't understand why Danny Pires, who had been my best friend since kindergarten, all of a sudden started yelling "Girls can't play ball!" to me at recess. I didn't understand why I no longer got invited to their sporty birthday parties at Grand Slam USA.

As I reflect back, it occurs to me that, at the budding age of 9, the boys in my class had finally soaked up that meathead au jus. The antiquated, hurtful narrative that boys are better than girls, particularly at sports. The messages had been pumping at them in toy commercials, sports broadcasts and history textbooks where boys get to be adventurers and girls get to cheer for them and bring them pitchers of water.

I had successfully fended that off, simply by competing. So it stung when all of a sudden my times and performances weren't enough to prove that I belonged in the game.

I definitely didn't cry about it then or now. But every time I don't get the invite to play pickup. Every time someone sees me as just an undersized girl who doesn't belong on the field, on the court, in the conversation. Every time women and girls in sports get marginalized, discounted or left out, it adds more fuel to an already raging fire. No wonder I'm burning up out here.

Healthy, unhealthy, who gives a f---? The point is, this is how I sublimated all those feelings. I'm still in this race, still fighting to prove to people who don't even think about me that they were wrong. That I'm tougher than they will ever be. That they'll never beat me.

Because there are no wimpy women in this house.

WHEN I WAKE UP FROM MY NAP, it's an absolute revelation. Unless you've been around toddlers recently, you might have forgotten what a 30-minute nap can do.

Don't call it a comeback.

Ricky puts an ice bandanna around my neck and drapes a wet towel over my head. Kalie hops in to pace me, and we begin climbing the second mountain section.

"You finally look like you're running Badwater!" Ricky says, 75 miles and 18 hours into the race. About damn time.

There must be something in the water Kalie sprays on me because we are cruising up these mountain switchbacks. At every turn, I look back and see another astounding view of the road behind me and the vast expanse I've covered on foot.

The landscape is severe and reminiscent of what you might find on Mars—craggy rock faces, a sky without clouds, questions of whether anything could sustain life here. With this as our dystopian bizarro backdrop, Kalie and I talk about life and nihilism, and how freeing it is to believe that nothing matters. Below us— yes, *below*—we hear fighter jets flying through Rainbow Canyon, a common training area for military pilots.

It's like being in a sci-fi movie. But this is real life. *My* life. What even *is* life?

Before you know it, I've conquered another 8 miles and we're at Father Crowley's Turnout at Mile 80.65. Jimmie tells me that Sally McRae, who will go on to win the women's race, left this parking lot crying. Judging by the piles of puke I passed on the way up here, I'm sure she's not the only one.

I feel strong but tired. I press on, running the flats and feeling cooler than I've felt since last night.

"Can I take this off?" I ask, offering Ricky the ice bandanna that has been refilled a thousand times and tied around my neck. I don't want to carry the weight, and I'm sick of being so wet. The chafing, you guys. It's inhumane.

"It's still over a hundred out, so no," he says, laughing. Bro, Death Valley really plays with you. It makes you think that 107 degrees is refreshing.

We get to the Darwin checkpoint at Mile 90.6 at 7:30 p.m. on Tuesday. We've officially exited Death Valley National Park and are moving into the backstretch of the race. I've been running almost 24 hours, but I still have another 45 miles to go before I can figuratively call it a day.

Time and space become amorphous and meaningless. The sun is up, but so is the moon. The landscape looks the same— desert to my left, distant mountain to my right. But way up ahead is a mountain range where I know there's a finish line. I just have to get there.

"Find it."

ALL DAY, THE SUN has been attacking me directly, but now she's trying a new tactic. Twilight, the silent killer. Through thousands of years of social and biological conditioning, the darkness tells me it's time to rest. But I can't stop now; I'm not even close to done with this race.

By Mile 95.6, I am a headless horseman. Twenty-four hours and 55 minutes into this race, and my body continues to make forward progress, but I'm not sure who's driving this thing. Everything feels strange and upside-down. And though I've never been drunk in my life, I feel hammered.

"I think I need a nap," I tell my crew.

"I want you to push to Mile 100 if you can," Ricky says to me. He's concerned that if I nap now, I'll lose ground and the runners behind me will leave me in the dust. Besides, goals are important and sometimes the urge to sleep goes away, right? So, I'm trying, y'all. I'm really trying to throw down these next 4 miles.

"Find it," I say to myself. But I just don't have it right now. Resistance is futile. But man, do I appreciate my team always nudging me on, believing I have it when I really don't.

The moment I hop in the passenger seat and close my eyes, your girl is zonked. Racked out. Unconscious. Gone in 60 seconds. But when Ricky wakes me up 30 minutes later, I pop up like a golden brown slice of toast, perfectly done.

"Start hunting," he says. Only two runners have passed, and all I see ahead are their vans' flashers. It's on.

BRENNA, KALIE, JIMMIE AND RICKY tag in throughout the next 20 miles, the night getting progressively darker and cooler as we get farther from Death Valley. The miles are a slow-motion blur as fatigue really kicks in.

Now that the temperature has dropped into the 70s, my body is no longer heat challenged, which means it's starting to perform other functions beyond just cooling off the engines. My digestive system is gearing back to life, processing everything I've consumed. My belly feels a little woozy every time I eat.

But I need calories. I can't make it another 20 miles on fumes and good intentions. So, everything is a balance. Everything is a struggle.

But I signed up for this. I wanted this. I still want this.

When I reach Mile 111 at 1:21 a.m., I walk to the van and matter-of-factly tell everyone that I'm taking a nap. "Wake me up in a few minutes," I say. There's a chance I'm asleep before my body even hits the passenger seat. But 4 minutes later, Ricky wakes me up, and girrrrrl, I'm telling you. That micronap? *Life-giving.*

We arrive at the Lone Pine checkpoint just before sunrise on Wednesday. I've gone 122 miles, and while I'd love to think that finishing is a foregone conclusion, the rest of this race is uphill. I've got 13 miles and 5,000 feet of vert between me and that finish line.

I suppose now is as good a time as any for blisters to develop on my heels. Those little motherf---ers sure know how to spoil a party.

Look, you probably have a lot of great people in your life who will be there for you when you need them. But if you don't have a Ricky, then you'd better go find yourself a Ricky. Someone who will clean up your blistered, pungent feet with no questions or complaints. True heroism.

Even in my condition—feral, sleep-deprived and light-headed—I know it's a scene. Me, kneeling across the passenger seat, eating a Pop Tart and dangling my heels out the door. Ricky, applying a tincture that stings so bad it makes me breathe like I'm in labor. I put on my third pair of shoes and prepare for the climb.

"You need to be *obsessed* with getting up these hills," Ricky says. He knows. He's been there. The second he says it, I'm locked in. No more lollygagging. We've got a job to do.

Good news. This ass and these thighs were built for two things: denim and climbing.

I POWER HIKE UP THE NEXT 3 MILES ALONE, my heart rate higher than it's been this entire race. Then Brenna and Jimmie rotate in, encouraging me, telling me I look strong, reminding me to swing my arms. I don't have the breath or the mind to hold up a conversation. I just nod along and keep grinding.

I hit the last checkpoint at Mile 131, and Kalie hops in to pace me to the finish. "Just keep going," she says. "Nothing else matters right now." Her small voice and quiet energy feel like they come from within me.

I'm in angry mode. Anyone between me and the finish line is my enemy. And I'm not just saying that to add drama. I'm about to snap.

We hit a series of steep switchbacks, and I'm gaining on the racers in front of me. I pass them on a turn, running in a burst that takes the wind out of me. The air is thin, the hills are steep and I'm running on empty. I'm in a dissociative state—between awake and asleep, alive and dead, here and gone. My nutrition is right at the brink.

I don't want to crash. I've come way too far to fail now.

"IT'S JUST A FEW MORE SWITCHBACKS," Jimmie says to me when I ask him for the third time how much farther I have to go.

I stare him right in the eyes and say, *"That's not helpful."* It's as if he's a customer service agent denying me a refund and not my very good friend who flew all the way out to the middle of nowhere to support me. As if him not knowing the precise distance from this arbitrary point to the finish line is a personal attack. As if he's sabotaging me on purpose.

So now I'm yelling. At my support crew. The four people who have kept me alive this entire time, tending to every blister and bellyache. Upon reflection, I'm the worst.

But you have to understand. At this point, I've been on my feet and sweating for 37 hours. My mind is foggy; my body is a disaster; and I'm so tired that I don't even have the cognitive function to regulate emotion.

I have less than a mile left of this life-sucking 135-mile race, and I want to cross that finish line running. I'm browning out, from sleep deprivation and an insurmountable caloric deficit, and I just don't have the legs to kick if I don't know how much farther I have to go.

Then Brenna comes bounding over with a big smile on her face. Who could possibly smile at a time like this? We're dying out here, Brenna!

"There's a woman up ahead, walking slowly... You can pass her!" she says. She believes in me and knows I'm competitive. But I'm beyond all of that.

As much as I like Brenna, I don't have the same relationship with her as I have with Jimmie. So I snap at him instead.

"I don't care about one single human being right now."

I think I was referring to the woman up ahead, but with such a blanket statement and stank attitude, I can't be sure. Honestly, I don't even remember saying it. But my crew can corroborate that I am possessed by an inner beast.

Finally, I see the finish line and the aforementioned woman, talking politely and appreciatively to her crew as they approach the tape.

I swear I love my crew too, but I've got a funny way of showing it. They get out of the van and join me in running toward that finish line together. I take off. It's maybe 100 meters, but it's everything I have left. I've still got some fast-twitch muscles ready to fire, and I cross the finish line not just jogging but running hard. When I go back and look at the race data, I'm the sixth-fastest person and the fastest woman in that 4-mile stretch. Is that an excuse for being a heinous zombie? Probably not. But to my crew, I'm sorry and you're welcome for the memories.

I DON'T CRY AT THE FINISH LINE. I don't feel overwhelmed or overjoyed. In fact, I don't feel much of anything other than wiped. After taking some photos and thanking my crew, I lie down on the pavement and close my eyes.

We did it. We actually did it.

It took me 37 hours, 37 minutes to get from start to finish, of which I spent 64 minutes napping, at least 120 minutes singing and 25 minutes yelling irrational things at my poor, wonderful crew. I polished off 4 liters of Coke, 11 packets of Pedialyte, a pineapple and a container of strawberries, two sweet potatoes, four protein shakes, two packages of gummy watermelons, a jar of pickles, a cup of ramen and two emergency McDonald's hash browns.

We spend about an hour at the finish line, but I'm not sure why. I'm minimally conscious, trying to eat a pancake but instead just fondling it. I put my head down on the picnic table and try to remain human.

Later that day, my team checks into our Airbnb, where I finally take a shower and wash off the sweat, stink and dirt that gives me that "girl raised by wolves" vibe. As the hot water hits my raw, chafed skin, I scream a little. OK, fine, a lot. But it's worth the pain to feel clean again. I curl up for the most important two-hour nap of my life.

That evening, the five of us head to a sleepy café in a sleepy town. It's just us, rehashing stories from this magical adventure as the sun sets behind that mountain ridge near the finish line.

That's when the dream starts to feel real.

I didn't know that you could feel cathartic and giddy at the same time, but here we are, laughing our heads off as I start to feel a warm, proud glow.

My crew fills me in on the things I missed while I was running. How mean and angry I was, how hot and sweaty and tired they were. But we did what we came to do, so the low points become the high points. That's how we'll always remember them.

Because we really did this thing.

I thought Badwater would show me how tough I am. But that's not what this was about. Badwater doesn't test your toughness. It's not a f---ing truck commercial.

When you're out there, you see people breaking down. Marching to the finish line with vacant eyes and a cramp-induced lean. Puking and crying and speaking in tongues.

Where do they muster the strength to pick themselves back up time and time again?

I knew before I even started the race that it would change me. Because I've done some hard things, but I've never seen myself on the other side of that line. Running Badwater was the only way I knew how to get to the truth, to ask questions I didn't know I had about myself.

Are you ready to see your insides laid bare? Do you actually want to know who you are when it all falls down? Can you trust other people to hold you together mentally and physically when you have nothing else left? Are you OK pooping in a bag next to someone you want to respect you when this whole thing is done?

I left pieces of myself out there. Things I thought I was are now just sitting in a discard pile somewhere between Mile 90 and the finish line. But I found new pieces, new answers, new reasons. And though I'm still not done figuring out how it all fits together, I know I wouldn't trade this feeling for anything.

I remember hearing an episode of the podcast "Invisibilia," in which anthropologist Renato Rosaldo discussed his time studying the Ilongot tribe, from a remote area of the Philippines. Rosaldo described a word, a feeling—*liget*—that didn't have a direct translation from Ilongot to English. It wasn't sadness, joy, fear or anger, exactly, but it could be all of those feelings or attached to them. It most closely translated to "high voltage."

Liget is primal, intense, all-encompassing and difficult to describe. After Badwater, I can relate.

It was like I experienced the entirety of human emotion all at once.

Love and pain. Terror and triumph. Anger and affection.

Humble but invincible. Close to dead but never more alive. And very, very sweaty.

I've always been a little bit terrified of letting go because it's scary to think of what might happen. But I learned that to prove myself I didn't have to be fearless. I just had to fear less.

I had to get comfortable being completely exposed—to my crew, to the elements, to the possibility of failure. To the unthinkable fear that I'm not good enough, not tough enough. That those boys might have been right about me.

I had to run headfirst into that fear, and why not add a haboob while you're at it. Because you might have to let it all in so you can let it all out.

Badwater showed me that it's not toughness or effort that sets me apart or defines me. It's my willingness to step into the arena and risk it all. My vulnerability is my superpower.
I just had to go out there and find it.

A plucky tomboy from the great state of New Jersey, **Kelaine Conochan** is a freelance writer whose work has appeared in *ESPN The Magazine*, *espnW*, *Runner's World*, and *Washington City Paper*. Her most recent project is *Recognize*, a podcast that investigates why coverage of women's sports is so crummy and what we can do to improve it. She currently runs (both her legs and her mouth) and resides in Washington, D.C., where she would happily sub on your sports team in exchange for trail mix.

I Flew to Texas to Watch Bull Riding on an Aircraft Carrier During COVID

MATT CROSSMAN

FROM *Experience* • JANUARY 6, 2021

The bull's name is Foghorn Leghorn. He is roughly 1,600 pounds of brown and white spotted mayhem, a thickly muscled mass of bovine boisterousness with a look on his face that drips disdain. Or maybe I'm reading into it. Regardless, I am relieved that there is a metal pen between me and this bull, who has been bucking off cowboys in the Professional Bull Riders for three years.

Grabbing onto the outside of that metal pen is a rising bull-riding star named Ezekiel Mitchell. He is 155 pounds, a lithe and flexible rag doll in chaps, equal parts intense stare and easy-going, dimply smile. Standing in the shadow of a World War II-era Air Force fighter jet, he discards his face mask for a helmet. Holding the rail, he quick-squats, once, twice, six times, stretching to prepare for the ludicrous thing he is about to do. He hops over the metal fence and straddles Foghorn Leghorn's back.

Mitchell slips his red-gloved right hand under a rope on Foghorn Leghorn's back and nods his head. That's the cue for someone on the other side of the pen to open it. The bull bursts out of the pen, and so does Mitchell, trailing above and behind him like a cartoon, left hand high for balance, right hand clinging to that rope. Mitchell hangs on for the bull's first two jumps. On the third, his hand slips. Now he's just along for the ride, and there's little chance it will end well. Foghorn Leghorn bucks again, gravity takes over, and Mitchell lands on his head. He turtles in the dirt for a blink, and Foghorn Leghorn rams his horns into him, then mercifully runs away.

Mitchell pops off the ground and circles around to the back of the bullpen, where he sits down and catches his breath. He's fine, or at least as fine as a man can be after he gets thrown off of a bull, lands on his head, and then gets rammed. Even by Professional Bull Riders standards, the crash is spectacular. It's historic, even, because of where and when it happened. Mitchell is the first cowboy in the history of the world to get thrown off of a bull …

On the flight deck of an aircraft carrier …

… in the middle of a pandemic.

As Mitchell walks to the makeshift arena to watch the rest of the event, I exhale, thankful he is OK. Standing on the deck of the *U.S.S. Lexington*, docked on the Gulf of Mexico in Corpus Christi, Texas, I ask myself, not for the first time, why did I fly to Texas to watch bull riding on an aircraft carrier as COVID-19 wracks the country, as a fall surge intensifies, as public health officials issue warnings and families drop their holiday plans?

And why are there 250 others on this boat, too?

The week before I left for Corpus Christi, I read *Fahrenheit 451*, about a future society so descended into frivolity that it burns books to avoid learning what's in them. At the risk of sounding self-righteous, I wondered if bull riding on an aircraft carrier as a deadly disease ravages the planet was evidence that we are, indeed, amusing ourselves to death.

But I learned on the aircraft carrier that bull riding wasn't really the point of all of those people getting together. Connection was.

The isolation we've experienced since March 2020 is bad for us. Perhaps the most insidious fact of the coronavirus has been that the best way to get through the pandemic emotionally and mentally is also the best way to catch the virus: by being a member of a tight-knit community. Figuring out how to be present with others, and what risks we'll take to do so, is the tightrope upon which we all have been walking.

"The reality is human beings are social creatures," says Daniel Aldrich, director of the Security and Resilience Studies program at Northeastern University, who has extensively studied the relationships among social connections, death, and disasters. Early in the pandemic, Aldrich gave interviews in which he criticized the term "social distancing" because he thought it sent the exact wrong message. He prefers "physical distancing."

Aldrich points to research showing that participation in a community is crucial to helping humans endure disasters. If we all locked ourselves in our homes and never left, that would kill the virus. But we would pay a steep price for losing our social networks, because it's not a zero-sum game, no matter what histrionic Twitter scolds might say.

"We need to have these networks; we need to feel connected," Aldrich says. "We will do dumb things or expensive things or risky things to get those connections satisfied."

After Mitchell's ride, I walk a lap around the fenced-in riding area. I face the dirt, with the gulf behind me. A woman wearing a U.S. flag vest leans against the fence. She waves a sign that thanks PBR (Professional Bull Riders, the sport's sanctioning body) and announces today is her 70th birthday.

Her name is Jan Bernard, and she has been a huge fan of bull riding since 2011. How huge? She can recognize the top bull riders by getting a quick look at their rear ends.

The source on that tush tidbit is Lloyd Bernard, Jan's husband of 50 years—and also her chauffeur, luggage handler and travel agent. This year alone, Jan and Lloyd drove their white 2015 Dodge Durango more than 40,000 miles to attend 13 PBR events, most of them after the shutdown. They wear masks everywhere they go, use copious amounts of hand sanitizer, clean their hotel rooms themselves, and bypass restaurants that are too crowded.

After each trip, they quarantine at home. All to watch cowboys ride bulls.

Why?

"See this red hair?" Jan says, smiling as she points to an amber bob of curls. "I have the temper that goes with it. If I have to stay home too long ..."

The rest goes unsaid, but the implication (confirmed by Lloyd) is that it would be unpleasant. But it's not just leaving the house that's important. What matters is who was there when they reached their destinations: People who share their passion.

When I talked to Jan and Lloyd on the flight deck the night before the bull riding event, a steady stream of people—from other fans to Ezekiel Mitchell to PBR CEO Sean Gleason— stopped to say hello. I half-expected Foghorn Leghorn to saunter over for an elbow bump.

I told Jan I was impressed the CEO knew who she was. Her hair glowed redder as she cracked, "He better talk to me. I pay his bills."

Indeed, she and Lloyd, along with 35 other fans, forked over $1,500 apiece to be here. With donations from Ford and Wrangler and other corporate sponsors, the one-hour event, held on Nov. 21 and broadcast on CBS the next day, raised $250,000 for military charities such as Operation Homefront, which supports military families. That stiff fee earned VIP ticketholders entrance to the event, meals, a couple of nights in a hotel, a COVID-19 test (which was required of everyone who got on the boat), tours of the *U.S.S. Lexington*, and a priceless immersion in a community of friends.

PBR, LIKE OTHER SPORTS, has allowed some fans to attend events for months. By design, the stands have not been full. But the slow trickle of attendance at such events will become a flood as soon as state and local governments allow it, and as people desperate for interaction feel safe enough to do so. "Every single venue, theater, movie, whatever, is going to be packed," Aldrich says. "There's such pent-up demand now for all those connections. It'll be nuts."

In the meantime, events that allow fans follow strict safety rules, some dictated by state and local regulations. Bull riders run the constant risk of getting their brains stomped out. It is an aggressive, swashbuckling, laugh-at-danger sport that celebrates its participants' ability to endure pain. So I wondered what PBR's protocols would be like. Answer: Stringent.

From the sport's return in Oklahoma in late April, through 20 events in 10 states, until the final bull ride on the *Lexington*, PBR employees and contractors were tested constantly and required to wear masks and stay within bubbles on the road and at home. The social pressure was as strong as the professional pressure—nobody wanted to be the reason that the virus spread and did to the season what Foghorn Leghorn did to Mitchell.

Those protocols were evident for the *U.S.S. Lexington* event. Before I flew to Texas, I was told, multiple times, that I would not be allowed on the aircraft carrier to cover the event until I passed a COVID-19 test administered by PBR. That applied to everyone—the Bernards, bull riders, and bartenders. Well, almost everyone. Nobody shoved a Q-tip up Foghorn Leghorn's nose. Masks were mandatory on the boat, even though it was outside and everybody had been tested.

After those precautions, we damn sure expected a spectacle, and a huge amount of work went into providing it. Onto the 872-foot-long flight deck, PBR hauled 300 tons of dirt and steel and 15 miles of copper and fiber-optic cables (for the CBS broadcast). Twenty dump trucks hauled up dirt to fill the 58-by-70-foot bull ring. The limited attendance included VIPs like the Bernards as well as local fans who paid $375 per ticket.

While the location was unique, the process was fairly normal. PBR rents dirt and builds and disassembles bull rings in arenas around the country, and has done so in Times Square and on California's Huntington Beach.

Getting the bulls onto the flight deck? That was new.

"HOW DO THEY GET THE BULLS onto the aircraft carrier?" my wife asked as she drove me to the airport.

I told her PBR would use an elevator normally used to take planes to the flight deck.

"Will there be somebody in the elevator with them?" she asked. This made her nervous, and rightly so. "I imagine the bulls are like velociraptors."

I told her I hoped nobody would be on the elevator with the bulls. But the more I thought about it, the more I wanted to ride on an elevator with a bull on an aircraft carrier, because once is the number of times I'll have a chance to do that, pandemic or no pandemic.

And that's how I've come to take that ride with not one, but seven bulls.

In truth, I'm not sure elevator is the right word. It's technically a platform lift on the side of the *U.S.S. Lexington*. I ride up with Foghorn Leghorn, Evil Intentions (no bull worth riding would ever be named Good Intentions), and five other bulls. They stand (maskless! not social distancing! breathing all over each other!) in a trailer pulled by a white Ford pickup.

I could reach in and pet them. I opt not to, just in case they are, indeed, like velociraptors.

The truck pulls onto the lift, and the truck and trailer are too long to fit. The driver turns slightly, so the truck and the trailer look like clock hands pointed to 12:35. Even with that adjustment, the very back of the trailer hangs off the end over the Gulf of Mexico.

As the lift carries us up to the flight deck, Foghorn Leghorn, Evil Intentions and the rest jostle for position. Their movements shake the trailer. Not a lot or anything, but seven bulls shaking a trailer that's hanging over the Gulf of Mexico …

"If I drop a bull into the bay, I'm dead," jokes Easton Colvin, a PBR media representative.

THIS ENTIRE EXPERIENCE is the brainchild of PBR CEO Sean Gleason. At mid-morning on the day of the event, Gleason and I talk at a round table a level below the flight deck. He wears a thin layer of scruff, cowboy boots and a cowboy hat. His dancing eyes make me think bull riding on an aircraft carrier in the middle of a pandemic isn't the wildest idea he's ever had, it's just the wildest one he has pulled off so far.

Gleason has wanted to buck bulls on an aircraft carrier since well before the COVID-19 crisis, when he saw a college basketball game on one a decade ago. This summer, he called a staff meeting and proposed the idea. "Do you think we can do it?" he asked them. "They all stopped and said, 'Well, hell, yeah.' I said, 'Good. Let's do it.'"

Now, a few hours before the event starts, Gleason is stunned at what his team has pulled off. "When I walked up and saw the crew laying down the dirt for the first time," Gleason says, "I'm like, *oh, holy shit, this is going to happen.*"

The whole event is a manifestation of PBR's slogan: Be Cowboy. "It's about getting up, dusting yourself off, getting back to work. It's cowboy ingenuity that got us back," Gleason says. "We dove in and learned everything we could possibly learn about this virus."

Gleason says the key to holding an event safely is understanding the difference between living in fear and living with danger. If we live in fear, he figures, we will cower in our homes. If we agree to live in danger, he thinks, we will face that danger responsibly—and take the necessary precautions.

"If it was all about the individual, none of my people would care if they caught COVID," Gleason says. They aren't worried about getting sick themselves. "But what they have learned, and what we will continue to preach, is it's not about you. It's about the person across from you."

I don't want to overstate the heft of a conversation about bull riding on an aircraft carrier in the middle of a pandemic, but our talk was full of two precious commodities: reasonableness and hope.

"The protocols we put in place have worked since Day 1," Gleason says. "We've had test after test after test, and result after result after result, to prove that what we did—stepping out and being forward-thinking with a safe and responsible return—was the right thing to do."

The first reason Gleason wanted PBR to get back to bucking bulls was that most people who work in the industry only get paid if events happen. The second reason was to give fans a sense of community that isolation had ripped away from them.

His third reason? "It's our way of giving the finger to 2020."

IF GLEASON WANTED TO FLIP 2020 THE BIRD, Flint Rasmussen, PBR's rodeo clown, wanted to point at it and laugh. With clown paint on his face and sneakers on his feet, he entertained the crowd in between rides with a mix of singing, dancing, and stream-of-consciousness commentary.

I probably missed some of his references because I was laughing, but I caught obvious nods to the movies *Titanic* and *Top Gun*. I mean, *of course* he ran to the bow and pretended to be Leonardo DiCaprio as the King of the World. Even Foghorn Leghorn could see that one coming.

When Rasmussen saw Jan Bernard's sign announcing it was her birthday, he flirted with her, offering to be Maverick to her Goose. Then he turned serious, or as serious as a rodeo clown can be on an aircraft carrier in the middle of a pandemic. "From me to you, thank you for coming to this shindig," he said. Then he sang "Happy Birthday" to her, and her hair glowed redder still.

Matt Crossman has written more than 40 cover stories for national magazines. In pursuit of stories, he has spent a summer trying to get his first hole in one, hiked with Green Berets, gone to dog mushing school, and come in last in a spelling bee, though that last one wasn't on purpose. His claim to fame, if he has one, is that he is the only writer in the 126-year history of *The Sporting News* to appear on the cover. He had to shove a plastic car in his mouth for the photo shoot, but that hasn't stopped him from bragging about it.

Simone Biles Chose Herself

CAMONGHNE FELIX

FROM The Cut • SEPTEMBER 27, 2021

Simone Biles has a keen air sense, the ability to let muscle memory pilot against the brain's logical judgment. She can clear her mind and think of absolutely nothing. Catlike in her reflexes, she locates herself in space and lands on her feet every time. This has been the mark of her genius since childhood, the thing that made her different. Watching her is like trying to catch light. You think, *Did that just happen?* She flies higher and is more nimble than her competition, with more room for failure because what she attempts is that much more difficult. She has beaten the records of her idols—Nastia Liukin, Shawn Johnson, Alicia Sacramone—and they think she's the undeniable greatest too. She's what superheroes are made of, except she's made of bones and muscles that strain and break.

This time, though, the break wasn't a bone; it was something in her spirit, an injury that could not be explained by CAT scan or X-ray. The past few years had been the most trying stretch of her personal and professional life. In 2018, Biles revealed she had been sexually abused by former USA Gymnastics doctor Larry Nassar; the organization she was winning medals for had covered up his crimes. Still, going into the Tokyo Olympics in the summer of 2021, after a successful competitive year, she expected things to go as they always did. Then, on the fifth day of competition, she pushed off the vault and discovered she couldn't see herself in her head, couldn't see the map of the floor in order to land. It wasn't just unexpected—it was terrifying. She immediately withdrew from the finals. "My perspective has never changed so quickly from wanting to be on a podium to wanting to be able to go home, by myself, without any crutches," Biles tells me over brunch at a hotel facing the south side of Central Park in early September.

Today, the 24-year-old gymnast is radiant and relaxed, her face lightly dressed with makeup. She's wearing a crisp white T-shirt that looks like it was pulled straight off a Uniqlo shelf. She suggests mimosas. It's 10 a.m., but why not? The ease of postseason Simone Biles is an art. In the months when she's competing or preparing to compete, she's focused, regimented. Today, she seems more open to going with the flow. Life is no less busy, but the stakes are much lower. She has just begun rehearsals for Athleta's Gold Over America, a nationwide gymnastics tour that she stars in; in a few days, she will present at the VMAs and walk the Met Gala red carpet. We chat about matcha and Telfar. In conversation, she is reflective and warm and has a bighearted laugh. It is easy to see why little girls scream when she walks into the room.

While Biles is generally honest about her feelings, she is skilled at presenting them in a rehearsed package. When we approach the subject of Tokyo, it begins that way. "You know, there have been highs, there have been lows," she says, sending her gaze up toward the ceiling as she considers the stakes of the discussion. As she continues, she no longer seems interested in being quite as careful. "Sometimes it's like, yeah, I'm perfectly okay with it. Like, that's how it works. That's how it panned out." She flips her 1b-colored, bra-length jumbo box braids over her shoulder. "And then other times I'll just start bawling in the house."

Biles is naturally inclined toward humility—she likes people to know she is a glass-half-full kind of girl—but when she talks about the narratives that critics spread during Tokyo, her indignation builds. She recounts the absurdity of some of the assumptions the public made about her performance, Twitter threads accusing her of giving up because she just didn't feel like competing. "If I still had my air awareness, and I just was having a bad day, I would have continued," Biles says. "But it was more than that."

After training for most of her life for these Olympic Games, after a grueling season, after years of discussing her abuser publicly—how could anyone think the Games went the way they did because she just didn't *feel* like showing up? How could they think that after all this time, all this effort, she would travel all the way to Tokyo to just quit?

"Say up until you're 30 years old, you have your complete eyesight," Biles says. "One morning, you wake up, you can't see shit, but people tell you to go on and do your daily job as if you still have your eyesight. You'd be lost, wouldn't you? That's the only thing I can relate it to. I have been doing gymnastics for 18 years. I woke up—lost it. How am I supposed to go on with my day?"

BILES KNOWS SHE IS THE GREATEST. She has had four gymnastics elements named after her—one on beam, one on vault, two on floor. With a combined total of 32 Olympic and World Championships medals, she is the most decorated gymnast of all time. "It's kind of unheard of to win as many things as I have," Biles says. "I don't physically understand how I do it." She seems genuinely bummed she can't answer the question. Is it mental? Is it physical? If she knew what it was, she could bottle it up and sell it. "No," she concludes. "It was a God-given talent."

For an athlete of Biles's ability, the mind remains the most important organ. It tells the body what to do, and the body remembers. Anything that shakes that clear-mindedness is a life-risking liability. Biles has always been able to power through possible mental roadblocks in gymnastics and in her personal life. She powered through when she ended up in foster care after being taken away from a mother who struggled with addiction.

She powered through thousands of hours of grueling training; through injuries like a bone spur in 2013 and a shoulder strain in 2015. She powered through years of sexual assault and through endless attacks on her spirit as she relived that assault publicly.

The *Indianapolis Star* broke the news of Nassar's longtime abuse of hundreds of young women and girls in 2016, followed up by another report revealing USAG knew about his conduct and had covered it up. Before then, the Biles we knew was quieter—diplomatic to everyone and singularly focused on the game. She showed up to meets, beat her competitors graciously, and went home, thanking everyone for a good time. The months that followed were difficult. "It was hard to be in the gym mentally some days," she recalls. She kept the abuse to herself for two years; when she spoke out about it in 2018, her voice was a knife in the discourse. "I've felt a bit broken," she wrote in a Twitter statement, "and the more I try to shut off the voice in my head, the louder it screams." Every day for months, this was her life: headlines and news chyrons with her name next to Nassar's, public events where she'd sign autographs for little girls in one moment, then address USAG via broadcast in another. Something in her self-perception shifted at this point; she was no longer willing to be gracious. You could see it in her eyes in 2019, ahead of the Nationals in Kansas City, when reporters asked her about the cover-up, as she tearfully lambasted USAG: "You had one job! And you couldn't protect us." She was no longer okay with being a champion ghost. She wanted those who caused her harm to see her as human.

Amid all of this, she never lost a meet. And in some ways, she felt stronger than ever—the gym had become her safe space away from the world, and she was at the top of her game, even landing the Yurchenko double pike, a move so difficult no other woman has attempted it. While she trained for the Olympics, she went to therapy, where she learned coping mechanisms and to listen to how she was feeling day to day. By the time the Games rolled around, Biles recalls, she told her therapist, "I'm good enough to go. And they were like, 'Yes, you're good enough to go and do your stuff, but you have to come back.' And I was like, 'Nah, I'm good.'" She felt the wound had been closed, the injury fixed.

She stepped onto the flight to Tokyo with confidence. But there were variables she didn't anticipate this time: COVID testing, breakthrough cases. "There was no crowd, no parents," she explains. It was going to be harder, mentally, to get into the game. Once she arrived, anxiety set in. *Everything will be okay*, she thought, but she had a nagging feeling that things were not *right*. The coaches went through the typical pep talks, reminding each person of their unique purpose on the team, but the words weren't landing with her the way they usually did. "Leading up to it, I got more and more nervous," she says. "I didn't feel as confident as I should have been with as much training as we had."

The trouble started after qualifiers. She fumbled event after event. Biles and her coaches moved frantically to find fixes. They tried using foam pits and surfaces that might make her feel safer. Nothing worked. "I was not physically capable," she says. "Every avenue we tried, my body was like, *Simone, chill. Sit down. We're not doing it*. And I've never experienced that." Biles is known in the sport for her independence. Even among coaching staff, she is respected for her ability to self-moderate, to pull back when necessary. But rarely does she pull back because she *can't* do something. Things were already a bit rocky in the qualifying meet, the first event of the competition, where she fumbled the dismount on beam. By the time of her vault performance, two days later at the women's team final, Biles knew something bigger was off. She went for a 2.5 flip and only completed a 1.5. It wasn't just a technical error. She had the "twisties," which is when an athlete's mind and body lose connection and muscle memory fails to kick in. Let any gymnast describe them to you, and it will sound like a unique hell: 1988 Olympian Missy Marlowe called them "a nonserious stroke." "It's so dangerous," Biles explains. "It's basically life or death. It's a miracle I landed on my feet. If that was any other person, they would have gone out on a stretcher. As soon as I landed that vault, I went and told my coach: 'I cannot continue.'"

With her coaches, she put together an alternate strategy that would ultimately deliver Team USA the silver in the team finals. "I'm sorry, I love you guys, but you're gonna be just fine," Biles re-assured her teammates afterward, hugging them one by one, like a mom dropping her children off at soccer camp. "You guys have trained your whole entire lives for this ... I've been to an Olympics; I'll be fine. This is your first—you go out there and kick ass, okay?" She texted her teammate MyKayla Skinner, who had spent the Games in the stands and was set to fly back home to Arizona the next morning. She told her to cancel her flight— Skinner would need to replace Biles as an alternate. "Are you sure?" Skinner texted back. "Yes, you're staying," Biles replied.

Biles had been expected to win five golds this year. Even the ads for the Tokyo Olympics implied she would sweep on the podium. It was supposed to be her purpose, and just like that, it wasn't anymore. "If you looked at everything I've gone through for the past seven years, I should have never made another Olympic team," Biles says, her eyes filling with tears. "I should have quit way before Tokyo, when Larry Nassar was in the media for two years. It was too much. But I was not going to let him take something I've worked for since I was 6 years old. I wasn't going to let him take that joy away from me. So I pushed past that for as long as my mind and my body would let me."

SITTING AT THE BIG DESK on the floor of the U.S. Senate, Biles is dressed smartly in a pink plaid blazer and a white undershirt. She's there for a Judiciary Committee hearing on the FBI's handling of the Nassar investigation in September. The jumbo braids have been taken down and clip-ins installed, her dark-brown hair shiny and straight with just a little body up at the roots. From the outside, she looks ready to take on the world. "Before we entered the room, I was in the back literally bawling my eyes out," she tells me the day after the hearing. "And then, of course, you have to pull yourself together and go out there, be strong for just that moment."

She begins her statement by recounting her significant contribution to the history of sport in this country. "I am also a survivor of sexual abuse," she continues, "and I believe, without a doubt, that the circumstances that led to my abuse and allowed it to continue are directly the result of the fact that the organizations created by Congress to oversee and protect me as an athlete, USA Gymnastics, and the United States Olympic & Paralympic Committee, failed to do their jobs."

As she talks about this, her voice breaks "Sorry," Biles says in a low whisper. She continues, detailing the rage she felt when she learned, in 2016, that her teammate had told the former head of USAG Women's Program she suspected Biles had been harmed by Nassar too. While an investigation was under way, and others had been informed, neither USAG nor the FBI contacted her or her parents; Biles was not told about the investigation until after the Rio Games.

It has been nearly seven weeks since Biles returned home to Houston from Tokyo. Logically, she knows she made the right call. Some days, she feels certain of that, other days, she's just heartbroken. "It's like I jumped out of a moving train," she says. As much as she wants to recall every emotion and impulse that led to the outcome in Tokyo, she can't. How do you process a split-second decision? "Everybody asks, 'If you could go back, would you?'" Biles tells me. "No. I wouldn't change anything because everything happens for a reason. And I learned a lot about myself—courage, resilience, how to say no and speak up for yourself." At first, it seemed as if her body had betrayed her. But it was actually looking out for her; it had lost the ability to be dutifully compliant.

As an athlete, everything is about timing. Three months to train for a meet. Ninety seconds on the floor. One minute on beam. If you tear a muscle, a doctor can estimate healing time to the day. But not for a spiritual injury. The ache is cavernous and hidden somewhere she can't touch. "I just want a doctor to tell me when I'll be over this," says Biles, letting out a deep exhale. When she has dealt with physical injuries, it typically required six-to-eight weeks of recovery. Maybe three months. "You get surgery, it's fixed. Why can't someone just tell me in six months it'll be over?" she wonders. "Like, hello, where are the double-A batteries? Can we just stick them back in? Can we go?"

She's back in therapy; she knows she can't set a timeline for healing anymore. "This will probably be something I work through for 20 years," she says. "No matter how much I try to forget. It's a work in progress." She's getting ready to tour with Team USA members, but she's no longer training; winning is on the back burner. Mostly, she is spending time with her boyfriend, the football player Jonathan Owens; her family; and her closest friends. She's going on vacation, taking thirst traps in Cabo, learning how to see herself and her own needs and desires more clearly. Early in her life, Biles developed a sense of maternal responsibility. She mothered her little sister when they were in foster care. She mothered her teammates to an Olympic win. It's time now for Biles to mother herself.

I FOUND MYSELF TWISTED UP in the gut listening to Biles's speech on the Senate floor, as I frequently was during our conversations, by what she has had to carry in her small body—all the responsibility that shouldn't be hers at such a young age. The person they bet their gold on had been left alone to suffer abuse. It felt violently familiar. Black women and girls—talented, genius, used up by institutions, forgotten about when we are the ones in need of protection. It's no wonder her body resisted.

I have a theory that if someone were to try and account for the exact amount of labor Black women have forcefully and freely contributed to the U.S. economy and culture, if America had to match us cent for sweat drop, it would be a number so great it would bankrupt all of this country's resources.

"As a Black woman, we just have to be greater," Biles says simply, echoing what many a Black female great has said before her. "Because even when we break records and stuff, they almost dim it down, as if it's just normal."

Those who follow astrology believe each generation shares a Saturn—an indicator of its unique lesson to learn, its "work to do." Every generation of Black women releases a generation of curses as it borrows from the lessons of the past and shapes the possibilities of the future. My grandmother's generation might say they were the last generation of Black women who hid—likelier to hide abuse, to hide desire, to hide their individualities. As a mentor of mine puts it, my mother and auntie's generation was the last generation of fools—inclined to stay in relationships they didn't want, to hold on to jobs that left them unfulfilled.

Biles's generation, which is also my own, is, I hope, the last generation of mules. We're more inclined to set boundaries—to say no to what we don't want, to whom we don't want, to what we don't want to do, to conventions, expectations, demands. Less likely to stay at jobs that make us unhappy, to accept the treatment our mothers and grandmothers were forced to endure. It's what all of my homegirls are telling themselves, one another, me. And if we've done it right, in the next generation, there will be no mules. We've done enough—the world will have to meet us on our terms.

Sometimes, and especially in the case of Biles, the payment for being the greatest to ever do it is the choice to not have to do it again. Biles tells me about the last book she read. Titled *The Subtle Art of Not Giving a F*ck*, by Mark Manson, it's a study in the obvious. "Life fucking goes on," he writes. "We now reserve our ever-dwindling fucks only for the most truly fuckworthy parts of our lives: our families, our best friends, our golf swing. And to our astonishment, this is enough."

"The girls were laughing at me whenever I was reading that, like, 'You are just so nonchalant about everything now,'" she recalls. "Like, 'This is so nice. How do you do that?' I said, 'Just read the book. You'll learn.'" Something about this slim orange book unlocked a door to self-efficacy. It gave her the permission to provide a little bit less labor, to offer Twitter less face time. She's giving less of a fuck about the cynicism of her haters; the expectations of fans, media, her coaches, her parents; giving less of a fuck about being perfect at the expense of her own health; giving less of a fuck about the demands that take her away from healing. She's giving one less fuck and giving one back to herself.

Biles knows there is a price to setting boundaries, and she's happy to pay it. "It does mean sacrificing some of that stardom," she says. "But at the end of the day, you can't have it all. And if you take care of your mental well-being first, the rest will fall into place." Being the girl who could show up for her team and support it in more ways than winning gold is pretty cool, too. This is the legacy she'd like to leave behind: one of moral fortitude and bravery.

In all her years of competing on a national stage, Biles had never been able to just watch. "I've always made the finals. I've never sat in the crowd," she tells me. "I've always wanted to see myself, like have an out-of-body experience, and I feel like God gave that to me. I got to watch the girls and my competitors compete. I was wowed by what they did, like, *How are they doing that?* Like, *How amazing is this?*" That feeling alone, she says, made it all worth it. Because she has already lived her dream—in fact, she got to do it twice. "Making it this far? It was one in a trillion."

I ask her if she thinks there's someone out there right now, someone who could be the next one in a trillion. She pauses. "I think that's definitely feasible," she begins, then reconsiders. "But at the end of the day, to accomplish everything I've done? That talent probably cannot be matched yet. Looking at my stats, especially in gymnastics, where it's so injury-filled—I've never had a huge injury stop me from a big meet. To be so healthy for so many years? That never happens. It'll be a long time for somebody to accomplish what I've accomplished."

And so Simone Biles gets to decide what it means to be Simone Biles now. She gets to decide what she gives up. It's up to her what comes next, if anything at all. She's not sure yet. She's figuring it out. But if she never comes back to competition, that will be just fine—and if she's got anything more to give, she'll let us know.

Camonghne Felix is an American writer, poet, and communications strategist. In 2015, she was appointed as Governor Andrew Cuomo's speechwriter, and was the first Black woman and youngest person to serve in the role. Her debut poetry collection, *Build Yourself a Boat*, was longlisted for the 2019 National Book Award. She holds an M.A. in Arts Politics from NYU and an MFA from Bard College.

The Depths She'll Reach

XAN RICE

FROM Long Lead • NOVEMBER 18, 2021

An old fisherman offers a diver some advice. You can go underwater in two ways, he says, taking a bit of coral and tossing it into the sea. Then he cracks a coconut and pours its milk into the water. The coral is still coral but the milk is now sea, he says. Be not like the coral, but like the coconut.

Adapted from *Manual of Freediving*,
by Umberto Pelizzari and Stefano Tovaglieri

A girl plays with her dolls on a third floor balcony. It is summer in the mid-1980s in Koper, a small Yugoslavian city by the Adriatic Sea. Beside the girl is a tub of water; fallen petals from her mother's plants float on top. When she climbs into the tub and splashes water onto the hot tiles, she creates, as if by magic, the sweet and musty scent of rain.

The girl submerges her dolls, one by one, to make them swim—her mermaids. She wants to know how moving underwater feels. Soon she will.

The girl's father walks her down to the beach and she wades into the tidal pool. She takes a breath, sinks beneath the surface, and propels herself forward with her arms. So entranced is she by this silent and liquid otherworld that she does not see the concrete wall inlaid with seashells. Her forehead slams into it. Blood curls in the salty water.

A woman stands alone on a narrow pedestrian bridge. It is the winter of 2010 in Ljubljana, Slovenia. It is night, and the water far below is dark and very cold. More than two decades have passed since her blood met water in the tidal pool, and she has since endured so much more pain, heartache, and loss.

The woman calls out silently to the universe.

I can't do this anymore.

If she climbs over the rails and jumps, it will all be over.

A diver floats on her back above a marine cavern with a travel pillow supporting her head. It is July 2021 in The Bahamas. She wears a thin wetsuit, a tiny headlamp, and a carbon-fiber fin that resembles a mermaid's tail on her feet. She is 39 years old and the best female freediver in the world. Only a few people—all men—have dived deeper into the ocean than she has on just one breath. Someday soon she may surpass them.

The diver's face is blank, and so is her mind. This is intentional: thinking burns oxygen and the air in her lungs must take her down nearly 400 feet into Dean's Blue Hole, where it is so dark that if her light fails she may as well be blindfolded. That same breath must also bring her back up out of the blackness, toward the spears of sunlight bursting through the turquoise water.

For 210 seconds, she will be suspended in the liminal zone between this life and the next. In a place where the water's weight will wrap her in a strong hug and shrink her lungs to the size of tennis balls. Where her heart rate will slow to 30 beats a minute, and her arteries will constrict to stop blood supply to her legs and arms. Where, if her oxygen runs too low on the ascent, she will black out and rely on the white-vested safety divers to pull her to the surface, call her name, and blow on her eyelids to stimulate breathing and keep her from drifting off further, toward death.

The diver has trained for nine months for this moment. Suffered. Held her breath for so long, so many times—underwater, while walking, lying on her bed—that she imagined when her mouth finally opened again, she'd inhale the whole sky. Dived so deep, so often, she was too tired to even put the key in the lock of her apartment at the day's end.

But wait—the time frame is wrong.

She has prepared for this not just for nine months but for all her life.

From a platform floating nearby, a safety officer in a pink, wide-brimmed hat begins the countdown.

— Four minutes…

— Two minutes…

— 30 seconds…

— Five, four, three, two, one…

— Top time!

The diver takes one long breath before noisily sipping air, like a fish reeled onto the sand. Eight little breaths, packing her lungs to their limits. Then, gently, she rolls onto her stomach and duck dives, following the guide rope down. She closes her eyes. With a few flicks of her tail, the mermaid disappears.

The announcer calls out again.

-- Alenka Artnik

-- Slovenia

-- 118 meters

-- World record attempt!

The Descent

Nearly 6,000 people have climbed Mount Everest. Only a few dozen have freedived 100 meters under the ocean. We are land animals, and unless we are taught to swim while young, open water evokes primordial fears. We panic when holding our breath. A sloth can manage up to 40 minutes underwater without coming up for air. The average human might last 60 seconds.

But offer food or bounty or glory and we can go against our instincts. Ancient trash piles of shells found as far apart as the Far East and the Baltic Sea suggest our ancestors dived the ocean shallows for pearls and shellfish thousands of years ago.

Who was first to go considerably deeper, no one can say for sure, but Haggi Statti is a reasonable guess. Diving for sponges had already cost the Greek his eardrums by the time an Italian navy ship lost its anchor near Crete in 1913. Statti said he would find it. He tied a float to one end of a rope, and a stone to the other end, which he clutched in his arms as he dived. On the seabed, 76 meters down, he located the anchor, secured it, and pulled himself up.

For decades, what Statti did seemed miraculous, perhaps even apocryphal. More than 40 years later, a French Navy physiologist warned that a depth of 50 meters was the absolute limit to which a human could descend. And beyond that, doctor? One will be crushed.

But then in 1962, an Italian spear-fisherman named Enzo Maiorca, having overcome his own great fear of the sea, freedived to 51 meters using a weighted sled to speed his descent and an air balloon to help him resurface. He emerged unharmed. Fourteen years later, his French rival Jacques Mayol made it to 100 meters using the same technique. Their exploits inspired the 1988 film *The Big Blue*, and with it, a generation of freedivers.

The girl on the balcony in Koper is not one of them. Her name is Alenka Artnik, and by the late 1980s, the Balkan state is collapsing.

One morning her mother Vida comes into the room Alenka shares with her older sister Tjasi and tells the girls the war has started. Ten days later it is over, for Slovenia at least, which gains its independence, though the rest of Yugoslavia descends into chaos.

For the Artniks, however, the chaos is at home. Vida was just 18 when she married Franc, a divorcé who, unusual for the time, was granted custody of his infant son, Simon. Handsome and athletic, Simon is 10 when Alenka is born. Before he finishes school, Simon is addicted to heroin.

Because drug use is taboo in Slovenia at the time, Franc and Vida are on their own with Simon's treatment. They help set up the country's first commune for addicts and talk about the dangers of drugs on television. They send Simon to rehabilitation clinics in Italy and then, for three years, in Thailand. He is clean when he comes home. His father Franc, who drinks, is not.

Franc has always been a proud, independent man, refusing to be recruited by the Communist Party. During the workweek he runs a successful plumbing business. On weekends he disappears for hours into the woods to pick herbs, wild asparagus, and mushrooms. The pine needles that fall from his clothes upon his return lend the family apartment the smell of forest.

But soon after Simon's troubles begin, Franc's drinking gets worse. He is drunk one week, sober the next. Some days he passes out in front of the apartment building. When Alenka, still in primary school, finds alcohol at home she pours it down the drain. Franc buys more. His business flounders and Vida is forced to find work cooking in a factory canteen.

She divorces Franc but they continue to live together. He sleeps in the living room and when Vida returns from work she immediately takes refuge in her bedroom.

At night Alenka hears her mother crying and worries she might kill herself. The young girl hugs her comfort blanket, pretending she is holding her mom, keeping her safe. To escape, she slips a yellow cassette into her tape deck and loses herself in the story of Heidi, the fictional Swiss orphan who goes to live with her grandfather in the Alps.

Simon relapses and police officers knock on the door looking for him. The son and the father, the drug addict and the alcoholic, fight incessantly.

At the beach in Koper where Alenka hit her head as a young girl, there's a kayaking club. The boats are narrow and unstable but very fast. Alenka is nine when she joins the club. On the sea she forgets her family strife. All that matters is her stroke, her breathing, the water. The now.

The club becomes her second home, a refuge. She trains every day—twice on weekends—and is selected for the national junior sprint kayak team. When she is old enough to be entrusted with a clubhouse key, she starts skipping class to paddle alone.

In 1998, Alenka drops out of school at age 17 and tells her parents that she wants to become a professional kayaker. It is plausible, but bullshit. Really, she just wants to get away.

Instead it is her mother, with whom Alenka has been so close, who leaves to live with another man. Alenka's sister Tjasi has already moved to Ljubljana, Slovenia's biggest city, and Simon is who knows where. Alenka is alone with her father.

Though neither of them know it yet, Franc suffers from borderline personality disorder. The rage and psychological violence that he once aimed at his wife and son are now directed at Alenka. He blames her for his unhappiness and failures, shattering what little confidence she has. As she tries to press forward with her life, she internalizes the pressure he puts on her. But she cannot reason with him. She feels helpless, desperate. She considers suicide.

I will jump from the balcony to punish you, she thinks. *To show you how much you are hurting me.*

Vida's new life continues to pull her further from Alenka, and in 2001 she remarries. The next year, tired of her father's emotional abuse, Alenka moves to Ljubljana, where she lives like a student, working in a skate shop to pay for a room in a shared house. She drinks and parties too much—a valve to relieve the pressure of her internalized trauma. She feels alone; a string of romantic relationships fails to pull her from her depths.

One night in 2004, Simon calls Alenka from a detox clinic. Too tired of his struggles and of her own life, she doesn't answer the phone. The next day, his body surrenders to the ravages of addiction. Vida, meanwhile, is diagnosed with cancer, and after a five-year fight with the disease, she also dies.

Disconnected from her family, Alenka feels unable to mourn her brother and mother properly, and Franc, still in Koper, has been tormenting her with manipulative behavior from afar. The weight of her family's struggles has pulled her deeper into despair.

She doesn't realize it, but by that wintery 2010 night on the bridge, she is drowning in grief. Nearly ten years have passed since Alenka first thought of jumping off the balcony to punish her father. And now, alone and looking at the water below, her remaining reserves of self-esteem are nearly spent.

But her distress call to the universe triggers something deep within her. She realizes that the burden of her family's struggles has pulled her, like a weight, to this dark place, this bottom. *I don't want this; it doesn't belong to me*, she thinks. *I cannot hold it anymore.*

So, like a heavy backpack, she takes the weight off and simply lets it go. Her troubles are far from over, but Alenka is no longer paralyzed by her past. She walks off the bridge and goes home.

The Turnaround
Salvation begins, as it often does, with an act of kindness. Twelve months after Alenka's night on the bridge, one of her ex-boyfriends invites her to swim with him at a local pool. He has taken up spearfishing and, to build stamina, swims underwater lengths with a group of men.

Alenka takes a breath and slips under the water, pulling forward with her arms. She is a child again, under the sea in Koper. *All the noise of the world has disappeared*, she thinks. *I am alone but also part of something.* For the first time in a very long while she feels at peace.

The following day Alenka buys a pair of fins and makes it as far without breathing as the best of the men. Keen to know more about this curious pursuit, she signs up for a short introductory course run by one of the country's best freedivers, Jure Daić.

Daić considers someone who is able to swim 75 meters underwater, three lengths of a typical pool, by the end of his weekend course to be an excellent diver. On the course's second day, Alenka swims one length, two lengths, three lengths, and keeps going. At 92 meters one of her fins falls off. Instead of ending her dive she turns around underwater, retrieves the fin, puts it back on, and completes the length. She is angry when she gets out, explaining she wanted to reach 120 meters.

Jaws drop around the pool. Most of the others did not make it to even 50 meters.

Who is this woman?

Daić wonders the same. Alenka seems eager to learn, peppering him with questions about technique. She has also casually told one of Daić's instructors some extraordinary things.

−− I hate my fucking life.

−− I am diving to escape the planet.

Curious to know more, Daić asks Alenka about her past and it starts to make sense—her unhappiness and intense drive. Compared to other top athletes he's trained, she doesn't seem to be physically extraordinary. But it seems to him that the mental strength Alenka forged through overcoming hardship has given her an obvious edge.

In many sports, 30-year-olds are approaching the ends of their careers. Freediving is different. Divers don't just need strength, flexibility, and extraordinary breath-hold ability, but also calmness, maturity, and self-knowledge. If they try too much, too soon, they are likely to burn out—or worse.

As the kayak club had been in her youth, the pool becomes Alenka's sanctuary. Every morning before work, she glides beneath the water's surface while swimmers churn up waves above. Very quickly—only a little over a year after her first freedive—she is breaking national records during competitions.

Though Alenka's self-confidence is improving, her heartache endures. Franc's psychological abuse continues as she starts freediving, but he eventually gives her emotional distance and tells her he is proud of her diving achievements. Soon after, however, he too dies of cancer.

In 2013, Alenka is selected for the Slovenian team, but she soon realizes that being the best in her country is very different from being the best in the world. So she trains even harder—too hard. Before the pool world championships in Serbia in 2015, her workouts are so intense she loses eleven pounds. By the time the contest starts, she is so tired she fails to make the finals. But instead of feeling the disappointment she expected—like when her flipper came off—she discovers she is content with failure.

This new self-knowledge changes Alenka's priorities. Instead of medals, she wants to make up for the lost years, to live more, to discover who she really is. So she has an idea: Go on an extended solo adventure to a place where she can dive in the ocean. If she's good at open-water freediving, cool. If not, at least she'll see another part of the world.

It sounds a bit crazy, she knows. She has only been on an airplane once before. Then again, what is she risking? Besides her sister, her close family is all gone. So, on the last day of 2014, Alenka leaves her job and embarks on a new life.

In the summer 2015, Alenka travels to Vis, an island off the coast of Croatia, where she intends to relax for several weeks. She meets up with some Slovenian friends who organize freediving courses in the sea. One of them is just about to start, they tell Alenka, with special instructors: Natalia Molchanova and her son Alexey.

Natalia, a Russian athlete nicknamed "The Machine," was a good swimmer from her youth. When she discovered freediving at the age of 40, she quickly dominated the sport. In the pool, she became the first female to swim 200 meters underwater, and the first to hold her breath for eight minutes. In the ocean, she became the first woman to dive deeper than 100 meters. At 53, Natalia is the greatest freediver in history—of any gender—and still holds most of the women's world records in the pool and ocean. Alexey, meanwhile, is starting to win men's events at age 28.

Is this the universe talking to Alenka again? She had met Natalia briefly at past competitions, but now she has the chance to know her properly and learn from a master. Alenka scraps some of her holiday plans and enrolls in the course. The two women bond over their fondness for cats. Natalia shares she has just learned to surf and expresses her love of the ocean. Diving in the pool is like jogging on a treadmill, Natalia had once said, while diving in the sea is like running in the forest.

In the island waters, Alenka comes to appreciate this difference. Our bodies are slightly less dense than water, so we float near the surface and need to kick hard to dive down. But the deeper we go, the more the water above squeezes us. As the pressure increases, so does our density. Eventually, it becomes too much, and we start to sink like a stone. There's no need to kick. Gravity takes us—we're in free fall.

Alenka surrenders to the pressure, and it's the most amazing feeling. As she descends, she is nowhere but in the present moment, and nothing above the service of the water—not even her own identity—exists. She is alone, but she feels connected to everything.

I am falling to the center of the universe, she thinks. *This must be what flying feels like.*

On her deepest dive with Natalia she reaches 49 meters and excitedly tells Alexey, a playful man with thighs like a wrestler.

–– OK, but it's not 50 meters, he responds.

–– One day I'll break the record, she jokes.

–– Really?

–– Yes, *your* record.

After the freediving course finishes, Natalia plans to stay on the island to train, but she receives a call from a wealthy couple requesting private lessons near Spain. Alenka accompanies Natalia to the ferry and waves goodbye. A few days later, Alexey leaves suddenly, too. When the divers on Vis—and around the world—learn why, there is disbelief.

Natalia is missing.

After her clients' class, she makes a dive—but never surfaces.

Despite a vast search, Natalia's body is never found. It is believed she was swept away by strong underwater currents.

Two months later, Alenka arrives in the Egyptian Red Sea city of Sharm el Sheikh with two brand-new suitcases, two wetsuits, and two sets of flippers. It is October 2015 and she is 34 years old. She takes a taxi along the desert coast to Dahab, a former fishing village that is now a diving hub.

Everything there is overwhelming: the desert, the heat, the language, the food. Alenka does not know a soul. But the water is magical. She swims out to the reef, teeming with fish, yellow, orange, purple, and blue. When she turns to face the shore and sees Mount Sinai in the distance and hears the calls to prayer, she feels like crying with joy.

Alenka rents a small, run-down Bedouin house. She seals the leaky sinks with silicon, paints the walls, and buys lamps and carpets in a bazaar. Two stray dogs and several cats move in.

In the mornings, she jumps on the back of a pickup truck with other divers for the short drive to Dahab's Blue Hole, an underwater pit more than 100 meters deep. From her pool training, she is strong and her breath-hold is good. The question is how she will cope with extreme depth.

A set of evolutionary responses known as the mammalian dive reflex offer us some natural protection underwater. Immerse your face in cold water and hold your breath, and your heart rate will drop automatically to conserve air. At the same time, your arteries will narrow, forcing blood to shift from your limbs to your vital organs. This prevents the lungs from being crushed, as deeper waters put immense pressure on your body.

But there remains the problem of the empty spaces inside us. At sea level, the pressure of water is defined as one atmosphere. Ten meters down, the weight of the water doubles it to two atmospheres. At 20 meters it triples, and so on. Most of our bodies are made up of water or solids, which cannot be compressed. But the empty spaces, like inside our lungs and inner ears, hold gasses and can succumb to the pressure.

As divers descend, the water's pressure forces their eardrums inward, causing a sharp pain. To avoid this, they must continually shift air into their inner ears as they sink. This pushes the eardrums back to the natural position, "equalizing" the pressure inside their head with the force pushing from the outside.

The simplest way to equalize is to close your mouth, pinch your nose and clench your stomach muscles, forcing air upwards out of the lungs. Deeper down, divers use more physically economical but technically difficult equalization methods involving the tongue, cheeks, and throat.

Experienced ocean divers can struggle for years to master equalization. But Alenka, relying on training partners, online diving forums, and her own intuition for guidance, has little trouble, and every day she goes deeper. By New Year's Day 2016, when the water has turned uncomfortably cold, her best monofin dive is 77 meters. She now knows she can handle the depths.

To conserve air as she sinks, Alenka must enter a meditative, zen-like state. One day, turning around to start her ascent, an image of her half-brother Simon appears, staring at her calmly, confidently, under the water. It is the face of a man who was never addicted to drugs, of the person he could have become. Simon's presence gifts Alenka with tranquility, and she uses that peace to smoothly push to the water's surface.

That night in her house, she tries to process what happened. For years Alenka had resented Simon for the pain he caused the family, especially her parents. Now, in floods of tears, she feels immense sorrow for all that he endured, all that he missed out on.

By the time Alenka leaves Dahab nine months after her arrival, she has dived down to 92 meters, just nine meters off the women's monofin world record. The 2016 world championship in Turkey is coming up, and Slovenia chooses her to represent the country at the event. She is the only diver from Slovenia to compete.

Still a complete unknown in the competitive ocean freediving world, Alenka stuns the competition by winning the monofin event with an 86-meter dive. In the bi-fin discipline, she also finishes first—and breaks the world record.

The Ascent

Freediving comes with mortal risk, mostly for spearfishers and recreational athletes, but also for elite ones, as Natalia Molchanova's death shows. Push too hard on the way down and you may suffer a "squeeze," the lung tissue tearing as it is compressed, forcing you to cough up blood. Mismanage the timing on the way up and you may black out as the brain shuts down in order to preserve the little oxygen remaining in the body.

Thankfully, due to strict protocols and the presence of safety divers, fatalities are extremely rare in freediving competitions, though they are not unheard of. In 2013, the American Nicholas Mevoli died from lung injuries while attempting a 72-meter, no-fins dive at Vertical Blue, a competition in The Bahamas that is the highlight of the year for expert divers.

Alenka receives her first offer to dive there in 2018, soon after becoming only the fourth woman to dive to 100 meters, behind Natalia Molchanova, and two athletes also on the Vertical Blue roster, Japan's Hanako Hirose and Alessia Zecchini, a 26-year-old Italian prodigy who started diving at age 13.

Like pole-vaulters, free divers must announce their targets before they begin. For each competitor, the organizers adjust the length of the rope, at the bottom of which is a plate covered with Velcro tags. For the attempt to be successful, the diver, upon surfacing, must hand a tag to the judge, make the "okay" signal with their fingers and thumb, and remain conscious with their head above the water for 20 seconds.

Alenka starts her Vertical Blue dives with a 100-meter plunge and completes it easily. A few days later, 103 meters. Then a meter deeper. If she can manage 105 meters, she will equal Zecchini's world record. On the live internet stream of the dive, the commentator remarks on Alenka's "perfect control, perfect technique" after she comes up.

Hirose and Zecchini also reach 105 meters. Each diver has another two dives to go deeper. But a voice in Alenka's head tells her to pause.

You need more time at these depths, she thinks. *You are strong enough to stop here.*

Hirose pushes on to 106 meters and then attempts 107 meters. On the ascent she blacks out. Zecchini tries for 107 meters and triumphs.

Alenka's decision to step away after such a comfortable dive puzzles other competitors. Why quit when you have a chance to win, to claim a new world record, and to raise your international profile? Alenka has no partner, no kids, and no job to return to. What does she have to lose?

But Alenka's personal descent has taught her something: When you've been to the very edge of the abyss and found what makes you want to return to the surface—to live—you have *everything* to lose.

If anyone had asked, she would have answered:

-- I feel too responsible to life to do something just because of my ego.

This is why Alenka has never experienced a lung squeeze, why she has been one of the very few competitors to have never felt the breath of a safety diver on her eyelids to coax her out of that breathless, mammalian state. This is why she still, to this day, has never blacked out.

She refuses to become a danger to herself.

But dangerous to her rivals? That will come.

The small sparkly stud Alenka wears beneath the left corner of her mouth is not a diamond. Winning a big freediving contest earns you a medal, admiration, and nothing more. She is burning through cash, and needs sponsorship to continue, so she applies to the Slovenian government for funding. To help elite athletes in sports with low prize money and limited commercial appeal, and in exchange for them promoting a healthy lifestyle, the interior ministry can put them on its payroll. This is how Alenka becomes a policewoman, without ever spending a day on the beat—or more than a few weeks at a time in her own home country.

In fact, Alenka stays nowhere for long and becomes a nomad, training in the tropics for the first half of the year to prepare for summer competitions. It is an enviable but lonely life, going from one place to another, always seeking out new training partners. In early 2019 on Panglao, an island in the Philippines, she meets a Swiss freediver, Florian Burghardt, who has taken a break from his job at a bank to get more serious about the sport.

He and Alenka talk, have coffee, and slowly fall in love. Burghardt spends the season with her, watching as she dives to 113 meters in Honduras, a world record depth matched by Zecchini in the same competition.

A year later, when COVID-19 becomes a global pandemic, the couple are back in the Philippines, stuck in a resort. The beaches are declared off limits so Alenka and Burghardt stock up on tinned tomatoes and pasta and olive oil and adapt their training methods. Alenka goes on what she calls "apnea walks," holding her breath while dodging the cows on the path.

In the resort's pool, increasingly cloudy with dirt, she holds her breath for 30 seconds and then swims ten laps—200 meters—underwater. Lying still in the water she improves her breath-hold personal best to 6 minutes and 40 seconds.

The pandemic quashes the 2020 competition season, but small, one-off events are held. In Kalamata, Greece, Alenka breaks the bi-fin world record, reaching 94 meters, but poor conditions scuttle her monofin dive. So, after a brief stop in Switzerland, where she and Burghardt get engaged, she flies alone back to Sharm el-Sheikh and announces her target: 114 meters.

The contest in Egypt is planned for two days, to insure against problems with the weather or water. Ahead of her dive, Alenka books a flight home for the first night of the competition. Tito Zappala, the Italian safety diver for the record attempt, hears Alenka's plans and he thinks to himself, fuck, she has it in her pocket.

And he's not wrong. When Alenka passes him on her ascent she smiles. The ease and control with which she completes her dive move Zappala to tears. It brings to his mind the story of the coral, the coconut, and the sea.

Alenka, he says, is milk in the water.

How does this happen? How do you go from having no confidence at age 30, to being the most assured, deepest female diver in the world just a decade later? From nearly taking your life, to making elite athletes shake their heads in astonishment at your achievements and lack of ego? From hating life so much to loving it so deeply?

These are questions people sometimes ask, and one part of the answer is that Alenka not only came to terms with her past— she drew strength from it.

–– It's because of the pain, she says. I surrendered to the pain, embraced it; that's when you get the big growth.

The other part of the answer is simpler. She trains like hell.

Alenka shares a small apartment with Burghardt in Collonges-sous-Salève, a French village near the border with Switzerland. It is winter, late January 2021, and there's snow on the nearby mountains. The pandemic has closed the local swimming pools, so she must train out of the water.

A contraption of bungee cords hangs from the ceiling of Alenka's living room. She jokes it looks like BDSM gear—it's not, but it is designed to deliver pain. She drops to the floor in a plank position, resting on her forearms, and then slides her feet into two resistance band loops that hang 30 centimeters off the ground. Then she kicks, feet together, dolphin-style, again and again and again until her legs burn so much she has to stop.

Another torturous workout device she employs is a half-moon bridge made of wood and typically used in pilates. Alenka uses it to increase the flexibility of her diaphragm and the capacity of her lungs. With her head almost touching the floor, she slips the bridge under her spine, stretching her back and the muscles between her ribs. Afterward, she lies flat, her knees raised, and inhales deeply, her chest bursting upwards like a balloon being inflated. Then, in an interminable exhale, the air rushes out of her mouth with the hiss of a punctured tire.

Weights. Squats while holding her breath. Lying on her bed with her mouth and nose closed for minutes a time, fighting the impulse to inhale—a technique known as dry static apnea.

In the evening Burghardt returns home from work. He and Alenka prepare dinner: pasta with mushrooms and sour cream and asparagus, a dish her father used to make. A green salad with raspberries on the side. Red wine from a bottle whose label reads *Seul l'avenir m'intéresse*, translated as "only the future interests me." An interesting choice, Burghardt points out, for athletes who must stay in the present.

What of the future though? Alenka is 39, becoming stronger, and diving more efficiently each year. The next major milestone for female divers is 120 meters. And while it will not be easy, it is reachable, she says, perhaps even in the forthcoming competition season, which begins with the Vertical Blue event in July. That would take the women tantalizingly close to the men's record, just 10 meters away. In 2017, the male-female gap was 28 meters, bigger than a six-story building.

The women's surge is partly due to the rivalry between Alenka and Alessia Zecchini, and partly due to catch-up. In the past there were far fewer serious female freedivers than male; as this changes, women are getting closer to reaching their potential.

Can women challenge the men's record? Before Vertical Blue, Alexey Molchanov, Natalia's son, says he doubts it. Freediving's deepest man says he has not had any strong competition in recent years to push him, and he reckons he has reserves to go 10 to 15 meters farther.

But Erika Schagatay, professor of environmental physiology at Mid Sweden University, and an expert on freediving, says they can. Relative to body size, males have the advantage of larger lungs and spleens, which hold a reserve of blood. Females, meanwhile, benefit from a more spread-out fat layer, making it easier to adapt to the cold water found at depth.

More than 700 islands make up The Bahamas but most of its people live in just two, New Providence and Grand Bahama. The others are known as the Out Islands and most, including Long Island, receive few tourists. Rent a car before landing at Deadman's Cay airport and you might receive an email which also informs you the keys are in the gas cover and you can spot your red Ford Fiesta by looking to the right after the plane lands.

There is one road south, crossed by goats, feral pigs, and vast casts of red-and-black land crabs. Left, right, left, right, crunch. Soon, a dirt track winds its way to a turquoise bay with a dark blot at its edge: Dean's Blue Hole. Just a few strokes from the shore, the depth plunges to 202 meters, through a gap that opened in the limestone bedrock during a distant ice age.

In early June 2021, with Vertical Blue a month away, the world's top free divers—42 athletes from 21 countries—begin arriving at the beach to acclimatize. Alenka and Burghardt fly in from Honduras, where they have been training for four months, and rent a pink cottage overlooking the Atlantic.

It's hard to keep your depth goal a secret when everyone is practicing on the same rope, but even so there is a buzz of surprise when the opening day's schedule is published. Alessia Zecchini will attempt 115 meters, one meter deeper than Alenka's monofin record. Diving immediately afterwards, Alenka will try for 118 meters.

She spends the day before the competition visualizing the dive and watching an old, familiar animated series for children that she has discovered on YouTube. The stories and voices are identical to those she listened to on cassette as a little girl in her bedroom in Koper. She sings along with the theme song.

–– Heidi, *Heidi…*

On Vertical Blue's opening day, the first athlete to dive blacks out upon reaching the surface. After him, a few divers are successful and a few, unable to cope with the depth, turn back before reaching the bottom plate. The beach is soon a tangle of flip flops, fins, and pool noodles, used by competitors as a flotation aid during the countdown.

Before swimming out to the floating platform to wait for their turns, Zecchini and Alenka share a long hug on the beach. The Italian goes first. Her dive is smooth, and when she completes the surface protocol, the athletes treading water around the competition zone slap the water in celebration.

Then the rope is lowered by three meters.

Alenka floats on her back with a travel pillow supporting her head. The pink-hatted safety officer counts down. Alenka prepares to dive. The long breath. The eight lung-packing sips of air. The roll over. The duck dive. With a flick of her fin, the diver disappears into the blue hole, arms loosely by her sides.

Strapped to her four-pound neck weight, a dive watch with five alarms alerts her to the depth as she descends. When the second-to-last beep sounds at 68 meters, she kicks a few final times before submitting to free fall. Water rushes past her face, the guide rope comforting her as it slips past her right shoulder.

Hearing the final beep, the diver opens her eyes, reaches for the tag, and turns around, all in one motion. She stretches her arms in front of her, hands together, and kicks hard.

At the surface, an announcer watching the sonar screen narrates the ascent:

-- 80 meters…60 meters…

The first safety diver swims down to meet her. Now, the second.

-- 29 meters. Diver in sight!

The diver bursts through the surface, grabs the rope with her right hand and removes her nose clip with her left. She makes the "okay" sign, and smiles. She takes the tag out of her hood, where she stashed it, and passes it to the judge who flashes a white card, signaling a successful dive.

-- Rock'n roll, she says.

Alenka celebrates with Burghardt by going for an omelette and coffee at a roadside cafe. She's happy but not triumphant. The idea that she is better than anyone else because of the record is total bullshit, she says. People cannot understand that for her, 118 meters is just a number, a logical consequence of her training.

— The outside world wants egos and fights and titles, she says. It's not easy to be unaffected. But it's possible.

Four days later, Alenka becomes the first woman to break 120 meters. Then, on her final dive of the competition, she goes two meters farther. In little over a week she has advanced the women's mark by eight meters, to 122 meters. Only Alexey Molchanov has been deeper at Vertical Blue, extending his world record to 131 meters.

With just nine meters of breathing room between him and Alenka, Alexey now has competition in the monofin event. What she said to him in jest six years ago, at the very start of her ocean-diving career, no longer sounds like a joke.

— One day I'll break the record.

— Really?

— Yes, *your* record.

If you or someone you know are in emotional crisis or have had thoughts about suicide, free support and coping resources are available. Certified listeners with the The National Suicide Prevention Lifeline are available 24 hours a day, seven days per week at 1-800-273-8255. The Crisis Text Line is a free, confidential texting service, also available around the clock, for people experiencing emotional crises. Trained crisis counselors are available by texting 741741 in the U.S, by texting 85258 in the U.K., and by text at 50808 in Ireland. The Crisis Text Line also offers services in Spanish.

Xan Rice was formerly the foreign correspondent for *The (London) Times*, *The Guardian*, and the *Financial Times*, and features editor for the *New Statesman*. His work has also appeared in *The New Yorker*, *The Atlantic*, the *Guardian Long Read*, *Granta*, *Popular Science*, and Long Lead.

Let Us Appreciate the Grace and Uncommon Decency of Henry Aaron

HOWARD BRYANT

FROM ESPN • JANUARY 23, 2021

When I first reached out to Henry Aaron to tell him I was interested in writing a book about his life, he did not want to talk to me. He was convinced the public had no interest in him, except to have him serve as their proxy to criticize Barry Bonds as Bonds neared his all-time home run record. Henry's titanic statistical achievements cemented, he was tired of the constant misinterpretation of his worldview. The journalistic response to his critique of race relations had turned him inward. In print, he saw himself portrayed as bitter, always bitter, when in fact he was merely telling the story of his life—answering the questions he was asked. When we first spoke, he was resigned to the idea that people did not want to really know him. Instead, they wanted him to reflect a sense of their own better selves. His perspective of his greatest moment—breaking Babe Ruth's all-time home run record—was somehow less important than theirs, and his view that the greatest moment of his career finally ended the worst period of his athletic life complicated their enjoyment that the night of April 8, 1974, brought them. The public reduced the effects of his own journey to him simply being bitter without cause.

I asked him whether he wanted to be known. "Yes, I do," he told me. "But whenever I say something, the writers get it wrong. Then they try to correct it, and then I have to correct the correction, and finally I just decided it wasn't worth it. Don't say anything. Keep to myself. If you don't say anything, they can't get it wrong."

Henry's critique was central to his life, and the critique was a simultaneously gentle yet ferocious indictment. Over the course of his 86 years, America asked him to do everything right. It asked him to pull himself up by his bootstraps: Henry's father had built the family house with saved money and leftover planks of wood and nails he scavenged from vacant lots around the Toulminville section of Mobile, while he had taught himself to play baseball. America asked him to put in the hours and the hard work and to not complain: Henry played 23 seasons and never once went on the then-disabled list after his rookie season ended three weeks early because of a broken ankle. No special favors. No handouts. America asked him to believe in meritocracy, the meritocracy of the record books and the scoreboard.

America asked him to do all of the things, and when he did them, he found himself at the top of his nation's greatest sporting profession through the merit of statistics. In return, the FBI told him his daughter was the target of a kidnapping plot. For nearly three years he required a police escort and an FBI detail for himself and his family. He finished the 1973 season with 713 home runs—one shy of tying Ruth's record—and believed he would be assassinated in the offseason. He had received enough letters to convince him so. He received death threats from 1972 to 1974—all for doing what America asked of him.

He was unconvinced a writer would take him seriously, because over his lifetime precious few had. As he seemed to warm to the idea—or at least not view it hostilely—he asked me a question I would never forget: "How many pages will it be?" It seemed so odd—yet the question was self-explanatory and my response would telegraph to him how seriously I took the project. Biographies of towering figures in the classically grand tradition are thick. They are doorstops. They are meaty paperweights that sit on the bookshelves whose girth scream importance—even if 95% of the population never finishes them, even if I was thinking, "Mr. Aaron, the only thing worse than writing a lousy book is writing a really long, lousy book." To him, big people got big books, and because he did not yet have one, he did not think people cared. Henry wanted to make sure I was willing to put in the work to understand a life.

He possessed an uncommon decency, a quality in short supply today. His decency convinced him no one was interested in him, not because he did not believe his life was important, but because he was not an anti-hero whose deep flaws, scandal and misdeeds made him more marketable. He was just a solid person. No jail. No arrests. No substance abuse, falls from grace, or mistresses.

Henry understood at once his place in the world and how his talent had created a different lane for him. The people who once dismissed him, and his people, made exceptions for him because he was The Hank Aaron. He was rightfully distrusting of them. He watched the change in how America viewed him as his talent kept proving its cultural racism wrong. And instead of his constant defeat of its presuppositions, the culture did not change, but in its eyes, he did. Henry became *dignified.*

In the African American story, *dignity* is such a sly and deceptive word, simultaneously complimentary and condescending, and dignity was attached to Henry like a surname. Its affixation to him, of course, said more about his world than it ever did about him. For what was called dignity was simply an acceptable response to hostility, and it was easier for writers and broadcasters, fans and executives to concentrate on his response to hostility than the hostility itself. It is a common expectation of African Americans that they be more conciliatory and not

vengeful, invested and not apathetic, constantly brave and aspir-
ing and *dignified* in the hostile territory of indignity. When he
smiled at the hostility, he was dignified. When he did not, he was
bitter. *Dignity* has always felt like code for treating white incivility
as inevitable behavior, of not ever punching the punchers.

His life seemed to mimic his career, a long, triumphant
marathon where in the end his values proved sturdier than the
temporary sensations of the moment. And through all the years—
like hitting 20 home runs for 20 straight years—he was still there.

There was a hidden fear I felt for my own family that I also
felt for him: the worry that Black people in their 80s and 90s
would die before the 2020 election, and during the last part of
their lives they would bear witness to both the elation of an
African American president and a hostile response so severe it
was reminiscent of the previous backlashes to Black success. I
was with Henry at his house in Atlanta on Oct. 1, 2008. After we
had finished talking, he and his wife, Billye, were heading to the
polls to vote early for Barack Obama, the act of doing so its own
statement. Her first husband was the late civil rights activist and
Morehouse College professor Dr. Samuel Woodrow Williams,
and before his death in 1970, Billye had long been part of the
Atlanta civil rights movement. The Braves moved to Atlanta after
the 1965 season, and Henry met with Andrew Young, Ralph
Abernathy and Martin Luther King, Jr., and told them he did
not believe he was sufficiently doing his part in the movement.
King and Young assured him that as a Black pro sports star in the
South, his role was significant. To cast a presidential ballot for a
Black man 42 years later was for them a major emotional event.

When Henry and I last saw each other, in Atlanta in early
2018, this—along with tennis ("Do you think Serena will get
another one?" he asked) and the NFL playoffs—is what we
talked about. And he reminded me of his father working at the
Mobile shipyard during World War II, when white workers rioted
because African Americans were being hired, taking what they

believed was theirs and theirs only. Henry was dignified, but he never forgot what was done to his people and by whom.

He never mentioned not surviving the vicious presidency of the past four years, but I worried about it for him, as I did for all the Black people of his generation for whom the vote was something some had literally died for—a vote that today was being strategically suppressed and delegitimized. When I wished him a Happy New Year a few weeks ago, he was grateful for surviving, and excited for Georgia. What he saw in the country reminded him of where it had been, of how deeply the past had wounded him, and he feared seeing the past in the future. We talked about losing Joe Morgan and Jimmy Wynn, Tom Seaver and Whitey Ford and Bob Gibson and Lou Brock and Al Kaline with pain and absolutely no hints that day that he and I would never speak again.

Before we hung up the phone, he said what he always said, "Call, any time. I love when we talk," and I said I would, but I also knew the truth: I never called him nearly enough because he was the great man, Henry Aaron, and one does not respect an invitation by overstaying one's welcome. Now, that time cannot be recovered.

When he was behind Ruth, he was ahead of America. When he passed Ruth, America still had not caught up to him—and now, respected as royalty, I asked him if there was ever a quiet moment when he could sit back with an umbrella in his drink and revel in triumph, that he indeed had made it. He said yes so many times, delighted in the happiness he had not felt in 1974, making bitterness the inappropriate adjective it always had been. He challenged baseball and had reconciled with it. He was an unquestioned immortal, no longer slighted. Jeff Idelson, former president of the National Baseball Hall of Fame and Museum, saw to that, as did his friend and former baseball commissioner, Bud Selig, who made it clear to all underlings at MLB that Henry was a made man, not to be harassed. President George W. Bush awarded him the Presidential Medal of Freedom.

In 2009, Henry, his wife, Billye, and I were sitting in a conference room at the Hall of Fame in Cooperstown. I was trying to comprehend the historical arc of Henry Aaron, and told him he represented so much of the Black American aspirational journey. I said to him, "You went from your mother hiding you under the bed when the Klan marched down your street as a toddler to sleeping in the White House as the invited guests of the president."

"No, no, no, Mr. Bryant," Billye Aaron interrupted me with a proud smile. "We didn't sleep at the White House. We slept at the White House *twice*."

Howard Bryant has been a senior writer for ESPN.com since 2007 and the sports correspondent for NPR's *Weekend Edition Saturday* since 2006. He is the author of 10 books and was a finalist for the National Magazine Award in 2016, 2018, and 2021.

Felipe Ruiz Took the Ride of His Life Working as Tommy Lasorda's Assistant

BILL PLASCHKE

FROM the *Los Angeles Times* • FEBRUARY 1, 2021

He was always there, but he was never there.

For the last six years of Tommy Lasorda's life, Felipe Ruiz accompanied him from the shadows.

He would drive the black SUV that ferried Lasorda to countless public appearances.

He would stand near Lasorda and keep the line moving during endless autograph sessions.

He would sit near Lasorda next to the dugout during games at Dodger Stadium, later helping him navigate the stairs and crowds when it was time to leave.

Look closely at photos of the gregarious, white-haired Lasorda and you will often see a gently smiling dark-skinned man looming behind him, always behind him, always there to laugh at his jokes and brush food off his collar and smooth the increasingly rocky path for baseball's aging ambassador.

The 33-year-old former home security salesman did his job so quietly and efficiently that few knew his role, and fewer knew his name. Lasorda didn't even call him by that name, referring to him as "Flip," or "My right-hand man," or simply, "My guy."

For six years Felipe Ruiz was an anonymous part of the rich pageant that was life with Lasorda, the unknown half of the Dodgers' oddest of couples, officially his executive assistant, unofficially his prop master and set dresser.

Then came the evening of Jan. 7, when it became clear this relationship was about much, much more.

Lasorda was resting at his Fullerton home after an extended hospital stay for a failing heart. He was suddenly hungry. He craved ice cream. He called for his guy.

Ruiz was there. Of course he was there. He slept in a chair next to Lasorda during Lasorda's extended hospital stays. He later moved in with Lasorda to help care for him during the pandemic.

On this night, as always, Ruiz heeded the call. He ordered out for the ice cream. He procured a cup of rainbow sherbet. He carefully spoon-fed it to Lasorda, who kept asking for more, and more, until he finished the entire serving of the brightly colored dessert.

Shortly thereafter, Lasorda's heart stopped. An ambulance rushed him to St. Jude Medical Center, where he was pronounced dead at the age of 93. Driving frantically behind the flashing lights, Ruiz broke down in tears upon realizing the magnitude of the moment.

He was losing more than a boss, he was losing family. While it seemed like he was behind him, he was really by his side. All this time everyone thought Ruiz was behind the curtain, Lasorda had actually been pulling him onto the stage.

In the end, Felipe Ruiz was so connected to Tommy Lasorda that the world's greatest eater called upon him to share his last meal.

"He was my best friend, my life mentor, my father, my grand-father," Ruiz said. "He didn't treat me like an employee, he treated me like a son."

No shadows here, only light.

THIS UNLIKELIEST OF PARTNERSHIPS BEGAN, appropriately, as a joke.

"A total joke," Ruiz said.

In the summer of 2015, Ruiz was installing a security system in a modest Fullerton house when Lasorda came home. Ruiz, a former junior college baseball player who was born in Torrance and had Dodgers season tickets, was star-struck.

"I couldn't believe I was actually standing in his house and that this was actually him," Ruiz said.

The old manager was impressed with the security setup and asked the dazed kid a bunch of questions. Before the dazed kid left, he handed Lasorda his business card and impulsively made a crazy offer.

"I told him I lived in Fullerton and had season tickets and if he ever needed a ride to Dodger Stadium, just call," Ruiz recounted. "I said it for fun. I never dreamed he'd ever call."

A week later, Lasorda called. He needed a ride to a game. Ruiz ran out of work and drove him to Dodger Stadium in the company minivan. A few days after that, Lasorda called again. He needed a ride to the doctor. Ruiz left work again and drove him.

For the next six months, as many as three times a week, Ruiz drove Lasorda all over Southern California. He did it for free. Frank Sinatra would be blaring from the dashboard, Lasorda would be telling stories from the backseat, and that was compensation enough.

"Are you kidding me?" Ruiz said. "I was living my dream."

Little did Ruiz know, Lasorda was in the process of changing executive assistants, and one day he put his prospective employee to the test.

Ruiz picked up Lasorda in Fullerton at 7 a.m., drove him to breakfast, drove him to his Dodger Stadium office to answer fan mail, drove him down to Manhattan Beach for lunch and an appearance, drove him to Ontario to hang out with friends, stayed there with him during a long and late Italian dinner, and was finally driving him back to Fullerton at 2:30 a.m. when a question was shouted from the backseat.

"Lemme ask you something," Lasorda said. "Are you tired?"

"Yeah Tommy, we've been going all day, I'm pretty beat," Ruiz said.

"Damn it, at your age I was never tired!" boomed Lasorda.

A few minutes later Lasorda asked the question again. This time, Ruiz was ready.

"No, Tommy, I'm not tired, because we don't get tired!" Ruiz hollered.

Test passed. Relationship forged. At the start of spring training in 2016, at Lasorda's insistence, Ruiz was given a full-time job by the Dodgers and accompanied Lasorda to Camelback Ranch.

"It's amazing that Tommy took a chance on me," Ruiz said. "I wasn't some famous former ballplayer or somebody with connections. All I had to offer him was loyalty and love."

For Lasorda, that was always enough, and thus began the ride of Felipe Ruiz's life.

It was a journey that took him to 30 states, 20 baseball stadiums, and included a trip to Cuba that featured a Havana ditch digger who recognized Lasorda, dropped his shovel and ran into the street to greet him.

It was a ride that featured late-night calls to Ruiz when the remote didn't work, impromptu calls to Ruiz for rides to the hospital to visit cancer patients, and eventually a request that Ruiz answer his flip phone when he got calls from strangers.

"Felipe was Tommy's security blanket ... he was his bench coach," said Mark Langill, Dodgers historian. "He took care of this older icon with such dignity, any vulnerability Tommy ever felt, as long as he had Felipe, he knew he wasn't alone."

Through it all, few noticed Ruiz, but he never cared.

"It was Tommy's show, and I was lucky to be there," he said. "Besides, I was getting the best education in the world. I was learning at Lasorda University."

There were lessons about manners. Lasorda once scolded Ruiz for getting off an elevator ahead of two women, and Ruiz constantly heard him reminding autograph seekers to say "please" and "thank you."

There were lessons about toughness. Ruiz accompanied Lasorda into the Dodgers clubhouse before every home game and listened to him act like he was still managing as he scolded and praised and exhorted even the biggest of Dodgers stars.

Every famous Lasorda speech, Ruiz has heard dozens of times. Every inspirational story, he can repeat verbatim. In fact, when Lasorda's memory began fading in his final months, he would sometimes ask Ruiz to repeat those stories for him.

"The great man took me under his wing and taught me in so many ways that I've got to believe in myself, that I can do anything I want to do," Ruiz said.

Finally, in those last months, in the last baseball experience of Lasorda's hardball life, he taught Ruiz about resilience.

Ruiz accompanied the ailing and frail Lasorda to Texas for Game 6 of the 2020 World Series. After the Dodgers beat the Tampa Bay Rays and clinched their first title since Lasorda managed them in 1988, Ruiz helped take him to the hotel to rest for the return flight home. At least, he tried.

"Are you crazy!" Lasorda shouted when he realized what was happening. "We just won the World Series and we're going to bed? No way! I'm not missing the party! We're going back out."

So Ruiz took him back out to the team hotel where, with all the players in quarantine, Lasorda pretty much was the party. He held court. He kept the bar open. They did not return to their hotel until 6:30 a.m., barely in time to pack and prepare for their 9 a.m. flight home.

"That was Tommy's last hurrah, showing his love for the Dodgers until the end," Ruiz said.

Lasorda also showed his love for Ruiz until the end, eventually adopting Ruiz's family as his own. He showered Ruiz's three children with gifts, spoke to their youth league teams and even stopped by mother Irma's house on his 93rd birthday.

"God has a special place reserved for you for giving me this man," Lasorda told her. "Thank you for him."

Today it is Ruiz who gives thanks, for the lessons from the back of the car, for the experiences of associating with presidents and superstars, for Tommy being Tommy.

"I realize that all this time, he was coaching my life," Ruiz said.

Meanwhile, the Lasorda family gives thanks for Ruiz.

"Felipe would take a bullet for my dad," said Lasorda's daughter Laura. "Him coming into our lives was surely some sort of divine intervention. I truly believe he is an angel."

Shortly before Lasorda's death, the old manager made one last request of the dazed kid. Lasorda asked him to watch over wife Jo, Laura and granddaughter Emily.

"Whatever you do, take care of my girls," Lasorda asked him.

"I will, Tommy, I will," Ruiz said.

And so he remains today amid the immense silence of Lasorda's Fullerton home, helping to care for Jo.

"I don't know if this is my job," he said, "but I know it's my responsibility."

He was driving Jo on the freeway recently when, stuck behind traffic in the middle lane, he suddenly heard a familiar voice.

"Get your butt over there in the diamond lane!" barked the spirit of Tommy Lasorda.

Felipe Ruiz cried, then laughed, then veered left.

Bill Plaschke has been a sports columnist for the *Los Angeles Times* since 1996. He has been voted the nation's top sports columnist eight times by the Associated Press Sports Editors in the large newspaper category. He has authored six books and appeared in the movie *Ali* and the TV series *Luck*. He is tolerated by his three children, Tessa, Willie, and MC.

Living Nonbinary in a Binary Sports World

FRANKIE DE LA CRETAZ

FROM *Sports Illustrated* • APRIL 16, 2021

It was in the WNBA bubble—the Wubble—that New York Liberty guard Layshia Clarendon made the decision. The Wubble was a stressful experience for Clarendon. For one, they were living through a pandemic. For another, life at the IMG Academy in Bradenton, Fla., was very small. Clarendon shuffled among their villa, the gym and games, like *Groundhog Day* designed for a professional athlete. They had also left their pregnant wife at home. (Clarendon alternately uses she, he and they pronouns.)

In her little time off, Clarendon became the face—and the force—behind the WNBA's Say Her Name campaign, thinking about and talking about Black death on a near constant basis, busy with calls and webinars and brainstorming sessions. It was important work, and Clarendon felt called to do it, but it was draining, too. And there was another stressor that was draining Clarendon, one he wasn't posting about on social media or sharing in postgame interviews: He couldn't stop thinking about his chest.

Clarendon had no idea whether the WNBA would support their decision to have top surgery, a gender affirmation procedure that removes a person's breasts and reshapes their chest to be flat, but they knew they would have the surgery regardless of how the league responded. The medical decision was not the struggle for Clarendon; the challenge was in figuring out whether she would be accepted by a sports world that was not designed for nonbinary trans people like her; she'd quietly updated the pronouns in her Twitter bio over the summer, but this was something different altogether. In the binary world of sports, leagues exist for men and for women. Clarendon sometimes feels like both of those things and other times feels like neither.

"It was something for me that was causing a lot of mental health issues," Clarendon, 29, says of the worry about whether to move forward with top surgery and whether the WNBA would allow it—and what it would mean for his career if the league didn't. "It made being in the bubble even harder than it [already] was." It opened up a whole slate of questions that she had to consider, so after the season was over, she went to Terri Jackson, the executive director of the Women's National Basketball Players Association (WNBPA). There was no precedent for this, but Jackson was all in to support Clarendon.

It's generally considered bad form to focus on the particulars of trans people's bodies, but as a professional athlete, the decisions Clarendon—or any trans athlete—makes about their body are incredibly consequential. Careers can hinge on them. The questions Clarendon considered included: *What will the recovery look like and how will it impact my 2021 season? The league and my team have a right to know a lot about my body because it affects my play, but is there anything personal that the league can't ask me about? I know I am going to publicly talk about my top surgery, but what if another player has top or bottom surgery and doesn't want to share that with their team or the public? If the league doesn't support me, can I be fired?*

When I first spoke to Clarendon in December, a few weeks before their surgery, they were still trying to navigate these conversations with the WNBA. Luckily, they received the "full support" of commissioner Cathy Engelbert, as well as the Liberty and the WNBPA. On Jan. 29, the day that Clarendon announced her surgery on social media, coordinated statements went out from each of the league accounts, too.

It was a stark contrast to how the National Women's Soccer League responded when Quinn, a midfielder for the OL Reign, came out as nonbinary and transgender on Instagram in September 2020.

"I wanted to make sure that my identity was represented in my workplace, and in the public sphere," Quinn, 25, says now of the decision to post about their identity on social media. Their teammates and coach knew, but the public did not, which meant that Quinn had to deal with being misgendered in the press—having the wrong pronouns used—and feeling invisible on a daily basis. "I really wanted to be another visible person in the sports realm, especially playing at such a high level. I wanted to help others that were looking for people like themselves in sport."

Quinn's Instagram post made headlines. But while their announcement was met mostly with support from the public, the NWSL's official Twitter account took weeks to acknowledge the event, and the Reign's account took even longer. When the NWSL finally did acknowledge it, it was a quote tweet of the BBC's coverage of Quinn's coming out. In Quinn's first televised game after coming out, broadcasters got their pronouns wrong on-air.

The way the NWSL lacked explicit public support for Quinn after they came out was likely not ill-intentioned (the NWSL did not respond to multiple requests for comment). In the Reign's case, the team did what it thought was most supportive of Quinn.

"Quinn privately shared their plans with the club prior to their public announcement. We believed this was Quinn's information to disclose in whatever way they felt was right, and at whatever time they felt was appropriate," Reign CEO Bill Predmore told *Sports Illustrated* via email. "While we were available to provide support if requested, the club was not involved in the form or timing of the announcement. Our view was that this was the most personal of news to share, so unless our support was specifically requested by Quinn, we should not impose our perspective to help shape the message nor should our club serve as the messenger."

But it is an example of how unprepared most sports leagues are to support nonbinary athletes. The WNBA supported Clarendon as well as it did only because Clarendon advocated for themself behind the scenes for months. Quinn and Clarendon, alongside triathlete Rach McBride, are likely the only openly nonbinary athletes competing professionally in North American sports. But the number of out nonbinary athletes is only going to increase.

Trans athletes have become political lightning rods and targets of institutionalized oppression; already this year Tennessee, Arkansas and Mississippi have passed laws that purport to, in the words of Tennessee Governor Bill Lee, "preserve women's athletics and ensure fair competition." The focus on physiology and biology and arguments about "protecting women" predominantly impact transfeminine athletes and take away the humanity from people who just want to play the sports they love. In the highly gendered world of sport, it's binary trans people—trans women and trans men—who are most visibly fighting for their right to compete. But left out of that conversation altogether are nonbinary athletes, who do not identify with a binary gender.

"People's education level on trans people in general is extremely low," says Ashland Johnson, the president and founder of the Inclusion Playbook, an advocacy group working to bring about social change through sports. "When it comes to nonbinary people, it's sometimes nonexistent."

The existence of nonbinary people complicates a seemingly neat and tidy way of organizing athletics: men's sports and women's sports. Including nonbinary folks in the conversation requires a willingness to acknowledge that the way we currently categorize athletics is in need of an overhaul, and that leagues need to make accommodations for the nonbinary athletes who are already here.

THE CONCEPT OF NONBINARY GENDER IDENTITY is not simply a third gender category. Rather, nonbinary identity sees gender as a spectrum: A person can exist anywhere in between the binary genders or shatter the binary altogether. "Nonbinary" can mean neither man nor woman. It can mean both man and woman. It can mean a million other things in between, each personal to the individual.

Nonbinary people can be assigned female at birth (AFAB) or assigned male at birth (AMAB). They can be intersex—a term used to describe someone who is born with reproductive or sexual anatomy that doesn't fit neatly into the boxes of "female" or "male" as the categories are typically defined. Nonbinary people can choose aspects of medical transition for themselves, like feminizing or masculinizing hormones or gender-affirmation surgeries, or they might not medically transition at all.

"I've always known I was more than just a girl or a woman, but I didn't know what exactly I was," says Clarendon. "And so, identifying as nonbinary and trans in terms of the larger umbrella is really important to me. That gives me a place to belong and gives me community."

"Nonbinary" gives Clarendon a word to identify with, one that encapsulates the fact that they feel like they are "equally both," sometimes more male, sometimes more female, but definitely much bigger than "woman." "It's really important to me for that to be seen and for me to be whole," he says. "My gender is just too big to fit in either box."

Sports gave Clarendon the freedom to be herself even before she had the words to articulate her gender. As a kid growing up in San Bernadino, Calif., he didn't know what transgender or nonbinary was; all he knew was that he felt best when he was in his hoops clothes.

They didn't necessarily talk about gender with their team-mates, but they knew there were people like them in sports, who liked to dress in gender nonconforming ways like they did. "That feeling of belonging is invaluable as a young person," Clarendon says. "I loved the competitiveness of sports, chasing a goal, the camaraderie of being around teammates and how when I made a pass to someone and they scored it felt like we could accomplish anything."

Clarendon says that realizing that gender could be fluid and ever-evolving was life-changing. He first identified publicly as "non-cisgender" in an article for The Players' Tribune in 2015. But it took longer for them to embrace the idea that they belonged under the trans umbrella, requiring them to unpack some of their own internalized transphobia and seeing trans identity beyond the singular, dominant narrative of transitioning from one binary gender to the other. Last summer, during the WNBA season, she told teammates that she was changing her pronouns, and she quietly updated them in his Twitter bio.

McBride's process was a gradual one, too. Growing up in Tacoma, Wash., and later, Germany, they dropped hints to loved ones for over a decade that they had what they call "gender strug-gles." They first heard the term "genderqueer"—another term that describes someone whose gender lives outside the binary and can sometimes be used interchangeably with nonbinary—in their 20s and instinctively knew that was what they were, but didn't hear much about that identity outside of classes at the University of Ottawa. They didn't find another word to describe themselves, though, until about two years ago when they began exploring nonbinary identity and started talking publicly about it on social media before coming out in a 2020 story in Triathlete magazine. Last year, at 42, the Vancouver resident switched to exclusively using they/them pronouns.

McBride—known as the "Purple Tiger"—has been racing full-time as a triathlete since 2011 and was dubbed "the most interesting [person] in triathlon" by TRS Radio. They are a three-time Ironman 70.3 champion, have logged eight Ironman 70.3 fastest bike splits and are a two-time Ironman bike course record holder and a three-time course record holder—including the Canadian National Championships. But not being able to fully embody their true self during competitions made them feel like they weren't reaching their full potential.

"Just recognizing my gender identity has created a space for me to feel more comfortable at the start line, because my experience before was of feeling odd and like I didn't fit in and I didn't understand why," says McBride. "Now, I understand why and I can embrace that and I can still compete amongst the people I feel most comfortable with."

AS SOCIETY'S UNDERSTANDING OF GENDER SHIFTS and more and more athletes come out as nonbinary, leagues need to be prepared to accept them—not just in words, but with concrete policies. Most professional sports leagues in the United States do not have trans-inclusion policies, though that is beginning to change. The National Women's Hockey League, the first league to adopt one, created theirs out of necessity when Buffalo Beauts player Harrison Browne socially transitioned in 2016. The National Women's Soccer League and Athletes Unlimited both unveiled theirs in March.

Interestingly, the leagues we currently think of as men's leagues are actually more inclusive of trans and nonbinary athletes from a strictly rules-based perspective. MLB, the NHL, the NBA, the NFL and MLS do not have gender requirements for participants; anyone is eligible to play in those leagues. These leagues might need "to make sure [their] locker room culture is welcoming," as one league employee put it, but they wouldn't have to change any rules to allow trans or nonbinary athletes to play.

Therefore, it's women's leagues that will have to take a hard look at their existing policies. At the time these leagues were formed, trans and nonbinary athletes weren't on their radar. But allowing anyone who is marginalized by gender to play in the women's leagues stays true to their original goal: to provide opportunities for people who were being systematically shut out of professional sports.

It's something that women's leagues are beginning to think critically about. "Quinn's announcement showed us that we have some work to do (both as a club and as a league) to reconcile a league that has been primarily defined by gender with the reality that the definition no longer reflects the full range of individuals who are playing in our league," says Predmore. "I am optimistic that we'll find a new and better way to define our league in a manner that doesn't rely on gender, but instead is focused on the quality of the players, our values and the experience we provide to fans."

For AFAB athletes who aren't taking masculinizing hormones, women's leagues currently allow them to stay—Quinn, Clarendon and McBride are examples of that. But even that can be thorny. For example, they have to deal with being misgendered every day just by nature of being in a women's league. It also seemingly lumps them into the category of "woman-lite," when they're not.

There is no current equivalent out athlete for AMAB nonbinary people in men's leagues. "Sport is not safe for trans people, and it's certainly not safe for people in men's sports who do not perform a certain type of masculinity," says Chris Mosier, the first trans man to qualify for the U.S. duathlon team and the founder of TransAthlete.com. "There is a structure in sport that probably prevents AMAB nonbinary people from [openly] participating."

As MORE LEAGUES ESTABLISH trans-inclusion policies, they are likely to look to existing policies for guidance. But experts say these policies are not as inclusive as they may first appear. To understand why, we must first talk about testosterone.

There is a long history of sex testing in sports, often under the guise of protecting cisgender women from men who might infiltrate their division and win, despite there being no evidence that has ever happened. Over the last century or so, sex testing has ranged from intrusive genital exams to chromosome testing to hormone testing focused on testosterone, which is currently considered the one true indicator of competitive advantage. This idea has come about regarding trans women's desire to compete against other women, though research has shown that any "advantage" trans women may have gained through masculinizing puberty is not retained after one year of hormone replacement therapy (HRT) with feminizing hormones like estrogen.

But testosterone is a hormone that occurs naturally at varying ranges, even in cisgender women. Despite the shaky (at best) science, the International Olympic Committee currently ascribes to a testosterone-based policy, as do the NCAA and many other elite sports governing bodies. These policies require that athletes competing in the women's category have testosterone levels under a certain number. This can disproportionately subject Black and brown women, whose femininity is policed due to racist stereotyping, to challenges to "prove" their gender.

"There is no solid evidence for the 10 nanomoles per liter for this regulation," says Katrina Karkazis, coauthor of the book *Testosterone: An Unauthorized Biography*. "It is an arbitrary threshold the IOC chose but cannot be explicitly tied to evidence of a performance difference based on T levels."

The NWHL, NWSL and AU's policies also center on testosterone. This is often missed in these conversations—how testosterone is being used to exclude not only transfeminine people, but transmasculine people, as well. AFAB players are able to stay in the NWHL and AU as long as they are not taking masculinizing hormones—testosterone—as part of their medical transition. (The NCAA has a similar policy.) It might be called a "trans-inclusion" policy, but "it's inclusive in name only" says Karkazis. Testosterone, she explains, is "being instrumentalized towards a particular end. And that end is around exclusion."

Harrison Browne's experience makes that clear—he left the NWHL so he could start hormones. "Do I wish that I could still play, if I could play in the league right now?" Browne doesn't hesitate. "Probably, yeah. I'm still healthy."

And while Browne is a trans man and it could be argued that there were other reasons why a women's league was not an acceptable place for him, what happens if the next AFAB player who wants to take testosterone to more fully embody their true gender is nonbinary and wants to remain in a women's league?

"These are really important questions that I don't think enough people are asking in enough different levels and positions," says Clarendon. "Right now, you either fit in or you get lost. Like, you meet the NCAA or IOC standards that make you eligible to play on the men's or women's side, or you don't. Or you transition and you get lost, forced to move on with your life and mourn the career you had playing the sport you were assigned at birth. What would be your hope?"

The NWSL policy differs from the other two in that it allows for a therapeutic use exemption (TUE) for AFAB players who are taking testosterone but whose levels remain "within the typical limits of women athletes," which mimics the IOC standards. However, it does not explicitly allow for nonbinary players, despite having one currently playing in the league. (The NWSL did not return requests for comment about which advocacy groups it consulted regarding its policy.)

AU's policy stands out from the others in that it does not specify a testosterone level for transfeminine athletes who want to compete on women's teams, just that they must be taking testosterone-suppressing medication. This is a big win for trans women and AMAB nonbinary people looking to compete against women. It allows them to do so without policing what it means to be a woman, or forcing AMAB nonbinary people into the same standards women are held to, which could invalidate their gender identity. Mosier helped the AU draft its policy, and it's a step forward.

However, like the NWSL and NWHL's policies, AU's shows how the IOC's arbitrary guidelines are having a trickle-down effect that results in exclusion. "Our drug policy follows the IOC list of banned substances, which includes testosterone as a performing-enhancing drug," a spokesperson for AU told *Sports Illustrated*. "Additionally, because our policy on transgender and nonbinary athletes is not based on testosterone levels, it would be very difficult to implement a policy that allows testosterone use."

Not every AFAB nonbinary person will want to take testosterone. But some will. And it's not just trans and nonbinary athletes impacted by these policies. Not only are T levels incredibly variable person-to-person and day-to-day, "there's actually contrary evidence, meaning that sometimes it's the people with the lower level who perform better," says Karkazis. In other words, measuring someone's testosterone levels alone won't actually tell you anything about what their sports performance will look like. As they stand now, these policies will have the impact of potentially pushing out the very athletes the leagues currently claim to support, and that should be concerning to everyone.

CONVERSATIONS ABOUT HOW SPORTS should be organized are not new. There's this idea that "the possibilities for the future are to maintain the fully sex-segregated system or to abolish it entirely," says Elizabeth Sharrow, associate professor of public policy and history at the University of Massachusetts Amherst, and whose work focuses on equity, policy and Title IX. "But that is a false narrative." A false binary, like gender itself. "We have the ability to imagine participatory or competitive structures in lots of different ways," they explain. "But in order to do so we have to give up the notion that categorization for athletics is easy, or is most fair or justifiable when we base it on the question of sex."

Proposed solutions involve classing sports more like wrestling—by weight class, or by height for a sport like basketball—than by gender (Nancy Leong explores some of these options in her 2017 paper "Against Women's Sports"). These solutions are flawed, as well, but reimagining the way we think about sports in the first place will require blowing up everything we think we know about how they should look. Clarendon sees potential in widening the focus of women's leagues to include all people marginalized by gender, in line with the original reason they were created, while Quinn imagines an inclusive space being one that explicitly celebrates the identities of everyone who plays. Until the entire concept of sex segregation is seen as no longer functioning, nonbinary athletes and those who advocate for them are forced to work within the existing systems to make them more inclusive of people they were not designed to include in the first place.

If leagues truly do want to make themselves places that allow athletes to be fully themselves, they need to create the space for them to do so. There are some changes that can be implemented tomorrow, like including a player's pronouns on the team's media guides, just like they do for name pronunciation or position. That simple act could have potentially avoided Quinn's being misgendered on-air last fall, or McBride's having the wrong pronouns used "almost 100 times" during a race broadcast, something that was incredibly demoralizing. "It's just like little pinpricks, every single time I hear [the wrong pronoun]," McBride explains. "It's like there's just no effort given."

Teams and leagues could also normalize social media and communications staffs asking players what pronouns they want used for them on their social platforms and whether they have a name they prefer to use other than their given name. Offering uniform or kit styles that better align with a player's gender could be another option.

Browne says that when he came out, the NWHL's press team was incredibly supportive, but he wishes they had created a list of questions that were off-limits for reporters. That would have saved Browne from being faced with intrusive questions about his body. And true inclusion may also require leagues to grapple with their names—potentially being willing to drop the word "women" to describe their athletes, since it's not an accurate descriptor.

"The rigidity of sports goes against my identity, in that I find having an expansive gender very exciting," says Quinn. "There's ways that we are 'supposed' to perform gender, even in sports, like when it comes to our uniforms or the language that we use. And so those can be pretty restricting and can go against my identity."

Those changes are likely to have a positive impact on the mental health of nonbinary athletes, something that would benefit their on-field performance, too. Surgeries are often considered necessary for something like an injury, because that impacts an athlete's ability to perform. But for Clarendon, their top surgery was necessary, too, both for their emotional well-being off the court and their performance on it. Trying to compartmentalize their gender and their job was impossible.

"We're [never talking about] how hard it was to have breasts and go to the pool in a swimsuit top and the dysphoria that you're experiencing, and then how it affects your overall mental health," says Clarendon. "I'm a big believer that the healthier athletes are, the healthier products and commodities they are. ... Being a whole person makes you a better performer at the end of the day, which is what honestly coaches and owners are really worried about, because it's the entertainment business."

These strategies will also help the athletes who are not yet out, who haven't even grappled with the question of their own gender identity because it feels impossible to do so when their job is on the line. "Segregated systems suppress even the possibility of self-exploration for a lot of athletes," says Sharrow, "because it's frightening to imagine losing something you love or that is actually your sources of income just because the structures that govern suggest your identity might be impossible."

As it stands now, players who want to come out publicly are left to navigate the decision on their own. "I don't believe Layshia is the only one; she is just the only one who is open about it," says Terri Jackson, the executive director of the WNBPA. Without a formal support process, leagues are not equipped to have conversations with the press or address players' identities on social media channels. This lack of institutional support and precedent likely prevents other players from coming out.

"There's been so much talk about exclusion," says Quinn. But those conversations distract from what they see as the real issue, which is getting back to the reason people—including, and maybe especially, nonbinary people—play sports: "because we love connecting with our bodies."

One of the best parts for Quinn of being out publicly has been the new extended trans community that they've found as a result of sharing their truth openly. They began navigating their public identity largely on their own, though their Canadian national team has begun to have conversations about what a trans-inclusion policy could look like and the Reign has begun to be more publicly intentionally supportive. In February 2021, the team's social media accounts posted a graphic advertising season tickets with an image of Quinn next to the text "They play here" and adding pronouns for every player and coach to their website. That, combined with the WNBA's coordinated effort, is evidence of a shift. Life Time, a health and fitness company that runs athletic events, has implemented a third gender option, "nonbinary/genderqueer" for all in-person run and triathlon events for the remainder of 2021 and plans to offer it for their entire portfolio of events—both in-person and virtual—in 2022 and beyond.

But until sports as a whole are ready to have conversations about the ways in which they're organized, relatively simple changes would allow players to fully embody their own identities and remain in the leagues they feel most comfortable. While Quinn and McBride say there are ways in which being in a women's league sometimes rubs up uncomfortably against their gender, players like Clarendon, who says they "feel like both genders," are perfectly at home in a women's league, but are waiting for the league to catch up to them.

"I felt particularly proud [last] summer that it was a queer, nonbinary, Black person who was leading the social justice movement," she says of her role on the W's Social Justice Council. She just wishes the league would be ready to name that identity and own the totality of the identities under its umbrella. Because it's not just a league of 144 women; Clarendon's presence proves that. As vice president of the WNBPA and as one of the oldest players on the Liberty's young roster, he gets to be a voice for change and an example for the league's next generation, one that is perhaps ready to talk openly about gender and identity among its players.

Clarendon is also entering the 2021 season with the freedom of being completely, fully, openly himself. They will no longer have the stress of wondering whether their league will accept them, whether they will have to fight for inclusion in a sport they have dedicated their life to. Even still, she knows these conversations are just beginning.

"There are only going to be more people who come out. We've been here the whole time," Clarendon says. "My story is not that unique in that gender is an evolution. What is going to happen when Ryan Ruocco uses 'he' for me on a[n ESPN] broadcast? What if I go exclusively by 'he' tomorrow? Is the league ready for that?"

Frankie de la Cretaz is an award-winning independent journalist whose work focuses on the intersection of sports, gender, and culture. They are the co-author of the book *Hail Mary: The Rise and Fall of the National Women's Football League*, and their work has been featured in *The New York Times, The Atlantic, Sports Illustrated*, and many more. They live in Boston.

Say You Wandered into Kansas vs. Texas Not Long After Halftime. Man, Did You Luck Out.

CHUCK CULPEPPER

FROM *The Washington Post* • NOVEMBER 14, 2021

The radio kept telling of something too outlandish to resist, and it kept telling it to a bent mind barreling out of Waco from Baylor vs. Oklahoma and dodging through the loathed 101 miles down Interstate 35 toward Austin in 6 p.m. darkness.

It told how perpetually sad Kansas (1–8) had taken the opening kickoff, hogged the ball for a whopping 7:02, led 7–0 and soon led 14–0. Then it said eternally entitled Texas (4–5) had tied the game at 14, so okay, but then it said perpetually sad Kansas (22–116 since 2010), which had scored 66 points across nine previous first halves in 2021, had gotten a touchdown drive, a sack fumble, another touchdown, a pick-six and a 35–14 halftime lead.

This could be a case of a peasant walloping a kingdom. This could be a case of a nadir of Texas nadirs across the past 12 seasons sailing sideways with the four head coaches and the 65 losses howling at the 82 wins and the lavish resources. This could be a case of a 31-point underdog standing 0–56 in its past 56

Big 12 road games, celebrating on a storied field. Clearly there seemed no choice in life but to aim for Darrell K. Royal Memorial Stadium and park for free in a garage that had stopped bothering to charge and had tucked away its $25 sign. Clearly it became mandatory to walk the great Austin streets toward the lights as if in some trance.

Along Colorado Street, people here and there filed toward home. On a TV pinned to the trunk of a healthy tree, the latest Texas coach overmatched in a capital of underachievement, Steve Sarkisian, did a sideline interview in which he apparently noted "one of the worst sequences I've ever seen a team play that I've been a part of." Along E. Martin Luther King Jr. Boulevard, people filed out in mild droves. At some junctures, it grew tricky to dodge them. Some ushered home children, who might get reasonable sleep anyway.

Near the stadium, people in burnt-orange filed away. It seemed impossible to buy a ticket at that stage, even for the last kook who craved one. People filed away. Texas scored to make it 35–21, and the speakers played "Stayin' Alive." People filed away. You could sit outside and wait. People filed away, most jovially, maybe because they live in Austin and Austin makes people jovial. You could spot the Bevo van backing up inside the fence and wonder whether Bevo, too, might depart soon.

He would not.

Don't impugn Bevo like that.

Soon, you could enter the stadium with a nod, maybe even a nod of pity.

The Saturday already had brimmed as November Saturdays do. Kingdoms real or alleged or both had found peril, their coaches twirling on imaginary spits. Florida had trailed Samford 42–35 at halftime yet had decided to play the duration and won, 70–52, amid mass lampooning. No. 8 Oklahoma had run into a fence of a defense at No. 13 Baylor, prompting a double field-storming—one at 0:03, then a field-clearing, then another at 0:00, of which outstanding Baylor linebacker Terrel Bernard said, "We didn't know, really, what was going on." And then old No. 6 Michigan had gotten the big play it seemed to hunt across seven seasons under Jim Harbaugh, and it came from tight end Erick All, who caught a fine dink over the middle 47 yards from a Penn State end zone with 3:37 left, then romped to the right sideline and then up it for a 21–17 win.

Thus did Michiganders toast an Ohioan.

But here, here in the great Austin, this was batty stuff. The stadium had emptied slightly less than imagined. People reveled one after another in one of the pinnacles of American life: appearing suddenly on the big screen. They sang "Livin' on a Prayer," revealing again how those unborn during Bon Jovi 1986 know all the lyrics. Five shirtless guys in the cold spelled T-E-X-A-S on the big screen, and the "E" seemed to have done the best gym work. People stood on giant verandas near the bar, gulping from beer cans.

That damned cannon kept going off after scores.

Scores kept happening.

Where it might have seemed impossible to care about some dreary Kansas-Texas game, it had become possible to care about nothing else.

Kansas hero Jalon Daniels, the quarterback from Lawndale, Calif.—!—steered the Jayhawks 73 yards in nine plays for a 49–35 lead. Clumps of people filed out. Some 8:47 remained. More clumps of people filed out, including that one guy in the stylish shoes who sort of stomped and harrumphed out. Bevo remained.

Texas got it to 49–42, of course, and it grew sad to think of Kansas losing yet again after all this. Kansas played to win and missed a gutsy fourth and one from its 34-yard line. Texas got an unsportsmanlike-conduct penalty for a celebration comprehensively absurd. Texas threw an interception invitation toward the goal line, and Kansas got O.J. Burroughs's interception with 70 seconds left, and a tiny clot of college-aged Kansas fans down near the end zone went berserk, bouncing merrily off a nearby stadium wall in one case.

They chanted the common taunt toward grifters Texas and Oklahoma: "SEC! SEC!"

Some guy walked over and taunted them for having reached 2–8.

They were about to win, except they weren't.

Texas called its three timeouts, got the ball again and scored with 22 seconds left on Cade Brewer's fine reach-up grab of Casey Thompson's 25-yard pass up the right sideline. Overtime beckoned. The stadium, maybe half-full, maybe not quite, sort of rocked. People held up their phones to make lights in the tens of thousands. It did get noisy. The Texas cheerleaders swayed in both unison and a frenzy.

And holy Bevo mercy, if suddenly you looked back over the overhang behind the bar and out toward the street, you might see smatterings of people *hurrying back in!*

They were about to win, except they weren't.

The Longhorns they might even still love grabbed a 56–49 lead in overtime and incurred another unsportsmanlike-conduct penalty, preposterous in every single way possible, for celebration against *Kansas*. Kansas faced a third and seven on its possession, and Daniels ran a beauty of a quarterback draw to gain seven. Devin Neal plunged in from the 2. Coach Lance Leipold, guts established, went for two.

The wee group of Kansas sorts waited with looks that seemed knowing. Standing behind them felt strange, like maybe an intrusion upon someone's eternal pity party. Daniels took the snap and hurried right to escape surging edge rusher Ovie Oghoufo. It looked hopeless. Daniels let the ball fly from way back at the 18. That, too, looked hopeless.

Just then, though, the eye might have shifted to this daydream of a sight. There, just behind the goal line, waiting for the ball, stood a fullback. A fullback! Maybe no one even knew he was Jared Casey, that he hadn't caught a ball all night or all year, that he's from Plainville, Kan., 25 uncluttered miles due north of Hays. When the ball nestled into his gut and his teammates began falling zanily upon him, from tight end Trevor Kardell to receiver Lawrence Arnold to lineman Mike Novitsky, the dot of Kansans had just witnessed the damnedest 57–56 win anybody ever saw, so it bounced with a madness only sports can create.

By all means, do go to the stadium.

Chuck Culpepper of *The Washington Post* previously wrote for *Sports On Earth*, *USA Today*, *the National* (Abu Dhabi), the *Los Angeles Times*, *Newsday*, the *Oregonian*, the *Lexington Herald-Leader*, the *National Sports Daily*, the *Los Angeles Herald Examiner*, *the Suffolk (Va.) News-Herald*, and, beginning at age 14, the *Suffolk Sun* of the *Virginian-Pilot*.

Super League Rage, Ronaldo Mania and the Fight for the Soul of Manchester United

WRIGHT THOMPSON

FROM ESPN • SEPTEMBER 16, 2021

On the morning of Cristiano Ronaldo's return to Manchester, a small crowd filtered into an enormous stone and marble church for Mass. Most were old. A few still spoke with a faded Irish lilt. The priest read from the gospel about the folly of building on a foundation of sand. Once there were enough sinners in this parish, as many as 50,000, to need all six of the confessionals. Now only a few thousand remain. Few things feel more melancholy than a huge beautiful house of worship left without worshipers, a dying parish hanging on after the neighborhood it was built to serve has vanished.

The neighborhood is Collyhurst, a name which evokes for Mancunians a black-and-white movie reel of a bygone way of life. Two players on Manchester United's 1968 European Cup-winning team went to church here, Brian Kidd and Nobby Stiles. The mailing address for the church is 2 Nobby Stiles Drive. Stiles also won the 1966 World Cup with England. His teammate, Sir Bobby Charlton, called him "a dog of war," by which he meant a fierce, often brutal defender whose tenacity and violence made possible the beauty of Charlton, Denis Law and George Best.

He's my favorite old United player, and after Mass, his boyhood friend and teammate Brian Kidd met me for tea.

Kidd told me a story about being 15 and a youth player for Man United, assigned the job of cleaning the boots of the main squad players. All these muddy spikes would get tossed in a wicker basket and Kidd would drag it out of the tunnel at Old Trafford to the maroon wooden benches, and he'd sit there and clean and look around at the towering empty stands and terraces, dreaming of when his time would come. He laughs a bit at how silly all this sounds.

"I'm not being melodramatic," he insists.

He can still see the green grass and the rising tide of concrete seats, and he remembers imagining his own feet on that field, swelling with longing, with respect but most of all, with reverence.

"I'd be cleaning George Best's boots," he says. "Nobby Stiles' boots."

Nobby's father ran the Catholic funeral home around the corner from St. Patrick's Church. Whenever somebody would get shot on the screen down at the local theater, someone would call out from the seats in the dark, "Send for Charlie Stiles!"

Sometimes as a young boy Nobby would accompany his father to funerals and wakes. Once they walked into a house and Nobby realized he'd come face to face with the family of the great Jimmy Delaney, whose signing in 1946 made the city ripple in much the way Ronaldo's signing has in 2021. One of Jimmy's United jerseys hung on the wall. Nobby stared in awe. His father quietly asked Jimmy's niece if his son might, for just a moment, be able to wear it. The woman smiled, took the shirt off the wall and slipped it on young Nobby Stiles. He later said he could feel himself changing, a Bushido handshake, or as he put it, "a passage of the warrior robes of my tribe."

I LANDED IN MANCHESTER on Thursday morning for Ronaldo's first match with United, here to document a new celebrity arrival in a booming, modern city, which is also a city that always feels old and unable to escape its history. I love Manchester. A visit to this place might mean a late-night club with post-punk on parade, or a pint of bitter at a dying pub, soaring glass architecture in the Northern Quarter or a barren lot in Collyhurst. There are dozens of cranes in the air. There are ground-level fields of blight. One of those cities has to be real, I often think, and one has to be an illusion, but both are on display when the place cracks open to welcome the arrival of the world's most famous athlete.

Digital road signs that normally update drivers about traffic and commute times said, "Welcome home CR7." The club sold $60 million worth of his jerseys in the 36 hours after his signing was announced, according to a rough estimate by a consumer website. Those sales came from more than 100 different countries, from Greenland to Fiji, according to Fanatics. The top five were England, America, Australia, China and Germany. Only Manchester's slums celebrated Jimmy Delaney. Only locals could point you to 2 Nobby Stiles Drive. The whole world knows Ronaldo. At the stadium on Thursday afternoon, as fans gathered to buy Ronaldo scarves and jerseys and pose for pictures, at least three different languages were being spoken.

One of the scarf vendors grinned at his own quick industry.

"We don't mess about," he joked. "I got me granny up all night."

It's been a wild six months for Manchester United supporters. In April, the owning Glazer family joined other elite clubs from England, Spain and Italy to form a so-called "Super League," patterned after the American franchise model. JP Morgan stage-managed the debacle, which died only two days after it was announced. The reason it only lasted two days was in part because fans, particularly blue-collar fans already angry at the changes brought to their lives by globalization, exploded in protest. Anything that diminishes the local in favor of wealthy internationals is the perceived enemy of the British working class, whether that is the European Union or a football league, and no supporters reacted with more anger or purpose than Man United supporters. A group of them stormed the gates of Old Trafford and forced a match against Liverpool to be postponed. One of those protesting fans carried a sign that read, "Football: created by the poor, stolen by the rich."

With all this roiling, Ronaldo came onto the market.

He first became a star at Man United nearly two decades ago, and has always professed his unending love and gratitude towards former manager Sir Alex Ferguson. Just weeks ago, Manchester City looked like the favorites to sign the Portuguese star from Italian club Juventus, but neither United supporters nor the Glazer family could abide the idea of the superstar coming home to play for the *other* team in town. There was no choice. Manchester United outmuscled its cross-town rivals. Ronaldo credited Ferguson with convincing him to return to the Reds, the past forever prelude here.

Ronaldo might be from the insular island of Madeira, famous for its fortified wine and now for one native son, but he lives in a world defined by economies more than maps. All his mansions are the same, whether they're in a toney suburb outside Madrid, or Turin, or Manchester. He is his own nation state, borders merely invisible lines rushing beneath the white wings of his Gulfstream G200. More people follow him on Instagram than live in the United States. His life represents a perfect evolution of the new globalist class of humans who aren't tethered to antiquated things like countries. Even his love for Manchester, and the way he articulates that love—such as calling Ferguson his "football father"—feels not quite *of* Manchester—which is so defined by its sense of place—but shallowly adjacent to it, referencing not the unique history or power of the city or the club but his own sporting experience in both.

And yet he is completely a creation of Manchester. The global economy that makes his weird, extravagant life possible was born here. As the pop culture critic Luke Bainbridge has said, Manchester is where Marx met Engels, and is also where

Rolls met Royce. Communism and socialism were born here, yes, but so were globalization and free trade. Ronaldo endorses high-end companies like Tag Heuer, Coca-Cola and Nike. Savvy investors own shares in his image. He's as much corporation as person. It's quite surreal and yet somehow inevitable that a man like Ronaldo would arrive as the savior of a city like Manchester, because the forces that created him have also been battering his new, old home for as long as locals can remember.

On Thursday afternoon, two days before match day, a drizzle fell on Sir Matt Busby Way, which runs in front of Old Trafford. At the pub on the corner, a worker drilled holes in the smooth, old bricks, really leaning into his work, so they could hang a banner welcoming Ronaldo back home. Inside the stadium itself, the Manchester United Megastore had sold out of all its Ronaldo jerseys.

"Are you getting any tomorrow?" an elderly man asked.

"Hopefully," the man behind the counter said, in a voice that suggested he already knew the odds didn't look good. I stood in line behind him and when my turn came to buy a jersey, I told him I wanted number six on the back with the name Stiles. The elderly man approved.

THERE'S A FANCY RESTAURANT in the city center called The Ivy, where a group of club dignitaries gathered for a fancy lunch on that Thursday. Sir Alex Ferguson, the hero of the moment after his role in landing Ronaldo, arrived and smiled at fans. Manager Ole Gunnar Solskjaer looked relaxed. Even Ed Woodward made an appearance. He's the Glazers' head bean counter and the current focus of fan anger. His home has been attacked twice, and he hasn't attended a match at Old Trafford since the Super League debacle. He clearly still feels skittish. All the other famous men entered through the front door. The local paper reported that Woodward snuck in a service entrance around the side.

So it's important to note that the Ronaldo mania remained tempered by lingering feelings of alienation. For the past 16 years, since the Glazer family bought the team, there has been a growing rift that plays out in little and small ways in Manchester, almost daily. Dislike of the Glazers started when the family saddled the team with debt to get the deal done. That's acceptable, even smart, in the asset and wealth management game, but the fans immediately (and correctly) understood that with debt service, and the dividend checks the family would certainly draw, there wouldn't be the money needed to keep Man United at the top of the football food chain. All those fears came true. Today a teenager living in Manchester has no memory of a time when Man City wasn't the most successful and dominant team in the city. Ronaldo is intended to reverse that trend.

I met a lifelong United fan named David Hawkes, who said the Ronaldo signing has him spinning "like a washing machine," as he hopes all this optimism turns into wins. He described for me the conflicting emotions he's feeling about the way his club has been decoupling from local supporters and reaching toward the seemingly limitless pool of international consumers.

"The Super League thing hit me like a train," he says. "It really hurt me."

All this is old and personal. His family moved from the industrial slums north of the city, a place named Miles Platting, down to the coal yards of Trafford. His grandparents' house got hit in the same German bombing run that damaged Old Trafford. His wife said she thought he was grieving over the Super League.

"I think she was correct," he says. "United and my family histories are so woven into me that it was a grim feeling indeed. It's also partly mutated into anger, anger at the Glazers, the nation-state owners, the whole entitled globalization theme of the mega-rich who wish to become richer. Anger as well, if I'm honest, at myself. It's taken me far too long to really confront the truth of what is happening to United and to football."

Hawkes remembers exactly when he first loved United. It was February 6, 1958. He was coming home from school. The war had been over for 13 years and wrecking balls were finishing what

German bombers had started. Entire streets were being moved away, miles of vibrant neighborhoods turned into abandoned, grassy fields. The national rationing had only ended in 1954. People were just starting to reset their horizons.

"Make do and mend was so ingrained into them," Hawkes says.

Hawkes came home from school and even now he can barely describe the scene that greeted him when he walked through the door. He saw the coal fireplace in the small dining room and the easy chairs. The Bakelite radio his father built himself sat on the table and played the news.

His mother was "folded up" on the floor, weeping.

He asked what was wrong.

She told him.

An airplane carrying journalists, supporters and the Manchester United team, led by the great manager Matt Busby, had crashed while attempting to take off from the airport in Munich. Twenty-one people survived. Twenty-three died. They brought the bodies back in the rain and they stayed all night at Old Trafford. Thirty-thousand people stood outside, soaking wet, a working-class honor guard who just couldn't bear the thought of those beautiful boys in there all alone. Busby Babes, they called them. Something young and beautiful had been taken, and their death reopened the wounds of war.

The stoic Mancunians who kept so much inside attached two decades of fear, loss and privation onto these beloved angels in red. For weeks it seemed like all people did was attend funerals. Charlie Stiles, Nobby's dad, buried several of them. The dead men weren't strangers to his son. As an academy player at United, Nobby did all the dirty work expected of the up-and-comers. He loved it. His hero was Tommy Taylor, and he used to carefully clean his spikes after every practice and game.

"He got the Babes their bacon sandwiches when they played snooker," his son, John Stiles, says. "And when they died, he could never talk about it. Ever."

Busby survived. Charlton survived. They promised to rebuild, and this team rising from the ashes is when modern Manchester United was born. People invested their whole selves in the team. "Because of what happened to the team and to the city of Manchester," Hawkes says, "it was a spark. It became a cause. We are going to drag this team back to where it should be."

Hawkes voice cracks as he's telling the story. It's only been 63 years.

"I still feel it emotionally even now," he says.

IT'S STUNNING HOW MANY LOCALS of a certain age and social class, especially those with geographic roots in the north of the city, still get emotional talking about Munich. On Friday, I met my friend and poet Mike Duff at a pub on Oldham Road. He brought one of his mates, a fellow writer named Tony Flynn, and as a way of welcoming me to town, Tony sat down and started handing me gifts. An old boxing program from the 1930s. An antique hat pin from Old Trafford. But the biggest gift was a tribute to the players who died in Munich, listing their names and showing them as people here remember: strong, hard jawed and on the pitch. His mother and his older brother, just 11, were two of the many who stood watch in the rain when the bodies returned to Old Trafford.

"I saw grown men crying in the streets," Flynn says. "When you see grown men crying and you don't know why...", his voice fades.

Flynn calls Ronaldo "the prodigal son," and said his own son, Sean, still a true believer in things like loyalty, refused all along to believe he'd ever sign with City. Flynn can't afford to go to Old Trafford any longer, but he can't stop loving the club.

"I couldn't sever that umbilical cord," he says.

"It's like leukemia," Duff says. "It gets in your blood."

We're sitting around talking about the next day's match, and they're telling stories about the old neighborhoods, all factory and mill workers, all Irish, all Catholic.

A few pints in and they start cracking on each other. I love hearing Duff's stories about the time he did in Strangeways jail, or his former career as a shoplifter. Duff's work is all set in "the Heartlands," as he calls it, that area of northern industrial Manchester where he was born and raised. Once he visited Tupelo, Mississippi, and when he saw the childhood poverty of Elvis Presley, he immediately understood him as a brother, a comrade. The Super League didn't surprise him one bit.

"It's capitalism, isn't it?" Duff says. "Capitalism doesn't care. It's a Ponzi scheme that will one day fail. I'll be dead when it fails, but it will fail. My kids are angry and my grandkids will grow up angry. So sooner or later the Ponzi scheme fails but enough people have to get angry. And those United fans got angry. When they got angry they showed what people can do. They can storm the Winter Palace. They can storm the Bastille."

He grew up in one of the many Catholic parishes in the Heartlands. His was called Corpus Christi, a neighbor of the more powerful neighboring church and school St. Patrick's, where I went to Mass.

For generations the club dispatched scouts into the churches and schools. Nearly every single person who lived in this part of the city was Catholic, and nearly all of them were Irish. They were two and three generations into a new home, and they were caught between the island of their past and the city of their future, no longer Irish but not really English, families all intermarried and stripped of the sturdy markings of home, and about the only thing that bound people together was their love of the Reds.

"Everybody was educated through Catholicism into believing in Manchester United as well as our Lord Jesus Christ," Duff says. "I can remember teachers praying for Man United in European Cups."

He laughs and smiles.

"Never mind the poor and starving," he says. "Let's have three Hail Marys for Nobby Stiles."

I WOKE UP ON SATURDAY, put on my Stiles shirt and went to meet my friends for the match, United vs. Newcastle. Two of my favorite people in the world live in Manchester, Richard and Carmel, and they've been to Mississippi where I live many times. Whenever I am here, I spend whatever free time I have with them. They're family. Richard's grandson, Reece, is 15 and a Ronaldo and United obsessive, so I wanted to get them tickets. These were, without question, the hardest tickets I've ever tried to procure, but walking up to meet them, I had them in hand.

Richard wore his signed Eric Cantona jersey, the most beloved United number seven after George Best but before Cristiano Ronaldo.

"I've never been allowed to touch it," Carmel said.

Now we were all laughing at the grown man wearing an autograph.

"Did he tell Cantona you were 7?" their friend Phil cracked.

Phil's stepson, Max, pulled up a chair. I love big game days. This constant adding of people, everyone full of joy, looking at watches, the coming storm so powerful that not even this calm is truly calm. Reece, a teenaged boy, said nothing. Maybe a mumble. He's a good-looking kid, scored two goals in his last football match, and a mumble is about all you're gonna get.

Max works on houses and was recently involved in a gut job where they found, abandoned in the attic in seven or so boxes, a collection of Man United memorabilia. There were newspapers from the days after the Munich crash. There were old games on VHS. And the real prize: a collection of every game program from the 1930s to around 2010. He took them home.

Carmel's dad kept a similar collection. He loved United. When she started dating Richard, the first football fan she'd brought home, her mother took to him immediately. The second time Carmel brought Richard to visit, her mom disappeared into the basement and returned with her late husband's entire United collection, all his programs and even his treasured framed photograph of the 1968 European Cup team. That photo now hangs in a place of honor in their home.

Our half pints of bitter and lager arrived.

I caught Carmel smiling and shaking her head in wonder and joy, at this family moment, at this gathering of friends old and new, worlds colliding, the coming football match the excuse rather than the thing. She's as kind and funny a person as I've ever known, and I've come to see her as my platonic ideal of a Mancunian. She's working class. The city she's called home her whole life, turning down transfers to London at work, has always been defined by its contradictions, by an impulse to feel both love and alienation, often at the same time, and to not worry much if outsiders can't put together a coherent list of local values. The compromises are the culture. I like it when she describes the polyglot immigrant tangle of her family, complete with the disownings and religious feuds, with Italians marrying Irish, and Catholics marrying Protestants, living in and around the slums and housing estates of a big, gray industrial engine, unified by one thing.

"They were all Reds," she told me.

Her mother now has dementia. It's getting worse but for now she lives in the warm and happy past. She remembers all the music she and Carmel's father heard. Once she went to see Nat King Cole at a circus, and the air stank of elephants. She remembers her husband going to see United, and teaching Carmel to memorize the results and the team's starting lineup, taking her and her party trick down to the local curry house to impress the owners with her knowledge: Law ... Charlton ... Best ... Kidd ... Stiles ...

So when Carmel sees that poster in their house, the 1968 Cup Champions, she doesn't think about football, or trophies, but of her mom and of her dad. She sees the poster and thinks of home. For a long time, 30 years or more, she didn't go to Old Trafford. Before she met Richard, the last time she went was with her father. She was a nine-year-old girl. And when she returned all those years later, and rose out of the tunnel to see the pitch, she found herself emotional, because in some way she couldn't articulate, that father and that nine-year-old girl had been there waiting all these years for her to return.

ACROSS TOWN IN WORKING-CLASS north Manchester, at this exact moment, a fierce crowd of several thousand awaited the start of another football match. The F.C. United of Manchester is a small, local club who play in the seventh division of English football, a splinter cell, founded by alienated Man United supporters who were willing to trade size and prestige for a feeling they'd lost along the way. Their new club is often abbreviated as FCUM.

Club president Adrian Seddon laughed.

"It's not a coincidence," he said.

"The major event for us was Malcolm Glazer," Seddon says. "For a lot of fans it was a line in the sand. There was a lot of people who weren't happy with the way football was going. Local Mancunians were often priced out of going to football. This is one of the deprived areas of Manchester."

The Super League brought them attention and new members.

"I had my line in the sand 16 years ago," Seddon says. "Some people had it this year. I don't think it matters … if you get to your line in the sand, we're here."

They have a standing-room terrace in their stadium. There's a sign that reads "Making Friends Not Millionaires," and a banner of the famous Munich memorial clock that hangs on the side of Old Trafford.

"This is a club that appeals to Manchester United supporters," Seddon says. "But we are Manchester United fans who don't feel like we have a place at Old Trafford anymore. For us it's not a new team. It's a continuation of Manchester United—but the good bits we like from Manchester United."

They have a member's bar where normal folks can afford to drink. Every one of their players, and their manager, have other jobs. The supporters rented an old steam train to travel to an away match. They wear the same colors as United and they sing all the same songs. Their stadium, which they paid for themselves, is like a minor league baseball park and is located two miles from the spot where Manchester United was founded in 1878. Originally created as a kind of company softball team for the Lancashire & Yorkshire Railroad, Man United was by and for industrial workers. The team took the railroad's yellow and green colors before later changing to red, and more than a century later, when Mancunians protested the Super League, they lit flares that spewed yellow and green smoke.

The Reds used to be deeply rooted in this part of the city, and the FCUM's location is no accident. Nor was their decision to place Nobby Stiles at the center of their own nascent mythology. Stiles has a banner honoring him hanging from the owner's box at midfield, and the best youth player is given the Nobby Stiles Shield. His wife, Kay, and his children show up to present the trophy. In a lot of ways, Stiles is their patron saint.

"Nobby Stiles is probably the most famous son of this area," Seddon says. "He's from Collyhurst. This is his territory."

STILES WAS BORN IN A MAKESHIFT air raid shelter during a German bombing attack of Manchester and grew up in Collyhurst. He didn't like his fame. He never talked about football at home. There were no pictures on the wall. He even sold his World Cup medal. "If you walked into the house you wouldn't even know he'd been a footballer," his son John says.

Only when they went to their grandmother's house in Collyhurst and found the scrapbooks carefully preserved in the attic did John and his siblings really understand the legend.

"She saved everything," he says.

Brian Kidd said that Stiles was as gentle off the pitch as he was ferocious on it. "He had a lovely family he thought the world of, and that was his world," Kidd says. "The rest would be a sideshow."

Kidd sometimes finds himself driving past the Collyhurst street named after Stiles, to remember the past, to conjure images of the families who lived in these empty urban fields.

"It was the slums of Manchester," Kidd says.

These slums are where Man United were born and where its first fans lived. The whole of northern Manchester was once filled with some of the first factories ever built in the world. The loud, belching brick cauldrons shaped everything about the city, and much of the world we know today.

Those factories, most of them cotton mills, were rife with oppressive conditions for local workers. According to historians, child labor made the economy turn. Long after slavery had been officially outlawed in Britain, Manchester mill owners purchased kids from London orphanages and got a discount if one per dozen was mentally handicapped. Working mothers were encouraged by doctors to give their children opium and leave them home while they worked long shifts. Only 57 percent of kids lived until their fifth birthday. Friedrich Engels—who called Manchester "hell upon earth"—described "children deformed, men enfeebled, limbs crushed, whole generations wrecked, afflicted with disease and infirmity."

Over time, the world's first factory workers moved north and east into the rolling hills outside the city. Once known as Irish Town, it's now a beautiful park called Angel's Meadow. The trendiest neighborhoods are just next door. "They're bringing in IT people from London and they want nice places to live," Duff says.

The descendants of Irish Town—"blood of the Meadow," as Duff calls them—are now in the way of progress, which comes in the form of new condos and urban professionals to live in them.

"They don't want to live next to people drinking cans of cider on the street," Duff says. "Even though it's them people's area. They shift you out bit by bit."

As many as 70,000 people once lived here, in 1,000 houses, many alongside livestock like pigs and cows. Nobody had running water or toilets. The basements flooded so often that they were filled with dirt and condemned, but new arrivals with no place else to go often slept atop the dirt. This part of Manchester slopes downhill to the river, so every bit of human and animal waste passed through the meadow. The papers reported on all the toxic and tainted food. Tests revealed dirt in the tea, chemicals in the beer, sawdust in the bread.

Cholera outbreaks, called the Irish Fever by the local papers, ravaged the homes. After the second major cholera outbreak, just a few years after the Irish potato famine flooded the city with another rush of immigrants, the city tore down the slums—starting a pattern that continues today. They buried them right where they died, as many as 40,000, right where the slums had stood. The park got its current name because residents reported seeing angels standing guard at the entrance, watching over all the dead children. Generations of boys and girls flocked to the mass grave turned park, the only open green space in their lives, and that's where they learned to play football.

One of those kids was Nobby Stiles.

MIKE DUFF KEEPS A FRAMED PICTURE of Angel's Meadow above his bed. That's where his mother was born and raised. He believes we are all like coins passing through the world over and over again. That there's no such thing as time. The packed slums of Angel Meadow are still there in some multi-verse. He holds a hand-rolled cigarette.

"They *have* to be there, don't they?" he says. "Because they *were* there. And they have to be there forever. And the packed slums of tomorrow are there in the past ... They've already been built."

Here's what I think he means. There's a man who rides a bicycle around the old cotton mill neighborhoods with a boombox strapped to his side. The music pouring from the speakers the few times he rode past me was weird space age atmospheric post-industrial, like something you might hear while getting a deep-tissue massage from an alien robot. It's very, very weird. He's dressed like a street priest prophet shaman. These musical orbits feel divine. The man wears sunglasses. You cannot see his eyes. His given name is Barrington. His music is loud. Real loud. *Boom Box Barry*, they call him. He's cranked the volume up so high that when he passes close to you there's nothing but distortion. Just noise. Most people listen and maybe smile at him then go on about their day, so it's as if the music is coming from the city itself, an endless, eternal soundtrack that's only unmuted briefly by his presence. Like he's not playing music himself so much as he is allowing us to hear the music the city is already playing. I came to think that the noise was some kind of an ancient horn summoning the dead of Angel Meadow, who briefly walk amongst us until the boombox finally travels too far away. Bodies are suits for the soul, and cities are houses. Manchester is a city of souls. They sing, and they dance, and they ride a bike with a boombox.

"All the Manchesters are here," Duff says.

AFTER THE PUB, we were walking to Old Trafford through neighborhoods passing people of all ages wearing Ronaldo jerseys. The United academy administrators used to place youth players like Paul Pogba with local families. Richard and Carmel hosted several. The team liked the players to make this walk, to see the city they represented, to understand who would be pressed up against the glass once they got rich and famous.

I had a nagging feeling I couldn't shake. The people with me are long-time Reds, with Irish Mancunian roots, and yet it was near impossible for them to get tickets to go and watch their local club welcome its newest star. That felt broken, as if the local supporters were defending something from their opponents and also from their fellow fans. Carmel and Richard have always been generous with the parts of their city they love, hoping for nothing more than for me to love them, too.

We saw the lights to the cricket ground, and then we got to the quadrant, a wide square with a tunnel of trees in the middle, which is home to The Quadrant, a pub where locals meet up before heading to the grounds. Everyone wore their new Ronaldo shirts.

"All the number 7s," Carmel says.

Finally the white tubular superstructure of Old Trafford peaked up between the trees. The shortcut was coming up on the right, through the parking lot of the cricket stadium. From there it was just a few more minutes to Sir Matt Busby Way. It's one of the great streets in sports, a battalion of red, singing fans, the traditional vendors selling burgers and bacon sandwiches and full English breakfasts. There was a chill in the air, and grey industrial skies, which felt perfect.

We got to the shortcut, and across the street, we saw a blue historical plaque on a modest house. Richard had never noticed it before, and we both squinted to read the small print. It took our breath away. This was where Tommy Taylor was living when he died with his teammates in Munich. He got dressed here and went to the airport and never came back. His protege, Nobby Stiles, made a solemn ask after the crash.

"Can I have Tommy Taylor's boots?"

His request was granted.

STILES WAS THE LAST KING of Collyhurst, a man who outlived his homeland. Now the neighborhood exists mostly in imagination and memory. Displaced residents connect in message boards and social media groups. Nobby's son used to watch closely when Stiles would speak to people whose childhood neighborhoods had been erased. John came to believe that when they listened to his dad's stories, their long-lost homeland returned. Nobby would get raucous, standing ovations.

"Son," he'd say, "I don't know why."

"They love you," John would tell him. "That's why."

Stiles remains one of only three Englishmen to win a World Cup and a European Cup, but he didn't make a lot of money in his career. He took coaching jobs where he could get them, feeling guilty that his wife needed to work in a local department store so they could pay their bills. He spiraled. "When I didn't feel suicidal," he wrote, "I felt tired. Bone tired."

One morning, mid-1980s, he went to fill up his car with gas. The ATM coldly reported insufficient funds. In shame he went back home to scrape together enough change. That shame festered. A breakdown was coming, and one day it finally happened on the M6. After all his battles, Stiles didn't care if he lived or died. He closed his eyes and sped down the road.

When he opened them again, he saw a row of cones blocking his lane. He swerved at 70 miles per hour and hit a truck. Somehow they both came to a stop. The lorry driver got out. When he saw one of the nation's great working-class heroes in the other car, any anger dissolved. Kindness and concern entered his voice. Nobby never forgot that.

"I'm sorry, mate," Stiles said.

The truck driver responded with love. Stiles wasn't *them*. He was *us*.

"Don't worry, Nobby," he said. "How are you feeling?"

At home Stiles finally told his wife how worthless he felt. She pulled him close and asked him to take a walk. He told her everything. They laughed and smiled and opened a bottle of brandy, and the next morning, he wrote in his memoir, the telephone rang at his house.

It was Alex Ferguson.

He wanted Nobby to come back to Manchester United, to join Brian Kidd in coaching their youth team. For three years, from 1989 to 1991, two men from St. Patrick's coached Man United's famed Class of '92. Players like David Beckham and Gary Neville learned not just how to play the game but how to carry the spirit of places like Collyhurst. Every day the future stars listened to someone who'd gotten bacon sandwiches for the Busby Babes. Nobby connected them to the past and they carried that past out on the pitch.

"If they were gonna go out on a horrible, horrible night in Bradford," John Stiles says, "when it's pissing rain, and it's starting to get naughty, they'd f---ing love it. Gary Neville spoke about it. Me dad told 'em what it meant to be a Man United player."

A LOW, HOWLING NOISE HIT US just as we first saw Sir Matt Busby Way. Chanting fans lined up for a table at the Bishop Blaze, a cocaine lager pub of track suits on parade. A dad leaned down to his young son and pointed up at the statue of Best, Law and Charlton on the plaza at the end of the street. He whispered something I couldn't hear and, after I took a picture of them together for him, he told me this was the boy's first game. He wore a Ronaldo jersey. Everyone was wearing a Ronaldo jersey. The crowd sang, thousands of voices together:

"Viva Ro-nal-do ... Viva Ronaldo

Running down the wing

Hear United sing

Viva Ronaldo"

The last "o" in Ronaldo created that low, howl, like somebody blowing down the barrel of a gun. We all moved slowly down the long tunnel, lined with exhibits, tributes and old photographs of the men who died in the Munich crash, and of the men who lived and rebuilt the team. None of that is ancient history. Nobby Stiles knew them, and he and Brian Kidd were part of the 1968 team whose victory symbolized the club's rebirth. Together they coached the Class of 1992, who played with Ronaldo at the beginning of his career and instilled the love that made today possible.

Reece and I were sitting together in Section 120, so we made our way out of the tunnel through the narrow turnstile corrals and then down the steps to our seats. We were really close to the pitch. Row EE, just five up. A familiar smell floated in the air which I couldn't quite place. Then it hit me. I smelled grass.

I asked Reece a question.

He just nodded.

The starting lineups were announced and with them the words everyone here had been waiting to hear: "Number 7—and welcome home—Cristiano Ronaldo."

IT TOOK THREE DAYS in Manchester to see fans forced in public to reckon with Ronaldo's history. That moment arrived when a small single-engine airplane circled the sky above Old Trafford, carrying a banner that read:

"#Believe Kathryn Mayorga."

Mayorga is a Las Vegas woman who alleges that Ronaldo raped her in 2009. She went to the police shortly after the alleged assault but did not identify her attacker, and the police closed the investigation. In 2010, she agreed to a $375,000 settlement with Ronaldo and signed a non-disclosure agreement, but later went public with her allegations in 2018. After the Clark County district attorney declined to press charges in 2019, stating that the allegations "cannot be proven beyond a reasonable doubt," Mayorga filed a civil lawsuit. Ronaldo has maintained the encounter between them was consensual.

The first time the plane appeared, the crowd started singing "Viva Ronaldo."

Three more times the airplane appeared above the stadium, as the skies changed from gray to blue, and then it was gone. A few fans sitting around me pointed up, and that's the only reaction I saw or heard at the stadium. I didn't struggle to understand why corporations wouldn't really care about allegations, because shareholder value is capitalism's only ethic, an idea first put to use in Manchester. The desperate need in the city for nobody to bring up anything that might tarnish their new trophy was harder to understand, but only a little. Fandom has always been most of all an act of tribalism. Things can be explained away, or ignored, or used as fodder.

On the other side of the stadium, visiting Newcastle fans mocked the striker.

"Geordie boys, we're on a bender.

Cristiano's a sex offender."

For 45 minutes, the game remained 0–0 until the first half stoppage time when Ronaldo fielded the ball close to the goal and scored. I couldn't see it from my seat, but I heard two explosions of noise, a loud eruption when the ball hit the back of the net, and then an even louder collective "boom" when Ronaldo did his iconic goal celebration.

The crowd kept singing, and chanting, and cheering. The noise was a catharsis as much as anything, part celebration of the rebirth offered by a newly signed star, part prayer that this rebirth might be one that lasts. Our seats were near the Stretford End, traditionally the home of working-class United fans, and I kept looking at the faces around me. The past 16 years slipped from their shoulders. Alienation and decline were held at bay. Self-awareness and empathy were held at bay, too.

Loving something as deeply as the people in this stadium love United requires a lot of remembering, remembering Nobby Stiles and Busby's Babes, but it also requires a lot of forgetting, too. Forgetting Kathryn Mayorga. Forgetting that the Super League concept will almost certainly return. Forgetting all the times you swore you were finally done with a club that took your love and made you pay for the privilege.

For today the fans only live in a world they're creating, a world of imagination and hope, and in this world, the future is bright, the past is glorious, their hero was righteous and their rivals were vile.

ONE HALF TO GO. While Reece and I walk up to the tight concourse to get a steak pie and some snacks, hit pause on the madness and consider this contradiction and beauty. This stadium is packed. Some of the people, like me and many of the folks sitting around me, are from other countries. We are here for a lot of reasons, as are the millions watching all over the world. There is a planet full of human beings looking for community where they can find it. People everywhere feel alienated. Study after study shows that. In a world where fewer and fewer people go to church, they are also looking for communion where they can find it. Many people are finding both in an aspirational love for big football clubs like Man United.

Think about that for a second. Globalization crushed the working class of Manchester, which imperils the localism of this rooting community, and which is also a central driver of a reach to be part of the community offered by Manchester United. Now take it a step further. This tribe has always been supported by two load-bearing spiritual columns: longing for what is lost and hungering for what is to come. In the past six months, the city has roiled with anxiety over one during the Super League protests, and shouted in ecstasy over the other during the days leading up to Ronaldo's Old Trafford return.

That contradiction, so essential to truly seeing the city of Manchester, feels especially poignant in Section 120, Row EE, overlooking the same piece of earth where Brian Kidd once day-dreamed while cleaning the boots of beautiful comets like George Best and dogs of war like Nobby Stiles. Because some of the people here, like the well-dressed elderly woman sitting directly to my left, are from that vanishing Manchester. She laughed in delight when she saw my Stiles jersey. Just as his life represented the rise of working north Manchester, so, too, has his death rep-resented the fall. Nobby passed 11 months ago and some people were surprised he was still living. The last two decades of his life got lost in dementia. His family protected him. The man afraid of nobody was afraid all the time. He'd get fixated on a fear. His boiler was going to explode. Somebody was trying to break in. His memories were cruelly stripped away.

"When my dad's brain was examined," John says, "it was riddled with CTE. It was sad. And it is sad. There's hundreds and hundreds and hundreds more that are gonna come."

His family have become unlikely advocates, working to make football take care of the damaged men left in its wake. John wonders how a sport so rich could just abandon men like his father, who gave his whole heart to United and never even met one of the Glazers.

"This is a fight for the little man against big business," he says. "There is nothing more important."

There's a myth that everyone in Old Trafford is connected to that big business, and that those little men are all shut out. That's not true. Mancunians love United and the stadium remains swollen with those who figure out how to pay to get in. That's comforting. The fight between Mancunian supporters and the forces of globalization pushing them out and replacing them with rootless strangers hasn't been decided. It is happening in real time. The most important fights aren't won by great generals on decisive days, like in the movies, but slowly over time, a few grains of sand at a time until a world is washed away. Like so many places, Manchester is engaged in a mostly hidden war over what it means to be from here. Everyone can feel it happening, but almost nobody can name it, except of course for a rare occasion when we can compare Nobby Stiles' Man United and Cristiano Ronaldo's Man United. Then this complex thing is made small enough to hold in your mind, to touch and to name, to mourn, to turn away from, to celebrate, to love.

RONALDO SCORED AGAIN in the 68th minute, and he ran to the corner right by our seats. Reece cheered and screamed and jumped up and down, free and full of joy, as Ronaldo leapt into the air not ten feet away. We ended up all over the television broadcast during this celebration. The Mancunian woman by me

turned to smile, and I grinned back. Strangers were hugging and
jumping. United scored two more times, and each time Reece
jumped up and screamed. The whole grandstand shook. Each
song left an echo, which kept on ringing after the next song had
started, so it all piled up on itself into a twisted tangle of noise.

Reece and I were laughing and joking on the walk back up
the stairs and down the long tunnel filled with reminders of a
cold snowy day in Munich. Everyone met back at the statue of
Best, Law and Charlton. Sir Matt Busby Way was a joyous parade.
We got back to the quadrant and The Quadrant was packed. The
whole square sparked with activity, folks lined up at the chicken
place, and at the pub. I heard Reece quietly humming and singing
"Viva Ronaldo" to himself. We walked through the quiet arbor of
trees, in the shade, and then found a place to sit down and order
food and a pint. Reece and his granddad Richard parked next to
each other and looked at highlights of the game. They were both
smiling. Reece squinted at the screen.

"You looking for yourself?" Richard asked.

I looked over at Carmel. She was glowing.

"It's so cute, isn't it?"

She smiled at Reece.

"He's the apple of my eye," she said. "I could eat him up."

That's how we ended the day when Manchester once again
became the center of the football world. With friends, and laughter, and a basket of fried chicken and chips on a street alive with
something old and hard to understand. A passerby complimented
my Nobby Stiles jersey. Cars honked. A man hung out an opening
window and sang, "Viva Ronaldo!" We waved back and the sun
slipped slowly out of sight.

Wright Thompson is a senior writer for ESPN. He lives in Mississippi with
his family.

'Got Back to My Roots': Nia Dennis and the Groundbreaking Genius of #BlackExcellence

THUC NHI NGUYEN

FROM the *Los Angeles Times* • FEBRUARY 12, 2021

Nia Dennis placed her hands on her hips as she sashayed onto the floor. Her shoulders were relaxed. Her chin was held high above a glamorously decorated blue leotard with jewels covering her collarbone like layers of diamond necklaces.

After weeks of planning and practicing, the UCLA senior gymnast was finally ready to unveil her latest floor creation. She was nervous and excited. But with a medley of songs from influential Black artists ready to blare over the speakers, she was also proud.

Years ago, there were moments when Dennis, then a promising Olympic hopeful, wished she wasn't Black. She wished her hair didn't stick up. She wished the white chalk she used at practice didn't show up on her skin as much. She wished she fit in.

Standing on the floor with her hand over her heart waiting for the music to begin, Dennis was ready to stand out more than ever.

"I got back to my roots," Dennis said. "I know who I am as a woman and a Black woman at that."

That woman celebrated Black culture in a 90-second floor routine that took over social media with more than 10 million views in the first weekend. Her score of 9.95 clinched UCLA's season-opening win on Jan. 23 against Arizona State as she whipped her black ponytail through sassy dance breaks then refocused for effortless full-twisting front flips and soaring double backflips. Her teammates and coaches served as the ideal, socially distant backup dancers.

Stars like Missy Elliott, Simone Biles and Janet Jackson gave her shoutouts on Twitter. Seeing Michelle Obama's tweet floored her the most.

"Now that's what I call fierce," the former First Lady wrote on Twitter. "You're a star!"

With her second viral floor routine in as many years, Dennis made another appearance on *The Ellen DeGeneres Show*, and did interviews via Zoom on *The Today Show* and NBC. When retired NBA star Dwyane Wade introduced himself before asking a question on TNT's *Inside the NBA*, Dennis sheepishly covered her face in disbelief.

"What's your message?" the three-time NBA champion said.

Inspired by the Black Lives Matter protests that unfolded last summer, Dennis wanted to add her piece to the social justice conversation. Instead of leading chants at marches or holding a sign, the 21-year-old communicated with tumbling passes as sentences and dance moves as punctuation. The message was still perfectly clear.

Celebrate Black excellence.

A place for expression
BJ Das was the mastermind behind Dennis' routine, but UCLA's volunteer assistant coach and choreographer can thank Dennis' father Casey for one critical element.

With Dennis and Das hoping to add step dancing into the routine, Casey, who pledged Phi Beta Sigma at Ohio State, put on his UCLA sweatshirt and boots and sent short clips for inspiration. The intricate dancing Dennis performs during Missy Elliott's "Pass That Dutch" when she claps her hands and taps her chest while rocking forward and backward was taken from one of Casey's videos.

Seeing the personal touch in the final product was "exhilarating" for Casey.

Casey, a pharmacist, pledged the historically Black fraternity while searching for a place to fit in at the large university. The Sigmas, along with being known for their signature "Sigma Nutcracker" step, were noted for social activities, community service and preparing members for entering life after college.

To Dennis, Greek life is a "form of unity in the Black community." To Casey, it was a "support structure of like-minded people." It allowed him to grow into the man he is today, Casey added.

His daughter, who started gymnastics at 4 years old, struggled to find the same place to express herself.

Gymnastics was her main social circle. Almost everyone she spent time with there was white. They made comments about her hair, asking to touch it. They pointed out how chalky Dennis looked at practice when the white powder gymnasts use to prepare their hands and feet to grip the equipment contrasted with her dark skin.

The statements weren't meant with malice, but Dennis just wanted to stop being the topic of every conversation.

"A bunch of comments like that would always kill my confidence in who I wanted to be," she said. "I'm not even going to pretend like I didn't go through this phase when I was younger: I did used to want to be white."

Dennis was sometimes dejected when she came home from practice, but her mother Deetra never missed an opportunity to tell her daughter she was beautiful. At the time Dennis thought Deetra was just saying what moms were supposed to say. Only after believing the words herself did Dennis realize the importance of having her mother's influence.

"Not hearing those words has a bigger impact than hearing those words because you don't even think that way [if you don't hear them]," Dennis said. "To have her feeding those words into my ear, I was slowly, but surely believing them."

Although she can't speak during her routine, Dennis wants Black girls and women to feel those inspirational words when she performs.

"I aspire to inspire," Dennis said.

Before she became a two-time viral sensation, Dennis was just trying to inspire those close to her, none more important than her younger sister. Mya, 11, brags to all of her friends that her older sister is so famous.

Mya is Dennis' "why."

"I don't ever want her to be ashamed of the color of her skin or want to wish it was lighter or want to wish it was different," Dennis said. "I want her to always love the skin that she's in and to be confident."

Break the mold
Dennis soars above her teammates' heads in her first tumbling pass, tucking her knees toward her chest into a tight ball as she flips twice in the air. Her legs can power her more than eight feet in the air. They helped her win junior national titles on vault and floor in 2014. They were also sometimes the target of criticism.

With her muscular legs, Dennis was accused of not having "clean" lines in her gymnastics during her elite career, as if the curves of her muscles distracted from the perfect split of a leap or a straight handstand on the bar.

Like how NFL scouts have used stereotypes to evaluate players—white players are more often described as cerebral and hard-working while Black players tend to be described more on their physical attributes—gymnasts of color often fight against similar barriers.

"It seems that Black gymnasts are usually known for more power rather than grace," said former UCLA gymnast JaNay Honest, who is Black. "Gymnastics is a subjective sport and there's also this body type, which we've been trying to change the culture of it. You gotta be 90 pounds and thin and tiny ... but obviously a lot of females are just not like that and specifically with Black women."

A Pac-12 Networks reporter, Honest was on the broadcast for Dennis' viral routine this year. At a meet in 2019, she interviewed former UCLA gymnast Kim Hamilton Anthony, who was the first African American gymnast to receive a full scholarship to compete at UCLA. The six-time All-American and four-time national champion said she was told "gymnastics was a white girl sport." People told her to give up.

"I'm so glad to know there are other athletes who look like me who can see my tape and I was able to go before them and pioneer in the sport," Anthony said during the interview.

In 2012, 73% of Division I female gymnasts were white, according to data from the NCAA, 7% were Black and 20% were "other." In 2019, the percentage of white gymnasts fell to 65% while Black representation grew to 9%. Other races made the largest jump to 26%.

Before Dennis' popular routines, several Black gymnasts gained notoriety with unique floor routines. Louisiana State's Lloimincia Hall (2014) and UCLA gymnasts Sophina DeJesus (2017) and Hallie Mossett (2018) earned millions of views.

Yet for every viral sensation in college gymnastics, there are still Black gymnasts facing discrimination within their own teams.

Black gymnasts from several schools including Alabama, Florida and UC Davis spoke to ESPN in 2020 about the racism they faced in the sport in the midst of the country's racial reckoning following the George Floyd protests. White gymnasts used the N-word despite pleas from Black teammates to stop. One Alabama coach referred to a group of Black gymnasts standing together at practice as "the back of the bus." The Black gymnasts were asked to overlook the incident as "a joke."

Watching the protests unfold this summer was emotional for Dennis. She was frustrated, upset and angry to see the continued prevalence of racism, and especially police brutality. "I was honestly scared for my life," Dennis said.

After UCLA's season was canceled last year because of the pandemic, Dennis used the down time to undergo shoulder surgery to correct a torn labrum she was competing on for five years. While recovering, she couldn't partake in marches or protests.

She would speak out on her own time.

Loud and clear

Lyrics are not allowed in floor routines, but Dennis still wanted to say something with her musical selection.

The original list of possibilities for Dennis' routine included around 85 songs, said Das, who helped choreograph all of UCLA's routines this year. With help from music producer Jack Rayner, who was working in Australia at the time, the final mix included eight. It's still more than Das would normally use, but Dennis fought to keep each one.

They all have meaning.

"We didn't really settle," Das said. "We wanted to do it right and we wanted her voice to be heard."

When the music starts, Dennis drops to a knee and raises a fist, two simple gestures made iconic in the fight against racial injustice by Colin Kaepernick and Olympians Tommie Smith and John Carlos. Kendrick Lamar's "Humble" leads the mix. Dennis, who calls the routine "The Culture," picked the song because Lamar has long advocated through music.

Each artist included had a significant impact on Black culture, Dennis said, whether it was through music or dance. She hits popular dance moves like Soulja Boy's "Crank That" and the woah. The Columbus, Ohio, native heel-toes to Tupac Shakur's

"California Love" and flashes four fingers on each hand, paying homage to UCLA's "fours up" slogan.

The senior didn't want to leave without honoring the place that helped shape her.

"UCLA gymnastics is probably the best place to come," Dennis said. "I'm not trying to sound any type of way, but we celebrate each other's individuality and our differences and our cultures 100% and this is honestly the best place I could have gone to find myself."

Dennis said she has grown "light years" during her four years at UCLA. In the process, she's embodied different characters on the floor from the Queen of the Nile during her sophomore year to a majorette leading a band as a junior. But this final piece stands out because Dennis is not playing a character.

It seems fitting she will leave UCLA performing simply as herself.

"I just know that I have to stay true to myself," Dennis said. "That's always going to get me farther than anything else."

Thuc Nhi Nguyen is a sports reporter for the *Los Angeles Times* covering college sports and professional basketball. She previously covered UCLA, professional soccer, and preps for the Southern California News Group after studying mathematics and journalism at the University of Washington.

Paspalum Shadows

ANDREW LAWRENCE

FROM *The Golfer's Journal* • MAY 16, 2021

On Sept. 26, 1783, a great schooner shoved off from London. Though the name on her stern was French, the Union Jack flying just above left no doubt that the *Comte du Nord* was now a thoroughly English vessel.

Like the seafarers of her day, the *Comte* was hewn from impressive timber and sported colossal masts draped with great sails to harness mighty westbound gales. But according to slavevoyages.org—an international research cooperative run through Emory University that has been investigating the transatlantic trade since 1992—the *Comte's* most impressive feature was her 700-ton payload, a size that would be tested some two months later when she ported in Malembo, a modest harbor in the West African country of Angola. The *Comte's* captain, a notorious Liverpudlian trader named James Penny, listed on the ship's manifest 97 women, 131 girls, 197 men and 249 boys—all loaded into her lower holds for future sale.

Over the course of six months, Penny packed these captives onto the *Comte* head to foot like spoons for a 49-day Middle Passage to Charleston, South Carolina. Those considered for the voyage but deemed too sickly to make the trip were murdered on the dock where they stood. The cries of those on the ship cut through the crackle of the swells crashing against the *Comte's* groaning hull as the abducted were ripped from their families, customs and cultures of a native land on which they would never again set foot. Men were bound together by their hands and feet to prevent insurrection, while women, considered lesser threats, were granted freedom to roam on deck and help with the cooking—though not without risking sexual harassment, assault or outright rape at the hands of the crew. Daily rations might include yam, biscuits, rice and horse beans boiled to the consistency of a pulp, but the way it was served—in a single bucket to be shared among roughly 10 people—was as likely to lead to fights as infections.

Worse, the *Comte* had no commode for these men, women and children. They could either relieve themselves over the edge of the ship or do their business in buckets—which, with the size of the crowd, overflowed quickly. In addition to the excreta, the cargo floors were consistently glazed in mucus, blood and vomit. In rough seas, the *Comte's* portholes were closed, leaving the Africans in her belly gasping for breath and prone to disease. The whole mix made for a steamy, unholy stench that, to the sturdy nose of Alexander Falconbridge, a British slave-ship medic who authored the seminal abolitionist tome *An Account of the Slave Trade on the Coast of Africa* in 1788, "resembled a slaughter-house. It is not in the power of the human imagination to picture a situation more dreadful or disgusting." To help sop up the mess, the ship was bedded with grass pulled from the Angolan deltas.

Today, the same turf lines fairways and greens all over the world.

GORGEOUS COASTAL VISTAS and fickle seaborne gusts pull amateurs and major championships alike to the Ocean Course at South Carolina's Kiawah Island Golf Resort. "You can play this golf course four days in a row and not have the same wind," says director of golf Brian Gerard. But the thing they all never seem to forget about this course is its viridescent surface—made up of a single grass type called *paspalum vaginatum*, or seashore paspalum. It's virtually the same grass that once lined the hull of the *Comte du Nord* and the scads of other slave ships that crisscrossed the Atlantic between 1500 and 1870, during the largest forced human migration in recorded history. The sod has been a course feature for the past 13 years, with the Ocean Course making the transition to paspalum ahead of its maiden PGA hosting in 2012. Since then, all five of Kiawah's courses and its learning center have been converted to paspalum from Bermuda. "And the difference between managing the two [grasses]," says superintendent Jeff Stone, "is night and day. There's no similarity whatsoever."

Paspalum's currency lies in its playability—it can be cut to any length—and its uncanny knack for processing salt. Unlike Bermuda, "one of the least salt-tolerant Southern grasses," says Stone, paspalum has a number of mechanisms for dealing with salinity that are still only partially understood. Paul L. Raymer, the professor in charge of the University of Georgia's turf breeding program—staffed by the leading researchers on paspalum—has isolated at least three of those mechanisms: paspalum's selective uptake, its ability to partition off the sodium it does take up, and its lack of surface salt glands; unlike Bermuda or more resilient zoysia grasses, paspalum can actually store salt on the surface of its leaves. "We don't fully understand it," Raymer says. "We would love to identify key mechanisms in paspalum and then move them into crop plants like wheat and alfalfa so we could actually grow crops on salt-affected soils."

Not only does paspalum thrive on the brackish well-water sources at Kiawah, but it likewise has no problem weathering the hurricanes that batter this region with increasing regularity, many of them tracing the same path as the *Comte du Nord* and other slave ships; the South Carolina Lowcountry and Georgia's Coastal Empire alone have been hit with more major storms over the past five years (seven) than in the decade prior (zero).

Berry Collett, the director of golf at Sea Island (a three-and-a-half-hour drive south from Kiawah), well remembers the anxiety he felt as Hurricane Irma buzzed up the coast in 2017. He had

just finished tinkering with paspalum on the Seaside Course fairways and some practice greens and feared his three years of work
would be ruined. When the storm dumped more than a half-foot
of rain and more than 5 feet of coastal flooding on the course,
Collett assumed the experiment—part of a never-ending quest
to "knock the socks off " his guests—was a bust. Or at least he
thought it was until he flew a drone over the course on a cloud-
less day after the storm and scoped his cellphone viewfinder. "It
looked healthy as ever, pure green," he says. "I was amazed and
thought, 'Damn, that paspalum is some good stuff.'"

COLLETT TELLS THIS STORY on a postcard-perfect 84-degree
weekday morning in July as a 71,000-ton cargo ship called *Golden
Ray* sits capsized in the channel, unwittingly winking at the dark
history on these shores. You can see it clearly from Sea Island's
ocean-facing putting greens, which at a glance seem made of
Astroturf. But then Collett has one of his charges dig out a plug
of turf with a hole cutter. Set off to the side, it looks like a flourless
chocolate cake you might order inside the lodge for $14—only
the icing has been replaced by a millimeters-thick layer of grass
with blades that feel waxy to the touch. After Rory McIlroy's 2012
PGA victory at Kiawah, Stone recalls, "some women came up to
take pictures with us. One of the ladies goes, 'I just wanna take
my shoes off and put my feet on this grass. This doesn't even look
real.'"

Surely this impulse rings true to the Liverpool fan who
dreams of romping barefoot over the pitch at Anfield, or the
Chicago Cubs lifer hell-bent on having their ashes sprinkled
in the outfield. Every field sport, it seems, has its own intimate
romance with grass. In golf, though, the relationship is technical,
too—as important to the game as club selection. This particular obsession—how different strains can *completely* change shot
strategy—turns golfers into self-proclaimed turf experts. Roger
Federer would be hard-pressed to name the grass variety at
Centre Court Wimbledon as quickly as the average golfer could

rattle off all the grasses on which they've played. And paspalum is as deceptive a surface as it comes, the greens especially. "The primary difference," says Kiawah head pro Stephen Younger, "is it doesn't have grain. So the break, and the consistency of the break, is truer throughout the entire roll of the putt. When you have Bermuda grass, wherever the green is growing closest to the hole, it's going to have a more dramatic effect on how much the ball breaks. Paspalum really putts a lot more like bent grass. Some of our players that come from parts of the country that have bent grass can adapt to the paspalum pretty quick."

Tim O'Neal falls in the opposite camp. Though born and raised in Savannah, Georgia, the 48-year-old touring pro cut his teeth on Bermuda-sod courses along the Southeastern shore. His first serious encounter with paspalum wouldn't come until he received an exemption into the 2007 Mayakoba Classic in Cancún, and it threw him for a loop he can still clearly recall. "Going out to the putting green, the grass looked a little weird," says O'Neal, who's seen a bit of everything over the course of his 23-year career. "And then, rolling putts on it, I soon realized that, OK, I don't know what this is. It sits straight up and really grabs chip shots. It's so sticky. I didn't adjust to it that well. I had never seen grass like that before." He would go on to miss the cut.

It wasn't until we spoke that O'Neal, who is Black, came to realize how much deeper his connection to the soil was on that day. "I did not know that at all," he admits, his usually stoic interview voice shaken. "I had no clue where that grass came from."

ON JULY 18, 1784, after a horrifying seven-week journey that tracked the Northern Equatorial currents across the Atlantic, the *Comte du Nord* docked in Charleston. After quarantining in port, the *Comte*'s enslaved were auctioned off in city squares. Despite losing 63 enslaved people during her Middle Passage, the *Comte* still carried a haul worth £27,556.71 sterling, or roughly $2.5 million in today's U.S. dollars. According to slavevoyages.org, of the nearly thousand cargos to enter the port of Charleston between 1670 and 1808, this haul was the largest single shipment of enslaved people to the Americas. That it was received nearly a decade after the First Continental Congress banned the importation of Africans as a response to British oppression makes this gruesome chapter of American history all the more significant.

An estimated 10 million Africans were shipped to the Western Hemisphere between 1500 and 1870 on ships like the *Comte*, more than 5% of them landing at ports along the coasts of South Carolina and Georgia, where, in 1775, there were two enslaved Africans for every free colonist. And this human capital, which promised technical skill in addition to free labor, would not only set the foundation for a trillion-dollar agriculture-based economy that would position the United States as a global superpower, but also create a system of economic and racial inequality that abides to this day. As these enslaved people were processed and sold to what slavevoyages.org counts as 133 separate parties in the urban heart of Charleston, where transactions were conducted in the same manner as cattle auctions, they'd leave behind blades of ship bedding, this seashore paspalum, on the beach. That's where Ron Duncan, Raymer's predecessor at the University of Georgia, found it growing in the early 1990s. And when he collected more of it from Sea Island, Mexico, the Caribbean and Central and South America, it confirmed his theory that the grass had indeed migrated with slaveship traffic.

Meanwhile, the turf's potential application in golf made for its own saga. Research in this area goes as far back as the 1960s, with early distribution orders for Southeastern courses originating from samples collected from the 13th fairway of Sea Island's Marsh Course, where it was taken for a weed and an existential threat to the flourishing Bermuda. Nowadays it can be found at Emirates Golf Club in Dubai, Turtle Bay Resort in Hawaii, Hanoi's Tam Dao Resort and many other far-flung seaside locales. Kiawah, which credits the legendary architect Pete Dye for championing the species there, says its Ocean Course is the northernmost U.S. plot to go full paspalum. Meanwhile,

Sea Island features paspalum only here and there—for now. Its success with the salinity of the surrounding area has the team thinking a full change is in order. "Mother Nature is telling us we need to redo this whole course in paspalum," Collett says.

THE ADOPTION OF AFRICAN TURFGRASS represents yet another layer of cultural erasure in a larger game of gentrification. Coastal Georgia and South Carolina alone have come a long way. Three centuries ago, these lands were dismissed as barely habitable, what with their marshlands, insects and humidity so suffocating that plantation-owning families would retreat to pieds-à-terre farther inland during the summer months. So it figures that, during Reconstruction, freed slaves were awarded parcels of this undesirable land. Besides, who'd want to live here when the war-torn South was basically broke?

But then, in the decades following slavery's abolition in 1865, two important things happened: Georgia and the Carolinas legalized chain gangs, which comprised free Blacks rounded up on misdemeanor charges and leased to businesses to pave roads and work farmland, and air conditioning was invented. Suddenly, well-heeled whites who never would have lived in this sweltering climate were manipulating the tax code to cheat Gullah-Geechee descendants of enslaved people out of land that was rightfully theirs, to build posh resorts and gated communities. And, more often than not, the centerpiece of these pleasure centers—many of them still calling themselves "plantations" well into the 21st century—were golf courses.

The road to the Ocean Course at Kiawah Island alone has more checkpoints than Parris Island. On the August weekday morning I drove through, white couples and families walked and rode bikes on paths that dead-end a few miles short of a Black neighborhood in Charleston.

At Sea Island, the scene was much the same: middle-aged white men taking cuts at their own pace, women and children lounging out by the pool. The few Black faces were tucked behind

service counters and sentry towers; in a picture, you'd be lucky to
see one lingering on the fringe. "We like the *Gone With the Wind*
history," says Amir Jamal Touré, an Africana studies professor at
Savannah State University, "the nice, sanitized story of the happy-
go-lucky African. People don't want the truth because they come
here to play tennis and golf. We want to promote that. We want
people to keep coming back."

When I asked Kiawah Island's golf stewards if their players
have any sense of the history underfoot, the most Younger, the
head pro, could offer was, "I think when we sit here and talk about
it with you, that's great. That's a vehicle for getting the story out.
It's a cool story."

It's a lived story for O'Neal, the journeyman pro, who easily
calls up the moments when he was profiled while playing on
what was then called the Nationwide Tour. There was the time in
2000 when a locker room attendant asked him to leave because
they thought he was trespassing, or the time a year later when
a security guard asked him to vacate a players-only eating area
because he didn't look like one—and nearly succeeded until a
peer came to O'Neal's defense. "It's just one of those things you
always remember," O'Neal says. "I remember exactly what course
it was. I remember exactly where it was. I say it doesn't bother
me, but it's there."

The specter of the *Comte du Nord* is there too. It's a centuries-
long legacy of pain and suffering that fits within a single blade of
grass. And as incredible as it is that the paspalum that once lined
those great schooners still endures, one could also say the same
of the people who originally were forced upon it.

Andrew Lawrence is a features writer for *The Guardian*, where he covers culture
and sport. Prior, he was a longtime staff writer at *Sports Illustrated*, specializing
in motorsports. *The Golfer's Journal* is one in a slew of publications where his
byline has also appeared. Previously, he was honorably mentioned for his 2016
SI.com feature on the Jewish-Israeli Nascar driver Alon Day and his 2018 *Men's
Health* story on the dangers of youth football.

Rosalie Fish Wants to Be the Face of Change

MIRIN FADER

FROM The Ringer • JULY 23, 2021

Before every race, Rosalie Fish stares at her reflection in the mirror. She pauses a few minutes and thinks of Indigenous women. Women who have gone missing, who have been murdered. Those whose names she knows, those whose names she'll never know.

Aunts, cousins, neighbors, classmates. Women who had families, who had ambitions. Who had children, friends, dreams, desires.

She paints a giant red hand across her mouth, stretching across her cheeks. Red is the color that spirits, that ancestors, can see, according to some Native traditions. The hand over her mouth is meant to represent and honor the Indigenous women who have been silenced through violence—sexual violence, physical violence, psychological violence—an epidemic that receives little national attention.

"I had always known I was a target," Fish says.

When she closes her eyes, she can see the women's faces. Sometimes Fish, a member of the Cowlitz Tribe and a descendent of the Muckleshoot Tribe, thinks of her aunt Alice Ida Looney. Looney disappeared when Fish was 2 years old, and was found deceased 15 months later. Fish also thinks of Renee Davis, a Native woman close to her family who was six months pregnant with her unborn son, Massi Molina, at the time she was killed. Her mind drifts to Misty Upham, the Native Hollywood actress who disappeared and was later found dead when Fish was around 12.

Fish started running to cope. To clear her mind. When she steps outside her home, past the pines and the large cedar in her front yard, to go running throughout the Muckleshoot Reservation, where she lives, in Auburn, Washington, she can briefly distract herself from the fear that pierces her: that as an Indigenous woman, she, too, could disappear.

She signed a letter of intent to compete for the University of Washington's women's track-and-field team as a transfer in January. She had led Iowa Central Community College to the National Junior College Athletic Association cross country title in 2019, and finished fifth overall at the National Half Marathon Championships in 2020.

"Resilience and self-belief are the two biggest predictors of success at this level, which bodes well for Rosalie," says Maurica Powell, Washington's director of track & field and cross country, who coaches Fish.

Fish is accustomed to being one of the only Native runners in her sport. Hearing racist comments as she runs, as she shines.

She runs to raise awareness for the Missing and Murdered Indigenous Women (MMIW) and Girls movement. Indigenous women on some reservations are murdered at a rate of more than 10 times the national average of other ethnicities, according to Department of Justice data from 2008. In the United States, murder is the third-leading cause of death among Native women.

More than four out of five Indigenous women have experienced violence. The perpetrators of this violence are often never held accountable.

In an analysis of the nation's urban centers, the Urban Indian Health Institute division of the Seattle Indian Health

Board reports that Washington state has the second most cases of missing Indigenous women. Seattle, which is about 30 minutes north of Rosalie's home in Auburn, ranked first among cities nationwide.

That's why Fish often asks friends to text her to let her know they've made it home safely when they go out at night. She leaves her phone's ringer on the highest volume when she sleeps, just in case. And when she leaves her home to go run around the reservation, she sometimes leaves behind notes for her family that read:

"If I end up missing, I did not run away. And if something happens to me, and I lose my life, I did not take it."

FISH DRAWS INSPIRATION from runner Jordan Marie Brings Three White Horses Daniel, of the Kul Wicasa Oyaté/Lower Brule Sioux Tribe, who paints her own face as a prominent leader of MMIW. When Fish first saw Daniel, who ran the Boston Marathon wearing the red hand print, she was left in awe. Both women hope to bring awareness to the crisis of violence against Indigenous women, which is often undercovered by mainstream outlets.

"Our relatives go missing three times— in life, in the media, and in the data," Daniel says. "And readers must also realize how prevalent this violence is, the jurisdictional loopholes that make it difficult to prosecute, the institutionalized racism that exists within law enforcement, the misrepresentation of Native peoples in the media, in school curriculums and stereotypes that all contribute to the normalization of racism we experience and erasure of Native peoples from almost every conversation we have today.

"When I wear the red handprint, it is sacred to me," Daniel continues. "It is not a fashion statement nor a political statement. It symbolizes the violence silencing our relatives' voices."

The first time Fish painted the handprint on her own face, as a senior at Muckleshoot Tribal School in 2019, she was terrified.

Terrified at the negative reactions she knew she'd receive from spectators, opponents, officials. Sure enough, some said she should be disqualified from competition for deviating from uniform code. Others shouted from the stands:

"*Hey, what's on your face!*"

"Look at her war paint!"

"*That's so stupid. Just run!*"

But Fish can't *just run*. Not when she's experienced walking into her school's girls' bathroom and seeing "DIRTY INDIAN SAVAGES" written on the stalls. Not when she's been rejected from some invitational meets despite boasting top qualifying times. Not when she lives in a world that often looks the other way when women who look like her disappear.

THE FIRST TIME FISH, whose friends and family call her Rosy, realized she was "different," as she puts it, was in elementary school. She watched as members of her tribe performed traditional Coast Salish canoe family dances and songs on stage at a school event in Auburn. She walked up to join them, instinctively drawn to the beat.

Her shoulders, her waist, her feet, all knew what to do. Her head tilted back and forth, her smile drawn wide. Lost in song, she felt safe. Powerful.

She grew up hearing stories of how resilient her ancestors were. How she is a descendent of a vibrant people who persevered and danced, who sang and survived. She learned about her great-grandfather, George Cross Jr., and another family member, Henry KingGeorge, who were jailed for fighting discriminatory hunting and fishing laws. She felt proud when she heard those stories.

When she got off stage, though, her face flushed with embarrassment as her white classmates began to mock her. She regretted performing the dance and began to feel self-conscious. Ashamed. "For a really long time, I didn't really want to embrace the fact that I was Indigenous," she says.

Classmates continued to mock her as she got older. Attending a predominantly white high school, Auburn Riverside, for the first half of her freshman year, she often faced microaggressions and racist comments. She was sexually harassed, she says, as other students grabbed, pinched, and catcalled her. She felt violated, and blamed herself.

She felt isolated, not just in terms of her Indigenous identity, but in other aspects of her identity as well. "I had begun to realize that I was queer," says Fish, who uses she/her pronouns.

Things at home weren't much easier. At times, Fish's step-father would come home drunk, yelling. Fish suffered severe depression by age 14. She felt as if she would never belong at school, internalizing years of messaging that girls who looked like her had no place. She'd look at herself in the mirror, fixate on every part of her body, and think: *There is nothing to love about me.*

She ran occasionally, but didn't yet consider herself a runner. Every day she felt more alone. *Nobody wants to hear what I have to say.*

She was prescribed antidepressants, but began excessively using them. She felt as if she didn't have any value, as if she didn't deserve to take up space. She felt hopeless, and tired. So tired.

Then she attempted to take her own life.

Fish hadn't anticipated surviving. She was brought to the local hospital's emergency room.

Autumn McCloud, her mother, fearfully waited outside her room. McCloud, a member of the Yakama Nation and descendent of the Muckleshoot Tribe, tried to reconcile the past, the present. Her daughter's suffering, her own suffering. Old memories flooded McCloud: how scared she was of her own father, who heavily drank, so much that she and her siblings would hide in the laundry room, waiting until his rage subsided.

She thought about how she tried so hard to give Fish a better life, having gotten pregnant with her at 18. "I tried to make things better," McCloud says of her family's relations. "I tried to be the peacekeeper." And there she and her daughter were, all these years later, trying to understand how patterns repeated themselves. Patterns McCloud now realizes stem in part from the boarding schools that previous Native generations, including her own family, were forced into.

Thousands of Indigenous children in the U.S. and Canada were sent to these boarding schools in the 19th and 20th centuries to erase their traditions, languages, and cultures. Abuse of all kinds was rampant in the schools. Large numbers of children did not return, according to the Truth and Reconciliation Commission of Canada; more than 4,100 were confirmed to have died at the schools. The commission, established in 2008, called the practice cultural genocide. In May, the remains of 215 children's bodies were found buried at a former Canadian school.

Fish says her great-great-grandparents suffered physical, sexual, and psychological abuse in the boarding schools—trauma that would become braided into the fabric of her family for decades to come. "We are lucky to even be in existence," McCloud says.

After everything her family has endured, McCloud worried they could lose Rosy, too, after she attempted to harm herself. "I didn't feel safe bringing her home," McCloud says.

So they stayed at the hospital longer. An elder on the reservation, a man who performed spiritual work, came by to visit Fish. He was a friend of McCloud's grandfather—Fish's great-grandfather—and wanted to see if he could help nurture her spirit.

"Rosy," the elder said, "losing you is one of our biggest fears." She looked up at him, taking in the word *our*.

"I don't know if we can handle another child in the graveyard," he said.

Something in her felt seen. Accounted for. "He opened my eyes," Fish says, "to seeing myself not as an individual who was alone, but someone who was part of a community."

Once Fish returned home, she saw the way her mother, her siblings, her extended family, her community, banded together for her. They told her that she was worth living for. Worth loving.

She felt the kindness, the warmth, of her aunts and of her grandmother, in the smallest of moments, like draping a coat over her when they sensed she might be cold. "When I saw my community and my family doing everything they could to make sure I was all right," Fish says, "it was so overwhelming I almost had no choice but to feel love for myself.

"At that time when I didn't really feel like I had the strength or confidence to live for myself, I was able to find a way to live for others."

She started running every day, thinking it could help calm her down. Center her. It had been a hobby, not a refuge. But now, it was slowly becoming so much more to her. It made her feel safe. Seen. It brought her joy, peace. A sense of belonging. So she'd run. Run through the reservation, past the cedars, the neighbors waving as she whirled by. She became obsessed with the feeling of the wind hitting her face as she picked up speed.

She was a natural distance runner, able to run for miles and miles at a time. First two, then three, then more. She didn't seem to tire. As she built up even more stamina, more strength, she wanted to keep running, pushing past her limits.

Running gave her purpose. It became a coping mechanism as she began to focus on her mental health. Talk to a counselor. Slowly, she started to appreciate her body; the miraculous way bones and joints and muscles and organs worked together to propel one foot in front of the other, mile after mile.

To run was to look at the past, to look at everything trying to hold her down, and say: I am still here. *We* are still here.

FISH WANTED A FRESH START, so she transferred to Muckleshoot Tribal School. Though she was learning alongside other Native students, she competed in league meets against the biggest schools in the area. She was almost always the only Native runner.

Fish's coach, Mike Williams, would try to enter her into competitive invitational meets, but would often be denied. "Well, I've never heard of Muckleshoot Tribal School," Williams remembers hearing from officials. Williams is not Native, but he's been a part of the Puyallup tribal community for 15 years.

One official asked whether Fish even owned a uniform, as if she couldn't possibly have one because she lives on a reservation. Other times, officials suggested she run in the junior varsity division, despite her varsity qualifying times. "It was really frustrating," Williams says.

Fish grew even more determined, running seven days a week. "That was the only way I could prove to the people who had prejudice toward Native Americans that we were perfectly capable of competing," she says.

Fans continued to hurl racist comments at her, especially when she started painting the red handprint on her face before races. She'd find other slurs and hateful messages on bathroom stalls at different meets.

Sometimes Fish's confidence would falter. *Do I really deserve to be here?* Williams would remind her: "You belong. I know you can win. Show them you can win!"

You belong here. You deserve to be here, she'd repeat to herself. Again and again.

She began to shine, winning numerous Washington state titles at the 1B level, including the 800 meter, 1,600 meter, and 3,200 meter as a senior in 2019.

She felt pride when she would beat girls from much bigger schools, hearing, "Rosalie Fish, Muckleshoot, in first place!" every time she came around the drag. "Everybody was like, who is this?" Williams says.

Winning state meant a great deal to her, because she won the sportsmanship medal there, too. She dedicated the 3,200-meter race to the memory of Renee Davis.

Fish cherished how women in her community rallied behind her. And slowly she began to come out of her shell. Trust people.

Once, before a race, a staffer at her school named Jenel Hunter
came up to her, and saw that Fish hadn't put her hair up for the
meet. Hunter smiled. "Don't you have a race coming up?"
    "Yeah," Fish said.
    "You should have your hair braided. I'll do it."
    It was freeing, feeling loved.

BUT FEAR WAS NEVER TOO FAR BEHIND, always chasing her
no matter how fast she ran. She and a high school friend went to
the mall one afternoon and spotted an unhoused woman asking
for a few dollars. Fish only had a credit card on her. "Sorry," Fish
said, "I don't have anything."
    She took about three steps in the other direction, and a famil-
iar anxiety seized her. *What if she's in danger? What if she needs
a bus ticket? What's going to happen to her?* Fish sprinted back
to her car, rummaging through her things to find any kind of
money. By the time she had gotten back, the woman was gone.
    Fish looked grief-stricken. Her friend tried to console her:
"Rosy, this is impacting who you are. This is impacting the way
you think, the way you act."
    In some ways, Fish knows it always will. She cannot separate
herself from that woman. From Indigenous women. She doesn't
want to. They are her. She is them. And all she wanted for them,
for herself, was to feel safe.
    So she kept running. Kept trying to raise awareness of vio-
lence against Native women. But despite her success on the track,
Fish flew under the radar in terms of college recruiting. She had
her best marks as a senior, when college scouts had largely already
picked out their scholarship athletes.
    Williams reached out to Iowa Central Community College,
a nationally respected program. Within five minutes of receiving
Williams's email, Iowa Central coach Dee Brown responded. He
was interested. And he'd soon learn she was the perfect fit: "She's
so motivated," Brown says. "So focused, so hard working. She

doesn't want to let any one person, or any one team, outdo her. She's eager and hungry to be the best she can be."

Fish continued to race with the red handprint on her face as she helped the Tritons win the national title in 2019 and take second at the National Half Marathon Championships in 2020. She began to share her story with local Native kids and beyond, realizing that running gave her a platform. And, after watching Jordan Marie Brings Three White Horses Daniel use her own platform, Fish felt she needed to do more to use hers as more and more Indigenous women turned up missing. And she hoped that if she shared the depths of her own struggles, it would make other Native girls and women feel less alone as they grappled with their own.

The first time she spoke to an assembly of schoolchildren, she was shaking. It was difficult, remembering how isolated, how worthless, she felt as a 14-year-old before attempting to take her own life.

She was vulnerable, cracking herself open for so many to see. But then she thought about how she wished someone back then had told her: "You are valuable. You deserve to take up space." So she continued to speak.

"It's comforting to know that she tells her struggles," says Cedar McCloud, her sister, "so when people of similar identities go through hardships, it's not as isolating."

When Fish saw a little girl with long black braids in the audience that day, she felt something new: hope. Hope for the next generation.

"It was hypothesized that it would take eight generations in order to heal the trauma that was left from boarding schools," Fish says. "I'm the fifth generation. And my great-grandchildren could live a life of no trauma from the boarding schools if I continue to work, and I survive, and I make it, and I try to break these cycles."

That was part of the appeal of signing with the University of Washington, in a state with 29 federally recognized tribes. Her entire family was so proud. Less than 1 percent of all NCAA athletes are Indigenous. "I cried," says her mom, Autumn, who herself is a graduate of UW Tacoma.

Fish's great-grandfather, George Cross Jr., would have been proud too. He was a big Huskies fan. He'd often call UW "the best school in the world."

Cross was the eldest Muckleshoot male tribal member when he died in March at 84 years old. He used to take Fish and McCloud's grandmother, Rosalie Cross, whom Fish is named after, to the nearby White River.

When Fish was 6 years old, she would sit snuggled between them in their pickup truck. They'd eat sandwiches and watch the river glimmer as it caught the light. She heard stories of how sacred rivers are to her community, how it sustained them with food and water over generations.

For a moment, reflecting on these experiences, she feels peace. But then the anxiety returns. The women flood into her brain again. The women who still have not been accounted for.

Women like Alyssa McLemore, from the Aleut tribe, who has been missing from Kent, Washington. She'd be 33 years old now.

Women like Kaylee Mae Nelson-Jerry, who is Fish's cousin. Nelson-Jerry grew up in Muckleshoot. She has been missing from Auburn since July 2019. She is 22 years old.

LATELY, FISH AND HER MOTHER have been talking more about the past and the future. What has been swept under the rug. Fish reminds her mother that she, too, deserves to heal.

As they recently reflected on difficult moments in Fish's childhood, and discussed how scared Fish and her siblings felt at times, McCloud started to cry.

"Mom," Fish said, "I didn't mean to upset you."

"No, no, it's OK," McCloud said. "I'd rather we talk about it."

Fish leaned over and snuggled into her mom's shoulder for a side hug. McCloud was surprised. Physical affection is still somewhat new for her. Hugs between the two of them have always been a little awkward, McCloud says, because she hadn't grown up with physical affection, either. "It's not because I don't love you," McCloud once told her daughter. "It's that I don't always know how to."

On this afternoon, though, some thread between them had been untangled. They embraced a beat longer than either were used to. As they held each other, something in Fish shifted.

You belong here. You deserve to be here.

Mirin Fader is a senior staff writer for The Ringer, writing long-form human interest sports features. She's the *New York Times* bestselling author of *Giannis: The Improbable Rise of an NBA MVP*. Her work has been honored by the Pro Writers Basketball Association, the Associated Press Sports Editors, the U.S. Writers Basketball Association, and the Los Angeles Press Club.

Courtney's Story

DIANA MOSKOVITZ

FROM Defector • SEPTEMBER 13, 2021

Courtney Smith remembers the exact moment her life fell apart. She was alone in her home in Powell, Ohio, a suburb of Columbus. She knew that she did not want her kids there or with her ex-husband. She wanted them somewhere safe, so she sent them to stay with her dad. She closed the curtain and the blinds, and turned on the TV. It was July 24, 2018, and she watched Urban Meyer, then the head football coach of the Ohio State Buckeyes, give a press conference.

What she wanted and needed was for Meyer to tell the truth about what he knew had happened between her and her ex-husband, Zach Smith. Zach had been Ohio State's wide receivers coach until he was fired a day earlier, after college football reporter Brett McMurphy published a report about Smith being the subject of a protection order and having been investigated for domestic violence against Courtney in the past. At the time, all that was publicly known about what had happened between Courtney and Zach was the information contained in McMurphy's 789 words published on Facebook. To many people, especially those who aren't college football fans, Meyer's press conference might have meant very little; those who cared to watch it were probably only interested in seeing how gracefully or awkwardly he would handle questions about the report and Smith's firing.

But for Courtney Smith, the stakes could not have been higher.

Courtney watched Meyer's press conference, not just as the ex-wife of a football coach, but as one who had been as close as a person could get to being Ohio State royalty. She watched as a woman who had once learned how to orient every aspect of her life around football and her husband's career. She watched as a woman who had for years documented, both in her diary and with photos and screenshots, the verbal and physical abuse she said she had received from Zach. She would never forget the night in Florida when he threw her after they got into an argument, or the time in Ohio when he put his hands around her throat and only stopped because her father walked in. She watched as a woman who had finally said no, gotten her own home with the kids, filed for divorce, and enrolled in nursing school. She watched as a woman who knew that her life was about to change, because all the things she had tried for so long to keep secret for the sake of her and her family were finally being brought to light, and the last place she wanted to be was at the center of a salacious college football scandal. It was for that reason that she needed Meyer to tell the truth.

"'Oh my God, please tell the truth,'" she recalled saying as Meyer spoke. "I was on my hands and knees, going, 'Please tell the truth, Urban, please.'"

Urban Meyer would fail Courtney Smith that day, and he wasn't alone. Defector's conversations with Courtney and those who are close to her, as well as the examination of hundreds of pages of records from law enforcement, the courts, and Ohio State, reveal the many ways that people and institutions across Ohio acted to primarily protect themselves rather than Courtney.

Prosecutors did not present a 2015 domestic violence investigation of Zach to a grand jury. Police withheld public records that documented the abuse, all while rabid college football fans called Courtney a liar, bitter, and crazy. Ohio State left her twisting in the wind, even after she helped the school with its own investigation, not releasing the most damning proof about Meyer and his destruction of evidence until well after he had retired, ensconced in a cushy job as a TV football analyst. And then her ex-husband took everything that happened and used it to rebrand himself as a renegade college football expert, the kind who could tell you stories about what it's like to work with Meyer and complain about how the real victims of "the system" are men like him. This does not seem to bother any of the former Ohio State players who still associate with him.

Zach maintains that he never abused Courtney. When Defector Media contacted him seeking comment on this story and the documentation cited within, he said that there is no evidence he ever abused Courtney because all of the statements that were given to police were just "statements" and not what he considers evidence. He also said that the protection order was issued just as much for his own safety as Courtney's, and that his own recollection of what Courtney told him over the years does qualify as evidence. Finally, he said that anyone who ever said he did abuse Courtney must have been someone who was never around them much, and that every instance of abuse described by the documents cited in this story is "fabricated."

"I never abused her. There is no evidence. I never abused her," Zach told me.

I asked him why anyone should believe him. He told me, "I don't care if people believe me. I don't care if you believe me."

A glance at the football landscape might even convince you that nothing happened. Three years later, Meyer is a head coach again, this time in the NFL with the Jacksonville Jaguars. Ohio State is ranked among the top programs in the country. Football has moved on. But for Courtney, what happened wasn't just a few bad headlines or unfortunate days that could be easily papered over with well-timed press releases. It was her life. She still lives with the consequences of that day in July, even if the TV cameras are gone, even if Meyer is hundreds of miles away, even if Ohio State would rather stop talking about it.

How do you survive when life as you know it is falling apart? What do you do when it seems like every institution, nearly every person in a state of more than 11 million people, and even a member of your own family doesn't want to help you? Courtney Smith learned how.

ZACH AND COURTNEY met at the University of Kentucky. He was an undergraduate transfer from Bowling Green, where he had walked onto the football team coached by Meyer. She was a freshman from Ohio studying communications. They started dating, fell in love, and then Zach got a job with the football team at the University of Florida, where Meyer was the new head coach. Looking back, Courtney said she felt pressure to marry Zach, especially from her mother. After all, Zach was the grandson of Earle Bruce, the former Ohio State football coach who took over the team from the legendary Woody Hayes and also had served as Meyer's mentor.

After their engagement party, Courtney said she talked with her future grandmother-in-law, Bruce's wife, Jean. She gave Courtney a notebook and told her to write down everything that would happen to her. She also warned Courtney that being a coach's wife wasn't easy, and told her all about the challenges that she would face.

"She gave it to me and she said, *Are you sure this is what you want to do,*" Courtney recalled. "*I don't think you realize how hard it will be.*"

Courtney would soon learn all the unsaid but important responsibilities that came with being a coach's wife. There would be recruiting dinners, booster dinners, team dinners, all intertwined with scrambling for childcare, as well as possibly having to bring dessert. There would be away-game travel, bowl-game travel, and the Meyer tradition of the wives bringing candy for players after certain practices. There would be the expectation that at all these events, the coaches would look like good, clean family men, with wives by their sides.

But Courtney was so in love. The young couple married in June 2008, in a church in downtown Columbus, followed by a big reception at a nearby hotel, recalled one friend, who asked to not use her name for fear of retaliation. The wedding colors were silver and pink.

"I'll always remember Courtney peeking through the door to the reception," she said with a laugh, "and asking me, 'Do you think it's too pink?'"

Her friend told me that she had tried talking to Courtney about Zach in college. She didn't like how when Courtney started dating Zach, she saw her a lot less and it seemed like Zach was in charge. But when she tried to bring it up, Courtney didn't want to hear it, and her friend wasn't too surprised. She really was in love with Zach, and they had a beautiful wedding.

A year after the wedding was the first time Zach hurt her.

It started after a party hosted by Meyer and his wife, Shelley, in June 2009 at their home. The Meyers were the toast of the town; the football team had just won its second national championship in four seasons under Meyer, and Shelley taught in the university's nursing college. When the party ended, Courtney, who was about three months pregnant with her first child, was ready to go home. But her husband wanted to stay out longer with some other graduate students, she would tell police years later, as part of a separate investigation in Ohio. Courtney left alone and drove herself to their home near campus, according to the Ohio detective's notes.

Zach came home well after midnight, and he was not alone. With him was a woman who also worked at UF. Courtney heard them come home and peered out the window, where she saw her husband and the woman "all over each other," according to the Ohio detective's notes. When they came inside, Zach asked if the woman could sleep at their place, Courtney told police. She said no.

Courtney told police that she drove the woman home herself and then came home, where she and Zach started fighting. Zach, she told police, was drunk. He grabbed her by her T-shirt and threw her against the bedroom wall, she told Gainesville police. Years later, Courtney would tell officers in Ohio that Zach had a look in his eyes that night that she hadn't seen before. She said the way Zach changed was "like flipping a light switch."

Courtney called 911 that night because she was scared. The Gainesville police officer who arrived found Courtney crying. Her T-shirt had a stretch mark in it as if it had been pulled, according to the report, and police could see a red mark on Zach's right bicep. Courtney said it was from when she tried to protect herself after Zach picked her up. Zach told the officer that the mark was from breaking up a fight at a downtown club. Another officer took photos of the scene and of Courtney's injuries. The photos show her with bruising around one of her eyes. The arresting officer wrote in their report that Zach was the "primary aggressor," handcuffed him for aggravated battery on a pregnant female, and took him to a local jail, according to the report.

That night, Courtney called Zach's family; his mother as well as Earle Bruce hurried down to Florida, she said. The next morning, Hiram deFries, a former oil executive who followed Meyer from football program to football program and has been described as everything from a consultant to a confidante, told her she needed to drop the charges if Zach was ever going to coach again, Courtney recalled. Bruce arrived, she said, and told her he was going to talk to Meyer about what had happened. (Defector Media reached out to deFries for comment, but did not receive a response.)

"I was so distraught. I had not slept. I was pregnant," Courtney said. "And I have all these people telling me not to press charges and what am I gonna do? How am I gonna provide for my child?"

The only people who asked her how she was doing, she said, were the police officers and the paramedics. The case wasn't prosecuted, according to court records, due to "insufficient evidence."

Meyer knew all about this. He would later tell investigators hired by Ohio State that he had met with Courtney and

Zach and they told him that the arrest was based on "incorrect information." Both Courtney and Zach refuted this to university investigators, with both agreeing that Courtney never met with Meyer.

Afterward, police wrote that they gave Courtney a case number, a brochure for victims and witnesses, and a domestic-violence pamphlet. She told herself it was a one-time event. They were young and had a baby on the way. She could make it work. She knew that Zach was under extra stress because the pregnancy hadn't been planned. Yes, people at the football program knew, but a lot of people still didn't know what happened, including her little sister, Michaela Carano, back in Ohio.

"When he was coaching in Florida, oh my God, so fun," Michaela recalled. "He was always making sure I was included in the games, picking me up out of the stands, bringing me out on the field, always super kind ... I just remember loving it.

"And then, as I got a little bit older, I started to notice things. I think I was too young at the time to notice the bad stuff."

IN 2010, THE COUPLE MOVED more than 700 miles north to Huntington, West Virginia, after Zach got a job as the wide receivers and special teams coordinator at Marshall University under then-head coach Doc Holliday, himself a former Meyer assistant. The local newspaper did a profile of the new coach, and he gushed about Courtney, telling the reporter, "I'm fortunate to have a great wife."

One of Courtney's longtime friends visited her in West Virginia. It wasn't too long after the couple's son was born, and the friend remembers being able to tell that Courtney wasn't happy. She wasn't quite sure of why, maybe it was the stress of a new baby, or being in a new town, or having so little money. She just could sense that something was wrong.

A year later, the family of three picked up and moved again, this time to Philadelphia, where Zach got a job coaching wide receivers and special teams under another former Meyer man, then-Temple head coach Steve Addazio.

"But when they came to Columbus," the friend said, "it spiraled immediately."

They returned to Columbus in 2012 because Meyer had come back to Ohio State, where he got his first coaching job under Bruce, and he wanted Zach Smith, the grandson of his mentor, a man he once told *Sports Illustrated* was second in his life only to his father, on his staff.

THE VIOLENCE STARTED AGAIN in June of 2012, Courtney said. It usually would follow an argument, and the couple fought a lot about how Zach spent their money, Zach's infidelity, him sexting other women, and Zach's use of pornographic websites, per Courtney Smith and a Delaware County grand jury packet. Years later, when a Powell police detective would ask her to tell him when the violence began after their move to Columbus, Courtney answered, "There are so many but the first one I remember is when I was nursing my daughter."

According to police documents, Courtney was nursing her daughter when Zach came home from work. She told him that she would be with him in 15 minutes or so, after she put their daughter to sleep, which she did. With the baby asleep, she went downstairs to check on Zach and they got in a fight. He grabbed her arms, called her names, and pinned her against the wall, she told police in 2015. Then he let her go. Afterward, Courtney recalled to police that they both sat down at their kitchen table and talked about what happened.

Zach apologized to her, she said, and told her that it wouldn't happen again. Courtney felt like she had played a role in it, too, because she was always so tired and so busy.

It happened again a year later. In August 2013, they got in a fight around 2 a.m. after Courtney saw messages that she thought looked like sexting between her husband and another woman. When Zach woke up and realized what Courtney saw, she would later tell police, he grabbed the phone out of her hand and shoved her against a banister. They later stopped living together for about a month, Courtney told police, then got back together and she and Zach started seeing counselors. It was a counselor who first told Courtney to start documenting the violence.

In November, Courtney caught Zach texting with the same woman again after an iPad update started sending her his text messages, she would later tell police. Courtney chimed in on the text conversation. Zach later came home and confronted her, in front of their kids and Courtney's mother, she told police. After Courtney's mother left, the fighting continued. They moved into the bedroom, still yelling, but when Courtney tried to leave, Zach "grabbed her by the throat and pinned her against the wall," Powell police would later write in a report. Courtney couldn't recall everything he yelled at her, but one part was, "I'll destroy you," she told police. Years later, Detective Ryan Pentz with the Powell Police Department would ask Courtney what she thought those words meant. She said she thought they meant that Zach would kill her.

"Whenever they were together, my heart always, I would go to bed at night, and just think, 'OK, is she gonna call me in the middle of the night? Are they going to be arguing and fighting?' It's been this way for years," Courtney's mother, Tina Carano, would later tell Pentz. "And, you know, every time it did happen, she would call me and we would talk. I would even reach out to be, like, Why are you doing this? Leave your hands off of her. You have no right to touch her. Always lying about everything.

"So of course, he would try to deny it, but then he would end up admitting to it at some point, you know? And, I mean, it's happened in front of the kids numerous times. I know that he doesn't care."

COURTNEY AND ZACH SEPARATED then got back together. She moved in with her father and, when his lease ran out in February of 2014, Zach moved in there, too. It wasn't long after he moved in that Zach hurt her again, she told police. This time they were in the kitchen at her father's house and started yelling when Zach put his hands around her throat, she told police. When her father came home, Zach let her go.

"All I know is, when I walked in there, he seemed very, like embarrassed or taken back that I walked in," her father would later tell Pentz in an interview. "And then he just took off."

Courtney told police that Zach went to a bar, and she later found him passed out in his car. She took him back home. The next day was their son's birthday party, and she had to act normal.

At some point during their stay, Courtney's father talked to his then-son-in-law, he told police. Courtney told police that the talk happened after her father walked in on Zach with his hands around her throat. Her father told police that the conversation happened after an argument between the two that escalated so much it scared him. Both said he talked to Zach and told him to stop hurting Courtney.

"I made him promise me not to ever put his hands on her again, and he promised to do that," he told police in 2015.

"Did he admit to you that he was putting his hands on her?" Pentz asked.

"Well, he didn't say no. But when I said, 'Hey, no.' I talked about the relationship. And then over a year and a half ago, he agreed that he would not put his hands on her again," he replied. "So that's admitting that's what he did."

COURTNEY TRIED TO LEAVE IN 2014, but when her temporary job didn't become a full-time job, she worried that she didn't have enough money to do it, especially since she couldn't afford full-time daycare for her preschool-age kids. So she took Zach back, but was determined to come up with a plan to leave. She started saving money.

In September 2014, Courtney told police that Zach slashed new furniture she had bought with a butcher knife. Scared, she grabbed a knife and locked herself in the bedroom, where she called her mom, police would later document in a 2015 report. Two months later, they got in a fight in the upstairs bathroom and then the hallway, where Zach began strangling her, she told police. He threw her down a hallway, leaving her with bruises, police wrote. "[Zach] left after saying, 'I can't believe you have turned me into this,'" according to a Delaware County grand jury packet. Courtney took photos of her injuries.

While Ohio State romped toward its first national championship in more than a decade, Courtney turned inward. She stopped going to a tailgate specifically for the coaches' wives. On Jan. 12, 2015, Ohio State won the college football championship. It meant Urban Meyer had finally brought college football glory to his home state. That night, confetti fell across the stadium in Arlington, Texas, and players grasped copies of the premade front pages of the *Columbus Dispatch* with championship headlines. The infamously stern Meyer seemed happy as he hoisted the trophy. "The Ohio State Buckeyes are the first national champions of the playoff era," ESPN's John Saunders told the millions of people watching on TV. Even NBA superstar and Ohio native LeBron James was there. After the victory, Zach talked to *USA Today*'s Dan Wolken about Meyer. "He's the best head coach in the country," Zach said. "His program is based on real. Everything about it is the truth."

Courtney spent the night crying in their hotel room.

"That trip was when I knew it was over. I couldn't do it anymore," Courtney said. "He was getting more money and the more power he got, the more we won, the worse he got and it was horrible. I wasn't myself at all, and people knew it."

Two months later, in March of 2015, after a fight while on vacation in the Dominican Republic, Zach choked Courtney, grabbing her, lifting her off the ground, and pinning her to a wall, she told police. Then he let her go and left the hotel room for the night. Courtney was left gasping for air. He would later apologize in a text message, saying, "I'm so so sorry!!!!" after Courtney brought up what happened. Courtney would later tell police that Zach threatened to kill her "all the time" and there was so much violence "she could not even keep track of them all," according to their report.

Any doubts Courtney had about her plan to leave evaporated the night in June that she found Zach's other Google account. On this Google Drive she said that she found photos of naked women, as well as text messages between himself and other women, and photos of his erect penis in all sorts of locations, including the hotel where Ohio State stayed before home games (you can tell because not only is the interior of the hotel familiar, but the folder name included the phrase "game day"), inside the Ohio State Woody Hayes Athletic Center (you can tell because, just beyond his erect penis, you can see an image on the wall of a football player in an Ohio State uniform), and inside a White House bathroom during the team's victory visit to see the president (you can tell because he made sure to put a Seal of the President of the United States next to his penis). He also included videos of himself jerking off in the work shower in a folder called "work shower."

Courtney confronted Zach about the Google Drive, she said, and they got into an argument. This time, Courtney hit him in the nose, she told police. She eventually left the house, but not before she said Zach grabbed her by the arm and told her, according to a grand jury report, "If you go public with any of this, I'll fucking kill you."

The moment any person decides to leave an abusive relationship is extremely dangerous. It's when the chance of an intimate-partner homicide spikes, because an abuser will lash out at their loss of control over a person. And Courtney wasn't walking away from anybody—she was leaving an Ohio State football coach.

The couple officially separated in June of 2015. Courtney found a place for her and the children and left; she had faith she would figure out how to make everything work. She would enroll in nursing school. She thought that by physically leaving, the violence would stop. She did not foresee the ways Zach would still bully and harass her, even if they weren't under the same roof. In October, Courtney would become so tired, so frustrated, so out of options, that she would do what she had promised herself since that night in Gainesville that she would never do again: She called the police.

COURTNEY WENT TO THE POWELL POLICE STATION on Oct. 26, 2015. She had called the day before looking for help when Zach came over to her home and refused to leave, cursed her out, shoved her, and took her son while yelling, "I don't give a fuck about your neighbors," according to Courtney's witness statement to police. He told her to call the cops, she said, because he didn't care. She was brought into an interview room, where Officer Ben Boruchowitz talked to her, with his body camera on and rolling, and Courtney went over the years of violence she said Zach had inflicted on her. She also was open about why, after what happened in Gainesville, she "was so terrified from calling the police."

"Urban I feel like will do anything to protect his guy," she said. "He doesn't want anything to get out and look bad for his program."

Boruchowitz told Courtney that he didn't care who Zach was; he'd even arrested NFL players. If lawyers for Zach showed up, he advised her to not talk to them because "you are in charge here."

"Do I have enough evidence here, I don't know," Courtney asked him, followed by a long pause. The video of the interview has been pixelated, so I can't see what either of them are doing, but in the silence sits the weight carried by every person who has tried to leave an abusive relationship. It's a heaviness that comes not from doubt about what has happened, but from the knowledge that speaking up might only turn the world against you. The silence broke when Boruchowitz gave Courtney contact information for a victim advocate.

A few times during the conversation, Boruchowitz left to talk
to a local prosecutor and left his camera rolling.

"She's really petrified. And I really believe her," Boruchowitz
said. "I don't think it's one of these women over-exaggerating, I
think she's really afraid that he's going to kill her."

"She seems legitimate," he said during another call. "You
know, a lot of these people come in and say, 'I'm afraid he's gonna
kill me.' But she actually seems petrified. That he actually is going
to cause her harm. She says that he, on numerous occasions, has
grabbed her on the neck lifted off the ground, she couldn't breathe
and loses consciousness and then throws her on the bed. And
she seems, like, extremely shaky. Like, it doesn't seem like to me
she's playing it out."

"The only reason I even called you is I'm trying to think of
what we can do to protect her other than a civil protection order.
Because if there is a legitimate chance that he's going to come to
Powell and, and murder her obviously, I'd like to be consulting
with you about that," he said later. "We would like to prevent
the murder."

THAT SAME DAY, then-Delaware County Prosecutor Carol
O'Brien contacted Deputy Chief Stephen Hrytzik about
Courtney's case, according to one Powell police investigative
report. She told Hrytzik that a victim was requesting a protection order, but did not have it yet, and she wanted the police to
keep investigating. Hrytzik assigned Detective Ryan Pentz to the
case, and he was joined by Detective Darren Smith.

The following day, Courtney went to the courthouse as
instructed and met with a victim advocate and a prosecutor, she
said, but she decided not to apply for a protective order when
they warned her that, if she failed to get one, it could hurt her
chances to get custody of her children. A spokesperson for the
Delaware County Prosecutor's Office told Defector Media, "No
one with knowledge of the answers to your questions remains

in our office, so we cannot answer questions regarding the legal decisions made at that time."

Over the next few weeks, Pentz would interview Courtney, talk to her father and mother, and review hundreds of text messages sent between Courtney and Zach.

An officer writing a report has a lot of power to craft the narrative of a case; they can make a person look reliable or untrustworthy, give a person credibility or cast doubt. You can tell a lot about how detectives feel about a case by what they put in the reports, and what they leave out. Pentz and Darren Smith, in their writing, believed Courtney. As they wrote in the grand jury packet: "It was noticed during the two sets of interviews that [Courtney Smith's] story of the years of abuse did not vary much. The second interview was a much more descriptive interview because Detective Pentz gave her more of an opportunity to elaborate on the abuse, but the overall circumstances regarding the abuse stayed consistent."

Courtney's father talked to the police and verified her account of the violence that occurred when she and Zach were living with him. Her mother did, too. Years later, when Courtney's story became public, her mother would tell Jeff Snook, a man who once wrote a book called *What It Means to Be a Buckeye: Urban Meyer and Ohio State's Greatest Players*, that her daughter was never "intentionally abused" by Zach. When confronted by McMurphy about this, she admitted to sending text messages that talked about Zach beating Courtney but said they were her "trying to be there as a mother." She later wrote a Facebook post casting doubt on if she had sent the text messages at all.

When contacted by Defector Media for this story, Tina Carano said there was "no substantiated case of domestic violence," said Zach was innocent, and blamed the media coverage on the MeToo movement.

But in the privacy of a phone call between her and Pentz, Tina Carano told a different story. She backed up her daughter.

Tina Carano told Pentz that she knew Smith had been abusing her daughter for years, ever since they moved back to Ohio. Carano said she saw Zach speak disrespectfully to her daughter, calling her "crazy" and other "degrading things." She didn't see Zach hit her daughter, but he did admit to her that he had been violent and apologized. Carano recalled asking Zach to get help because she wanted the family to stay together. "But in the end, it's just one lie after another," she said. Her daughter sent her photos after the abuse, and in person she could see the bruises, she told Pentz.

"When you would approach him about the violence, what would he respond to you?" Pentz asked.

"He just said to me, 'I am so sorry. I know. I'm sorry,'" Carano said.

"He would apologize for his actions?" Pentz asked.

"He apologized a million times, over and over again," she said. "He said, 'I'm going to get help. I'm going to make this better. Everything's going to be OK.'"

When asked by Defector Media why she has changed her story from what she told police, Tina Carano said it was because her daughter wouldn't let her talk to Zach, which conflicts directly with her telling police she talked to Zach about the abuse as well as Courtney. She also said she was done answering questions.

What's clear is, in 2015, she unequivocally said her daughter was telling the truth and had been physically and emotionally abused for years.

"She feared for her kids and their future what they would have," Tina Carano said. "Had it not been for that she would have never taken it."

Carano told Pentz that she worried about Zach getting a gun. "Because he is that crazy. What's he have to lose at this point, is how I feel. And he's gonna be taken down. He's gonna take down the whole family."

"I think right now he is, at this point, somewhat stable, because he's trying to retain his job," Pentz said in response. "If he loses that job, I agree. I worry about everybody involved. Right? Because, that's where I think things could really start going bad."

IN BOTH HIS CONVERSATIONS with Courtney's parents, Pentz warned them that he did not have final say over what would happen to this case. From the beginning, Pentz knew this case was not a normal one. This was a high-profile case involving a prominent family and a powerful institution. In talking with Tina Carano, Pentz laid out exactly how an investigation works if you are a high-profile person in Delaware County or, really, anywhere in the United States.

"Any time we deal with a high-profile employer, or we deal with a high-profile person or something that's gonna get media attention, our prosecutor's office gets involved immediately. So they've been involved for a long time already, since she walked in this door pretty much, our prosecutor's office has been involved in this in some way, shape, or form," Pentz told her. "I'm a fact finder. I'm collecting facts. That's what I'm doing. And then I will take all my facts, and we'll put them together, and I will send him to the Delaware County prosecutor's office. They make a decision of whether or not goes to the grand jury, OK? The grand jury, which is made up of 12 citizens of Delaware County, will determine if there's enough evidence to proceed with charges. OK. So we don't actually make that choice. OK. They want to make that choice for us."

Police would eventually talk to Zach, along with his lawyer, Dennis Horvath. He claimed that in Gainesville, the injuries were due to him trying to restrain Courtney because she was the one lashing out and she had called 911 to hurt him. He claimed that Courtney had threatened in the past to go public with false allegations to make him look bad. He denied choking her, and said all he ever did was grab her arm. In their grand jury report, police would detail all the ways they believed that Zach Smith wasn't being fully honest with them.

"Regarding the interview with [Zach], Detective Pentz felt he was being deceitful about some of the interactions," the grand jury report said. "For example, about the alcohol and drug abuse, [Zach] said neither one of them had a drinking or drug problem, when there is clear evidence that Adderall and alcohol played a major role in their life. Also, when Detective Pentz asked him about the bruise on [Courtney's] arm and he replied she fell into the banister and down the steps. If [Courtney] did indeed fall down the steps, Detective Pentz believes the injuries would have been even greater. It's also the belief of Detective Pentz that this injury was not self-inflicted because of the location of the injury."

Zach Smith told Defector Media that whatever the police wrote in their reports about him was their opinion.

The detectives moved fast. In a few weeks, a 13-page grand jury report was ready. In his grand jury report, Pentz acknowledged that this was not a perfect case. The detectives could not find much physical evidence due to the amount of time that had passed. They had combed through the text messages and found many in which Zach apologized, but he didn't say for what. Pentz wrote that it did appear that Zach "admits to at least one occasion to picking [Courtney] up by the throat here in Delaware County and once while on vacation." The report ended with the following: "With the photos that exist and some of the admissions through text messaging and [Zach] admitting to placing his hands on her, it is asked for the case to be reviewed for Felony Domestic Violence and Felonious Assault."

The results of Pentz's investigation never made it to a grand jury. When the police documents were finally released, O'Brien told the *Dispatch* that the case wasn't presented to a grand jury because "we didn't find any felony charges that we thought we could prove." O'Brien did not go into detail about why.

And that was it. Criminal charges were never filed in the case, and a mountain of public records related to the investigation vanished from public view. Hundreds of pages of records, as well as hours of videos and audio recordings, would remain unseen by anyone, even Courtney herself, for years because then-Powell Police Chief Gary Vest insisted he could not release them to anyone. His reasoning? Releasing the records would identify Zach.

The Powell police department wasn't the only powerful institution that chose Zach's reputation over transparency.

"I was never told about anything ... I never had a conversation about that. I know nothing about that," is what Urban Meyer had to say on July 24, 2018, when reporters asked him if he had previously known about the 2015 investigation of Zach Smith for domestic violence. It all unfolded while Courtney watched, all alone, from her home.

According to Ohio State's own investigation, athletic director Gene Smith personally spoke to Meyer about the 2015 case. The final document included in that report detailed the events of a fall day when Zach Smith was called back from a recruiting trip to have a meeting with Gene Smith, Meyer, and others. The document said that during that meeting Zach denied hitting Courtney, and that Meyer warned him that he would be fired if he ever did hit her. Per the report, Meyer "assisted in arranging professional counseling for Zach at this time."

In fact, monitoring the 2015 case would become a family affair for the Meyers. By the fall of 2015, Courtney had told Shelley Meyer about how much she feared Zach. The two texted back and forth about it, according to Ohio State, with Shelley saying, "I am praying for you!!! I wouldn't listen to him anyway. He doesn't talk to anyone about you. I know the truth. Please take care of yourself and let me know what I could [sic] help." Shelley Meyer also contacted Powell police to try and get information about the case. Powell police told her she would have to wait like everyone else.

Shelley and Urban Meyer have insisted that she never told her husband about what Courtney was telling her. Perhaps. But the Meyers also have been very open in the past about how key

Shelley was, according to her own husband, to keeping his college football program's running. In a glowing *Sports Illustrated* profile, S.L. Price wrote that Shelley sat in on all of Urban's negotiations during his hiring at Florida and "quickly became the program's go-to resource for gray-area discipline problems."

"It's not uncommon for me to have a player meet with her, because she believes in counseling and I still don't know if I believe in it yet," Urban said of his wife, making sure to point out she was also a clinical nursing instructor. "All the way from learning disabilities to behavioral disabilities to substance issues, she is an absolute proponent of counseling. I'm more, Let's get 'em up at 5 a.m. and make sure that doesn't happen again. So there's a balance there. I trust her."

So why would Urban Meyer claim not to know anything about what happened in 2015 during that press conference in 2018? He'd been coaching for decades by that point, and surely he must have realized that reporters would be asking questions and digging into this. McMurphy, the longtime college football reporter who now is the Action Network's college football insider, offered this observation. These coaches are often the highest-paid public employees in their states—Meyer was set to be paid $7.6 million in 2018—and with that much money and that much power, they can start to believe they are bigger than the program.

"He's a head football coach at a university, and he's paid several million dollars a year, and those guys think they're bullet-proof. They're like gods. Everybody worships them in Columbus. They can't do any wrong," McMurphy said. "And that's also kind of how Urban's personality is. Most coaches have big egos, and that's why they're successful as coaches, but it's also why they fail in other aspects and that's a big reason."

There were a lot of other things Meyer and other high-level Ohio State administrators knew about Zach. The university's investigation revealed that in May 2014, during an out-of-town recruiting trip in South Florida, Smith spent $600 of his personal funds at a local strip club, with another coach and "one or more high school coaches" present, a potential NCAA violation. Brian Voltolini, officially Ohio State's director of football operations and unofficially Meyer's right-hand man, knew about this, the university's report said. Meyer claimed he didn't know the exact amount that Zach had spent. The university soon afterward added a morality clause to its coaching contracts. (This is the same month, Courtney later told Powell police, that she found out Zach had spent much of the money they had been saving at strip clubs and on escorts.)

In early 2016, Zach's spending habits grew so bad that assistant business manager Jennifer Bulla sent an email to Voltolini and Gene Smith about his blatant irresponsibility. In her email, Bulla wrote that the bank wouldn't explain to her why Zach's cards kept getting declined, and that Zach always had a different reason. "Things I recall are … lost his wallet and got all new accounts, the bank had his wrong mailing address so declined since data didn't match, the bank put his account on security hold due to suspected fraud and didn't alert him, etc. Unfortunately, when Zach is scheduled to travel with UM [Urban Meyer] and he needs a car we (Mark and I) know it's likely he will be declined."

By 2015 and early 2016, according to Ohio State, Zach Smith was regularly late to practice and workouts, missing scheduled recruiting visits but saying he had made them, having a sexual relationship with a football staff secretary who did not report to him, having sex toys delivered to Ohio State's athletic facilities, and taking sexually explicit photos of himself at various Ohio State facilities.

In June 2016, with the help of Meyer, Zach went to a drug treatment facility. An anonymous email, which was included with the Ohio State report, told investigators that Zach did not take it seriously and left early.

None of this was reported in Zach's personnel file. His 2015 file is all about getting better at recruiting. His 2016 file has a goal of "I should be the best asst. cch in America." His 2017 goals were to be the best in America at recruiting, leading the wide receivers unit, and being a staff member, in that order. Even if a reporter had heard rumors of Zach's conduct and put in a public records request, they wouldn't have found an ounce of evidence in these files. In the files, there is no trace of anger from Meyer, no suggestion of the athletic director wanting him fired, no evidence of concerns about job performance or his inability to pay for a cell phone, and no mention of him blowing money at a strip club. It's all positive feedback with room for improvement. The only hint of a problem is 2017, when under areas for improvement his evaluation mentions "personal matters."

That did not stop Ohio State from giving Zach Smith a raise of $73,400 that year, increasing his salary to $300,000 a year.

On Dec. 5, 2017, Meyer texted recruiting chief Mark Pantoni, saying, "Just checkin on zach smith. Make sure he is working." Pantoni wrote back, "I ripped his ass yesterday morning so he knows I'm all over him."

Twelve days later on Dec. 17, 2017, Courtney called Powell police, saying she had heard from a neighbor that they had seen Zach peering into her windows at 1:30 a.m. Zach was given a trespass warning over the phone by Pentz, the same detective who had investigated him in 2015. In a later police report, Pentz wrote that another violation could lead to a charge of criminal trespass for Zach.

A day before Christmas, Meyer sent a text message to someone—the recipient's name was redacted by Ohio State—saying, "Keep an eye on zach. He is not here. Need to make sure his guys play well. I will say something as well."

On Jan. 3, 2018, Zach called the cops, saying his children were being taken over state lines by Courtney when he was supposed to have them, which police closed out almost immediately, according to a Powell police report, possibly because Zach became belligerent when a dispatcher suggested he come to the station to file a report about this after he was done eating. That same day, hours earlier, Tim Kight, Ohio State's football's "leadership coach," sent a text to Meyer asking him to call when he got a chance about "something serious." Meyer wrote back, "Volt and I will meet with Zach next Wed." Two days later, Kight wanted to know if Meyer could talk. "Yes," Meyer wrote back. The thread went silent until Jan. 14, when Kight wrote, "Incredible, isn't it?"

Around this time, reigning college football powerhouse Alabama approached Zach about a possible coaching job. Despite everything, Meyer decided he needed to keep Zach on his staff. On Jan. 18, 2018, he sent Zach a text message: "After much thought, I want u to stay. I have personally invested far too much in u to get u in position to take next step. U need to step away from other situation and let's go in it all.... again."

Eight minutes later, he texted Zach again: "We got u thru the shit–now go b a difference maker in the staff room."

"Yes sir I agree," Zach replied. "They offered me the job and I wanted to sleep on it before deciding but it doesn't feel right. I love this place, my players and am loyal to you for everything you've done. I just want to grow and keep my career on track but I'm confident that's here. I'm ready to be a difference maker and ready to win it all again. I appreciate everything coach."

Meyer wrote back: "From this point forward... All grown ass man conversation, never again childish shit... use ur gifts and knowledge. Cell phone away-full engagement and become a coordinator. U have the ability."

"Yes sir. I will."

Meyer texted a redacted recipient three days later: "Zach smith was offered wr/passing game Coord at Alabama. Went there to talk to Saban. At first thought maybe he should go but then decided all that effort I've put (in) to him and it's Alabama. I told him to stay and he turned it down. Every f—- day it's something."

In late January, Meyer included Zach Smith in a list of assistants he texted to then-university president Michael Drake, saying he needed help retaining them because they were being recruited by other programs.

IT'S POSSIBLE THAT MILLIONS OF COLLEGE football fans would still to this day not know who Courtney Smith is if it had not been for the events of Dec. 17, 2017, the day she called the police and Zach Smith received a trespass warning.

On May 12, 2018, Zach violated that warning given to him by Pentz and trespassed on his ex-wife's property. It would not be, in the long history of violence documented by Courtney and Powell police, the worst thing Zach did. It would be, however, the action that gave police and prosecutors enough evidence to feel that they could charge him with a crime. That charging document became a public record, and generated a case on the online court docket that anyone could see. And suddenly everything Courtney Smith had been fighting for all this time—making sure Zach kept his job, keeping her personal horror out of the public eye, ensuring everything at Ohio State football under Meyer's reign looked like a family friendly bastion of morality—was set to collapse. It only took a few weeks.

Word quickly got around about Zach's case. A friend of Courtney's told me that the first she heard about something happening with Zach wasn't from Courtney, but from other friends who follow websites for Buckeyes superfans. A tip came in to McMurphy, who had been laid off about a year earlier from ESPN as part of a company-wide staff reduction. Even though he didn't have an outlet, he started working the tip, eventually finding the records in Gainesville. And he called Courtney.

McMurphy was not the only person calling Courtney. She estimated she started getting calls and emails from seemingly every reporter who cared about Ohio State football, or just college football in general. She ignored them because that's what everyone around her was telling her to do, including her then-attorney— just stay quiet and focus on the court case. But that advice didn't seem to apply to Zach's supporters.

In the weeks and months that followed McMurphy's original report and Meyer's press conference, radio airwaves and the internet would be flooded with people desperate to defend Zach.

A representative example is Kyle Lamb, whose only relevant experience as a COVID-19 data guy for Florida Gov. Ron DeSantis was, in the words of the *Miami Herald*, "spreading harmful conspiracy theories about COVID-19 on the internet." He described the reporting about Zach as "irresponsible," vaguely gestured to concerns about "credibility," harped about changing details in the early stories while reporters were still trying to figure out what was going on, bemoaned that Zach couldn't win a libel lawsuit, and admonished fans who "shouldn't be judging him for what he says on Twitter," considering what Zach had been through.

The news of Zach Smith's misdemeanor charge first became public on July 18, 2018, when Ohio State writers started reporting on a court hearing scheduled that day in Zach's case. The court hearing got canceled after the news broke, but that didn't stop Zach's lawyer, Brad Koffel, from hopping on local radio station WTVN, where he's also a legal analyst with his own show, and defending his client.

The entire interview wasn't even 10 minutes long, but Koffel and the host managed to pack in just about every defense of Zach imaginable. The host, who goes by Woody, asked questions like, "Then why did she file trespassing charges other than to make him look bad?" and leapt to conclusions like, "Almost sounds like it was a setup."

"I've never been divorced. Thankfully. I've had friends and I'm sure there are many listeners that have ex-wives and ex-husbands," Koffel said in response to Woody's question about the trespassing charges. "And I think the motivations probably speak for themselves."

The segment ended with Woody saying, "Brad, thank you so much. I mean, this kind of thing happens all the time. But when you have a high-profile position, and the headline is out there—you know, that's why we're having this conversation. And at least we know he picked a good lawyer."

This is, perhaps, one of the biggest advantages Zach had. It wasn't just that he was the grandson of an Ohio State football coach, or that Meyer was mentored by that coach, or that he worked for one of the most powerful institutions in the state. It was that so many men could look at Zach and relate, because Zach peddled a narrative that catered to them: that the real problem wasn't himself or his actions or the countless chances he had been given. The problem was an evil woman had come around, weaponized his children, and ruined his life. It would later turn out to be a very popular message.

COURTNEY GOT A PROTECTIVE ORDER two days after the canceled court hearing. In her application, she wrote about what had happened between 2015 and 2018 that still caused her fear. She wrote that she once found a webcam under her couch that she believed Zach had used to watch her. She wrote that Zach had hacked her email, WiFi, and remotely accessed her laptop.

"The stalking and harassing never stopped," she wrote. "Zach contacted any male he thought I was dating, sending them threatening messages through social media accounts. He never followed the shared parenting plan and would tell me he didn't have to because he knew I couldn't afford to pay for an attorney."

The stalking and harassing got worse, she wrote, when she started dating someone seriously for the first time. She wrote that she once saw Zach standing in her boyfriend's backyard, watching them all eat dinner. He threatened to get her boyfriend fired from his job.

"He constantly harasses me and threatens through text messages and phone calls when he does not get what he wants," she wrote. "It's Zach's way or no way."

Meanwhile, Meyer was scrambling to make sure the revelation of Zach's misdemeanor charge wouldn't affect his recruiting class. On July 20, in a group chat with offensive coordinator Ryan Day and Zach, Meyer wrote, "[Redacted] texted me about Zach and the legal issue. Asked if he was ok. Says he hasn't heard from him in awhile. We need to keep recruiting [name redacted] as if he is not committed. Need to stay on this!"

"Yeah I haven't hit him up since Monday – was letting this shit blow over for a couple days. But I got you. Just hit him now," Zach wrote back.

"I also reached out to his mom and dad just now," Meyer responded. "We can't let people use this against us."

Zach texted again, saying he'd reached out to most of the parents and kids today and so far so good. Meyer sent the group a response from someone expressing sympathy for Zach. The message said, "Were it not OSU this is not news."

"He is a good man — our guy. He can reach out if he chooses but we are good. Just hopeful for better days. Pass to him our regards," the anonymous person wrote. "Hope you are well."

"These are elite people, my guy!" Zach exclaimed.

Day had a conversation with someone whose name is redacted and reported back, "He is great. No need for Zach to reach out to him for an explanation."

Three days later on July 23, McMurphy's report on Facebook about the arrest in Gainesville, Courtney's protective order and the more recent trespassing charge was out in the world. It quickly went viral.

That same day, Gene Smith sent a Facebook link to Meyer. Meyer responded, "Wow. Will discuss." Smith wrote back some suggestions for how to handle it; maybe they should send Zach to an employee assistance program, and Meyer responded that he was "not sure how to do this." Gene Smith told him that he would handle it with the help of someone from human resources, Voltolini, and public relations. The PR team whipped up a statement that read, "We are not going to comment at this time on the situation regarding Zach Smith. This is a personnel matter and we don't typically discuss such matters publicly. We are continuing to monitor."

The scrambling over Zach continued. Minutes later, in a group chat with Meyer and Voltolini, Gene Smith said that he had spoken with Zach about using the employee assistance program to help him "develop a management plan for his ex-wife and managing his children." Voltolini said he would meet Zach that day. Later, someone texted Gene Smith and Meyer saying they had confirmed that Zach would not be alone that night, and would be with his family. Gene Smith wrote back, "Thank you."

At some point, Meyer got a text from Kight, the leadership guru, with a quote about how "the Christian faith is for competitors. It is for warriors and fighters."

Later, Meyer got a text from Shelley: "2 things … u can always use Gene as part of reason for not giving the receiver position too. And … I am worried about Zach's response. He drinks a lot and I am just not sure how stable he will be. Afraid he will do something dangerous. It's obvious he has anger/rage issues already."

Near the end of the day, Urban sent a message to his staff: "All-I made a decision to release Zach from staff. Core value violation and cumulative issues. 'Win the Moment'-most important thing is team and players at this time. Zero conversation about Zach's past issues. We need to help him as he moves frwd. Team and players!! Thx. Will discuss plan when I return Wednesday."

What stands out the most from that day, from all those text messages, is how nobody talked about Courtney. She was always the ex-wife, or an unnamed problem that needed managing. Nobody in the text messages from that day asked how she was doing, or if anyone was checking in on her. In more than 200 pages of text messages covering a period of years, I only found her name used once.

After Meyer spoke to the press on July 24 and insisted that he had no prior knowledge of the 2015 incidents, he got back to texting with his confidantes. At one point he got a message from defensive coordinator Greg Schiano, which provided an update on how Zach was doing, followed by "WIN THE MOMENT!!!!"

Meyer wrote to Kight, asking for his thoughts on the "info that is in media."

"A thought," Meyer wrote. "All legal issues with Zach will b dropped. So I will have to answer why we released him. We know answer. Yet I won't share all the other issues. Thoughts?"

Kight wrote back with a suggested statement, which reiterated how often domestic disputes are "he said/she said," and called Zach's violation of the protective order a "bad judgement." Meyer wrote back saying he heard, incorrectly, that there was no protective order, forcing Kight to correct him based on what he had read about the case. Meyer said that someone from his staff had checked with the police and there was nothing in 2015, and the problem was Courtney's lawyer was releasing stuff, which, even if that were true, ignored how much Zach's lawyer talked to the media from the day the story broke.

"Scary," Meyer wrote to Kight, never indicating what he actually had to be afraid of.

"Faith and courage," Kight responded. "Remember Elijah and Jezebel?"

"Absolutely," Meyer wrote back. "Fatigue, doubt, fear overcame by Faith."

"LIFE CHANGED THE NEXT DAY, everything went crazy," Courtney said when recalling what happened after Meyer's press conference. "I had to prepare to move. I didn't know how I was going to finish nursing school. I had the *Today Show, Good Morning [America]*, everybody calling me."

She took that advice from Jean Bruce and started writing everything down. She felt like she had to. So one day she picked up one of her daughter's unused notebooks, light blue, spiral bound, adorned with purple-maned unicorns, clouds, and shooting stars. In the weeks and months to follow, she kept writing down notes. She wrote down a note to get hospital records of her panic attacks, notes about seeing former Ohio State players trashing her online, her thoughts on what Ohio State's investigation was missing, lists of people she needed to talk to for court, followed by a reminder to buy ink for her printer, and the ingredients she needed to make meatloaf one night. She grabbed a sticky note every time she remembered something about what

Zach had done to her. One day she put a pen to a sticky note and wrote just one word: "Lies!"

Her lawyer at the time told her not to talk to anybody, she said, though she now regrets not speaking out sooner, because nothing was stopping Zach, his lawyer, and his defenders from speaking out. Things got so bad that her lawyer told her she needed to leave town because she wasn't safe, Courtney said, so she took her kids for a weekend trip to stay with a friend out of state.

"The reporters were beating on my doors. I know the reporters were beating on his doors, but I didn't want the kids exposed to that," she said. "We just bolted. We left."

The day after Big Ten Media Days, on July 25, Ohio State received two public records requests from the student newspaper, the *Lantern*. According to Ohio State's investigation, the request asked for "emails and text messages, as well as any call history, between Urban Meyer and Zach Smith from July 18, 2018 through July 24, 2018 and between Oct. 25, 2015 and Dec. 1, 2015, and the same communications between AD Gene Smith and Coach Meyer for the same dates for any materials 'pertaining to Zach Smith.'" The requests went to an Ohio State lawyer who then emailed Gene Smith and senior associate athletic director Diana Sabau, telling them to get the appropriate text messages and emails. A day later, the same lawyer, senior associate general counsel Julie Vannatta, asked two people on Meyer's staff—longtime Meyer loyalists Amy Nicol, who was director of internal operations for football, and Voltolini—to "go get [Coach Meyer's] phone and check his text with Zach."

No one checked the head football coach's phone.

COURTNEY KEPT TALKING TO MCMURPHY. On Aug. 1, McMurphy published his second Facebook post about the story. It answered the question everyone in college football was asking in its opening sentence: "Text messages I have obtained, an exclusive interview with the victim and other information I have learned shows Ohio State coach Urban Meyer knew in 2015 of domestic abuse allegations against a member of his coaching staff." In the report, McMurphy quoted the text message between Courtney and Shelley Meyer, including more recent ones about Courtney's protective order (the one Urban Meyer thought she didn't have).

"Do you have a restraining order? He scares me," Shelley wrote to Courtney.

"Restraining orders don't do anything in Ohio-I tried to get protection order which is what started this whole investigation. And that should go through soon finally. It's hard bc you have to prove immediate danger. Legal system is tough. Basically you have to prove he will kill u to get protective order," Courtney wrote back.

"Geesh! Even w the pics?" Shelley asked. "Didn't law enforcement come to your place ever??"

That same day, Stadium, which would later hire McMurphy, published a 19-minute interview with Courtney. She did the interview because she felt like people were only getting Zach and Meyer's version of events, she said, and she was afraid of losing her kids. She wanted her viewpoint out there too.

McMurphy's second report dropped while Meyer and Voltolini were at the practice field. Voltolini saw it, called it "a bad article" according to Ohio State's investigation, and then talked with Meyer about whether the media could get his phone. They specifically talked about, according to Ohio State's investigation, "how to adjust the settings on Meyer's phone so that text messages older than one year would be deleted."

That day, Ohio State placed Meyer on administrative leave. He also spent the day texting with his then-agent, Trace Armstrong, A day later, on Aug. 2, he got a text from Armstrong asking, "U up? Laura and Colleen would like to be at your place at 11. They anticipate that they will need 4 hours with your phone. As well as some time with you and Shelley." Meyer wrote back, "All good. Available all day."

On Aug. 3, Zach sat for interviews with ESPN and a Columbus radio station. In the interviews he insisted that any injuries to his ex-wife happened because he was making defensive movements to remove himself from the situation. When asked how trying to remove himself could have led to bruises, Zach replied, "Well, I mean, I guess you'd have to be there." Zach said multiple times that never hit his ex-wife.

McMurphy heard the interviews, and he reached out to Courtney, asking if he could tweet out a screenshot of a text she had shared with him in which Zach apologized after she confronted him about strangling her. Courtney said yes. So McMurphy sent the tweet.

THE HARASSMENT STARTED almost immediately for Courtney and McMurphy. Courtney left town and came back, but she didn't feel safe when she came home. She withdrew. She felt afraid. It was impossible to open any of her social media accounts without getting barraged with threats from angry Buckeye fans, and she started to worry. What if one of those angry fans recognized her? Would they do something to her, or tell Zach what she was doing? Would they try to twist her words or take an embarrassing photo of her? There already were pro-Meyer protests happening following his three-game suspension by the university, attended by fans clad in scarlet and gray, holding homemade signs all in support of their coach. She withdrew from nursing school. She stopped socializing. She stopped going to restaurants. She even stopped going to the grocery store, instead using online ordering or having her sister get the groceries for her.

"My sister, she was too scared to go to Kroger, to go get groceries, so she would have me go," Michaela Carano said. "She was scared to leave her house, she thought people were looking at her. … She was just scared to go anywhere. It was so sad."

She was even afraid to buy alcohol. Both Courtney and her sister told me this: At one point, she was afraid to buy a bottle of wine because she was certain it would be used against her, proof she drank too much or was a bad mom.

"Every time I go to the grocery store and pick up a bottle of wine I'm, like, 'Oh my gosh, I can't even buy a bottle of wine. People are going to think I'm a drunk,'" Courtney said. "Do you know what I mean? You get so worried and paranoid. I am never going to be the same again. It's destroyed me."

McMurphy didn't live in Ohio, but that didn't stop rabid Buckeye fans from threatening him and his family as well. He got more than 2,000 messages on Facebook from Ohio State fans in 2018 after his reporting, he told me. The messages warned him to never enter the state of Ohio, brought up his daughter's name, and mentioned that they knew where he lived.

"I've been at ESPN, CBS, I was a beat writer, so you deal with rabid fans. I vote in the AP Top 25 poll so I'm used to the, 'You're an idiot writer because you didn't rank my team high enough.' You're used to that. But this, this stuff was a whole 'nother level," McMurphy said. "This was people threatening my life. This was people putting my home address on one of the Ohio State fan websites saying, 'Go get him.' This was people calling my wife's cell phone number and threatening her. This was people posting stuff on my wife's Facebook page threatening her."

I asked McMurphy why this story, and why this fanbase. The answer: Because Meyer won a lot, and winning makes people happy.

"Look, Urban is a great college coach. You can't take that away. And he won national championships and that's what the fans care about," McMurphy said. "If Urban Meyer was coming off a 4–8 season with a career .500 record, one, he would have been fired instead of just a three-game suspension. And I probably wouldn't have gotten all the hatred and feedback that I received."

This did not stop McMurphy's reporting. On Aug. 17, he published another story, this time not on Facebook but on Stadium's website. It said that Zach had ordered more than $2,200 in sex toys, male apparel, and photography equipment and had all the

packages delivered to the Woody Hayes Athletic Center. It also
reported on Zach taking photos of his penis while at the White
House and Zach having sex with an Ohio State staffer at the office,
and photographing it.

WEEKS LATER, AND NEARLY A MONTH AFTER Meyer had
been placed on administrative leave, Ohio State published the
results of an investigation done by outside counsel, which cost
the university $1 million. The results, to anyone who followed
McMurphy's reporting and what Courtney had been saying,
weren't terribly shocking. It confirmed the 2015 investigation
by Powell police. It confirmed the 2018 trespassing charge. It confirmed the protection order. It confirmed Zach's bad spending.
It confirmed his penis photos, which it called "sexually explicit
photographs." It confirmed the sex toys, and that he had been
having sex with a football staffer.

But this was not received as vindication. From the outset,
the investigative report itself admitted it was flawed. A review
of Meyer's phone, when Ohio State eventually got it on Aug. 2,
would reveal that the phone was set to only retain messages for
one year—as he had discussed with Voltolini. Investigators also
were unable to get text messages from Gene Smith, Voltolini,
and Zach Smith. The investigators also did not have access to
the Powell police records—because Powell's police chief refused
to release them, claiming he could not because of privacy. In one
interview, the chief went so far as to invoke Marsy's Law, a law
intended to keep crime victims informed of what is happening
in their cases, as the reason he could not release any records.

The *Dispatch* sued for the police records and won, but they
would not be released until December. By then, the national
media had moved on. The investigation by Ohio State had been
done. The university also did not release the hard copies of
Meyer's text messages, the ones quoted in this story, until a year
later, after Meyer had served a three-game suspension, retired,
and landed a cushy TV analyst job with Fox. Defector Media

reached out to both Powell police and Ohio State for comment on their decisions to delay the release of these records. This story will be updated accordingly if significant comment is received. (After publication, an Ohio State spokesperson told Defector Media in an email that "all public records were posted online as they became available.")

When Meyer announced his retirement, his wife sat down for an interview with ABC 6 in Columbus. She thanked Buckeye fans for their unwavering support of her and her husband through what she only referred to as "September."

"To Buckeye Nation—this program is our home. And the support we've gotten through all of August and all of September," Shelley Meyer said through tears. "It never wavered."

On Sunday, Meyer made his NFL debut in Jacksonville's loss to the Houston Texans. Defector Media reached out to the team to see if Meyer had any comment on this story, and will update if we receive significant comments.

HOW DO YOU SURVIVE YOUR life falling apart? You survive by having no other choice. After all the cameras left, after the reporters moved on to other stories, after Ohio State got a new coach, after Meyer triumphantly opened a restaurant six miles from where Courtney lives and got a new job in the NFL, Courtney still lived in central Ohio. She still had to finish nursing school. Her divorce was finalized in 2016 but, after Zach was fired from Ohio State, he asked the court for a reallocation of parents rights and responsibilities because he was traveling a lot less as well as modification of his child and spousal support. That wasn't wrapped up until late 2020, when Courtney became legal custodian of the children, according to court documents. (As of Sept. 7, she is owed more than $129,000 in child support. When asked about this, Zach blamed his lack of payments on Courtney.)

But she just kept going. One of Courtney's longtime friends said she cried when she heard Courtney had gotten her nursing license. She had no idea how Courtney did it.

"With everything you've been through, you've done this amazing thing," her friend recalls telling her. "Now you can provide for your family for the rest of your life. She's an amazing woman."

Firing Zach might have stopped him from being a legal problem to Ohio State, but it did not end his growing familiarity with the criminal justice system. He was able to plead down the criminal trespass charge, the one that tipped off all those reporters, to disorderly conduct, in return for Courtney having her protective order for three years, according to a memorandum of understanding. Then he got charged again. On May 9, 2019, Courtney got a call from her children's school saying Zach was trying to pick up their kids. Zach wasn't supposed to have the kids at that time, according to their parenting plan, so Courtney said she would come and get them. Courtney arrived, then Zach. The school's principal put Courtney in one room and Zach in another, she told the Delaware County Sheriff's Office in a witness statement.

"I asked him to come into the office to clarify the parenting agreement. Zach started to raise his voice, saying he was allowed to take his kids and I could not stop him. I brought him to my office, keeping the door open. I showed him the parenting agreement, stating he did not have custody of the kids until 6:45 p.m. on Thursday," principal Melany Ondrus wrote. "He continued to raise his voice, saying that was not my job and he would slap us with a civil suit. He said if he needed to call the cops he would, and I replied that would be my next step as well."

The ensuing investigation found that by being at the school, Zach had violated the protection order. He would be charged with one count of violating a protection order.

The same month, Zach launched his own podcast. It's best described as hours of talk about the extreme minutiae of Ohio State football as well as college football, from a guy who has some stories about Urban Meyer, all served with a heaping side of men's rights rhetoric, some of it directed at Courtney herself.

Lamb promoted the podcast's launch, and the show currently has 1,600 reviews on iTunes. He's leveraged his relationships with former Ohio State athletes for credibility, and hosted a tailgate on Saturday with former Ohio State wideout Braxton Miller. The show is widely heard in enough of the Columbus area that Courtney's sister had a friend who listened to it for a while. She said her friend stopped once she explained who Zach was, but the experience reminded her how little people still knew about what her sister had been through, because almost everything that was written or reported was about Zach.

"It was never from my sister's point of view, it was never from how she feels, like, about anything. I feel like it was all about him because he was the public figure. He was the one that people cared about because he's a coach. Everyone loves him. He's in this community," Michaela Carano said. "I feel like people didn't care about my sister because she's a nobody, she was nobody other than being his wife."

For Courtney, the show has meant she's changed her behavior. She tries to be careful about whom she befriends. She never knows if another parent is a fan of the show and what that means they've heard about her. She told me, "It has changed my way of living."

On Dec. 19, 2019, Zach was convicted of one count of violating a protection order. It was his second trial on the charge, after the first one ended in a mistrial. Courtney couldn't make it to the courthouse that day because she ended up with a nursing clinical that she couldn't reschedule. But she was allowed to submit a victim impact statement to the court, which the prosecutor read aloud for her. In her statement, Courtney described everything it took for her to walk away from her abusive marriage, the difficult years she went through, and the current social media taunting she still endured from Zach, who still spends time online telling just about anyone that he never physically hurt his wife, and any information to the contrary is just a pile of lies cooked up by Courtney in order to ruin him. (Courtney is not alone. He also spends plenty of time calling anyone he doesn't like, man or woman, a bitch.)

"I could stand here for hours giving everyone in this court-room examples of the kind of abuse he, his friends, his family, and his network have inflicted on me before and after the CPO was implemented. But one only needs to see his public social media accounts for a glimpse—and that word is underlined to be emphasized—of the intimidation and harassment that occurs on a daily basis," the prosecutor said, reading the statement for the judge. "I am still very aware of what he is capable of. And he has made every effort possible to keep my fear of him alive. I've come to accept that nothing will change unless the people he surrounds himself with will stop enabling him and he takes accountability and responsibility for the pain he has inflicted upon me and many others."

Judge Marianne Hemmeter sentenced Zach to 20 days in jail, with credit for one day he already spent, as well as an anger management class and three years of community control.

"Nobody, not you, not the president, nobody is above the law," she said at sentencing, later remarking, "I do take into consideration that a fine only would be very demeaning to the seriousness of the offense. Not only because there's a victim involved that I do find was afraid of you, but because it's demeaning to the system as a whole. Again, what point is a protection order if it's not enforced? What point is the criminal justice system? If somebody who violates a protection order isn't called to task?"

Zach served his 19 days in jail. He turned the entire case into a four-part series for subscribers only on his podcast, in which he called out various people—his lawyer, the prosecutor, the judge, and of course Courtney—as the reasons why he ended up in jail.

This is what still frustrates Courtney. There is no protective order to stop your ex-husband from calling you a crazy liar online, to his thousands of Twitter followers. "It does more damage," she said, "than anyone would ever know."

I REACHED OUT TO COURTNEY back in January with no objective. I just wanted to tell her that I was thinking about her. It was when the Jacksonville Jaguars announced Urban Meyer as their new head coach. She wrote back and told me that she was thinking of telling her whole story. In the course of talking to her, as well as her friends and family, over the course of months, I asked her several times if she was OK with doing this story. There's no ignoring what might happen with the Ohio State fans who still believe she was an evil woman out to destroy good men like Zach and Meyer, or even what Zach himself might say.

In every conversation we had, she came back to the same reason for going forward: She wants other women in abusive relationships, especially with coaches, to know they are not alone. She wants people to know victims of abuse don't come forward so they can get lots of money, but because they're afraid. She wants people to at least somewhat understand the hell that women go through and the power dynamics at play. She wants to talk about online bullying and the way it is used to hurt people. There is so much she wishes she had known before leaving her ex-husband, and maybe now this will help someone.

What gets her through every day is the same thing that has always gotten her through each day: her kids. They're growing up, already more quickly than she'd like. They are the reason why she left, because she couldn't imagine them growing up in a violent home. They are why she went to nursing school, because she hated the idea of not being able to care for them on her own. On the darkest days, she wakes up, drags herself out of bed, and gets through the day for them. Talk to Courtney for even one minute about her children and she will light up, because she is truly amazed at how great her children are.

They don't have a perfect life, but it's a good one, with a nice home, a dog, and signs with quotes that make Courtney smile scattered around. Her kids go to good schools, play sports, and have plenty of friends. Her daughter especially loves it when her aunt Michaela comes around. Despite everything, Courtney

Smith still has her close group of girlfriends, the kind she can sit around the pool with in the afternoon and tell jokes. All the fears that so many people tried to implant in her brain—that she couldn't leave her husband, that she needed to stay quiet, that she would be destroyed—are beaten back.

Courtney will tell you, like she told me, she has no idea how she got through it, but she doesn't have to know how. What matters is she did.

If you or someone you know needs help, the National Domestic Violence Hotline is available at 1-800-799-7233 or online at the-hotline.org.

Diana Moskovitz is the investigations editor at Defector Media. She previously worked at NFL Media, the *Miami Herald*, and Treasure Coast Newspapers, and spent five years at the sports and culture website Deadspin.

What It Was Like to Watch Naomi Osaka Up Close During Her Vexing 2021 US Open

KEVIN VAN VALKENBURG

FROM ESPN • SEPTEMBER 4, 2021

Naomi Osaka did not want to be cut off. She did not want to be rescued. Yes, she was crying in her US Open postmatch news conference, crying as she struggled to find the right words so she could share what was on her mind, but each time the moderator tried to end it, assuming Osaka didn't want to continue, Osaka overruled him. She was determined to get this out.

"Recently, when I win, I don't feel happy," Osaka said late Friday night. "I only feel relief. When I lose, I feel very sad. And I don't think that's normal. Basically, I feel like I'm kind of at this point where I'm trying to figure out what I want to do. I honestly don't know when I'm going to play my next tennis match. I think I'm going to take a break from playing for a while."

It was a stunning moment, and it might take on extra weight in the coming months—and years—if Osaka never plays professional tennis again. This isn't the first time Osaka has announced she needed to take a break from the sport. She was, after all, coming off an extended break that saw her withdraw from the French Open and skip Wimbledon. But this felt different. Sitting in the room, I wondered whether I had just listened to a retirement speech. Osaka was clearly hurting, but before she slipped out of sight, she was going to find the composure to tell the world something.

She was not OK. And she wanted to admit that.

"I guess we're all dealing with some stuff," Osaka said. "But I know I'm dealing with some stuff."

Ever since Osaka withdrew from the French Open after being informed she'd be fined increasing amounts if she didn't consent to postmatch interviews, it felt as if Osaka was asking, just for a while, to let her tennis speak for itself. At least until the world felt less awful for her and talking made her less anxious.

The more I thought about it, the more I realized: Was she really asking for that much? And what did it say about us if we cared more about the talking than the tennis?

Maybe instead of longing for sound bites, we might learn something by slowing down and observing, letting her physical gifts reverberate in our consciousness, because a perfectly struck forehand has a language all its own. So does a racket thrown in anger.

I made a vow to watch—to truly watch—Osaka move through time and space at the US Open. No questions, no quotes. I was just going to write what I saw.

What I saw, I now realize, was someone in pain.

I wonder if what I witnessed was an ending.

But also, maybe, a beginning.

Osaka's first-round match against Marie Bouzkova on Aug. 30 felt, for flashes, like a triumphant return to form. Despite all that had unfolded in the past last year, Osaka came to Queens as the defending champion. The last time she'd played a match in Arthur Ashe Stadium, she'd walked away with her second US Open trophy.

She was light on her toes as the match began, shifting her weight back and forth, trying to find her center. Most tennis players do this, unconsciously fidgeting to quiet their mind before the ball is in the air, the moment when they ask instinct and training to take over. But with Osaka, it has always felt a little deliberate, as if she is trying to persuade herself to keep moving and stop thinking.

Osaka's serve, arguably the best in the women's game, can look a lot like a lightning bolt racing downhill. I know this because, for one service game, I found an empty seat on the baseline behind Bouzkova, trying to watch it from her perspective. Osaka likes to blow air on her fingers before she dribbles the ball, likes to hold it up and nod to her opponent before she serves, a small reminder the start of a point shouldn't be a surprise. She closes her eyes as she tips her head back, just for a split second, then coils her spine as she tosses the ball into the air. Jumping off her toes, she springs into space, hammering her racket downward, sending the ball screaming over the net.

Bouzkova, a 23-year-old from Prague, handled these lightning bolts with more vigor than I might have expected, stepping into balls with a piercing two-handed backhand that made Osaka run and change directions, even flustering her occasionally. The flaws that would prove to be her downfall in her next match against Leylah Fernandez were there, but I wasn't smart enough to see them yet. Osaka wasn't moving well, not reacting to the ball as she once did. At 4–4 in the opening set, Bouzkova scraped together a break point and for a moment it felt as if we might have a competitive match.

It's then I saw it, the vast gulf between Osaka and someone like Bouzkova, a wiry and fast but also limited tennis player. A cold intensity washed over Osaka's face. She thundered a serve out wide, her right arm uncoiling in a blur, and Bouzkova flailed in desperation but could do nothing more than deflect it off the frame of her racket. Deuce. Another serve from Osaka, this time rifled up the middle, and Bouzkova's head sank as it sped by untouched. Advantage Osaka. She bounced on her toes and blasted a second straight ace by Bouzkova to end the game.

As the crowd erupted, Osaka looked more relieved than elated, letting loose a short scream. It ended well before the applause did. Bouzkova looked dazed. She would win only one game the rest of the match, rarely forcing Osaka to win extended rallies.

A couple of times, Osaka blew on her fingers as she was headed to her chair, and I pictured a gunslinger walking away from a shootout, deadpan and unfazed, like she was just glad it was over.

When the match ended, she spotted a little girl in the crowd who had been cheering for her. Osaka jogged over to her bag, rummaged inside and retrieved something, an Olympic pin she handed to the little girl. The little girl smiled, and so did Osaka. It was one of the few times she smiled all evening.

This has been a vexing season for Osaka. In February, she captured her fourth career Grand Slam title, winning the Australian Open for the second time, dominating the draw and losing just one set on her way to the title. But in May, she withdrew from the French Open, then decided to skip Wimbledon entirely. She lit the Olympic cauldron in her home country of Japan, but fell early in play. When she returned to play a tune-up in Cincinnati, she cried during her news conference. The isolation of COVID, she said, was starting to wear on her.

Osaka's serve can be lethal, and her two-handed backhand is efficient, maybe even underrated at times. But her forehand has long made me feel things. During her rise, it was as good a marriage of grace and power as anything in sports. Like a trumpet blast or a cymbal crash, it had a way of announcing its presence.

It was here, at the US Open, that her forehand first came of age. In 2017, as an unseeded 19-year-old, she thrashed the defending champion, Angelique Kerber, so convincingly in the first round (6–3, 6–1) that Osaka was almost sheepish afterward. Some of her forehands left Kerber looking overwhelmed. She needed reps to consistently harness it, but a year later, she would run Serena Williams ragged with the same shots on the same court to win her first Grand Slam title. It wasn't long before Osaka took over as the No. 1 player in the world.

Much has happened since, however. Now her forehand runs hot and cold. As Osaka gained more experience, she lost some innocence. She stopped playing fearless tennis. When she drew Fernandez in the third round after a walkover in the second, it felt like a dangerous matchup. In addition to being left-handed, Fernandez had nothing to lose.

Even on bad days, there is something mesmerizing about the way Osaka coils her body in anticipation of the ball, storing energy in her core before unwinding and unleashing it, pushing off the ground as she rotates so that both feet are often in the air at impact.

Every modern tennis player uses a version of this method to generate power, swinging the core instead of the arm, an evolution that, on the women's side, probably began with Steffi Graf before it was perfected by the Williams sisters. Serena, however, learned to generate power with her feet still connected to the ground, a technique that sharpened her accuracy and allowed her to change directions quickly. Osaka's power is like a mix of the hammer throw and the ballet, with little sautés after her best shots. The fluid, looping arc she makes with her right arm can be beautiful to watch, but it is also maddeningly inconsistent.

Osaka might have looked across the net at times against Fernandez and seen a version of her old self. It was Osaka who used to play fearless tennis, who pumped her fist between points and fed off the energy of the crowd inside Arthur Ashe. It was Osaka, once upon a time, who didn't let mistakes bother her, who watched others unravel while she remained composed. But the deeper into the match she went Friday, the more obvious it was that something wasn't right, either with her game or with her state of mind. Even after she broke Fernandez at 5–5 in the first set with a pair of majestic forehand winners, it didn't seem to help her relax.

In the second-set tiebreak, Osaka's anger bubbled over after each missed shot. She hit a forehand wide to fall behind 4–0, then slammed her racket into the ground, drawing a chorus of jeers from the crowd as she sheepishly walked to the net to retrieve it. She threw her racket again after losing the next point, receiving a warning from the chair umpire for her behavior. I was reminded of her US Open final against Serena Williams on this same court, when Williams infamously lost her cool as the match slipped away. Osaka spent much of the changeover before Friday's third set with a towel draped over her head, looking as if she was trying hide from the world, longing to be anywhere else.

Fernandez broke Osaka's serve in the first game, and from there, it was obvious it was only a matter of time. There would be no spirited rally. When Fernandez won a point in the second game with a shot that clipped the net, Osaka responded by firing the ball into the stands in anger. It became difficult to watch.

Osaka tried to compose herself between points, taking deep breaths and an extra second to fiddle with the strings of her racket while her back was to the court, but all that accomplished was drawing jeers from the crowd. When the match ended with another unforced error by Osaka, Fernandez pumped her fists with ecstasy, soaking up a standing ovation from the fans. Osaka gave her a brief congratulatory hug, then quickly packed her things and departed, throwing up a gentle peace sign as she exited the court.

An hour later, she was wiping away tears, but adamant that no one was going to stop her from saying what she wanted—what she needed to say. This might be it for her, at least for a while. It wasn't an answer to a question about her future; she volunteered the information unprompted. There were long bouts of silence as she tried get the words out

When she finished, Osaka looked relieved. She put her mask back on and got to her feet.

She drifted toward the door, never once looking back.

Kevin Van Valkenburg is a 2000 graduate of the University of Montana School of Journalism. He worked as an enterprise sports reporter and online columnist for the *Baltimore Sun* before joining ESPN as a news, features, and investigative reporter.

Beneath 9/11's Terrible Smoke, a Flash of Gold

SALLY JENKINS

FROM *The Washington Post* • SEPTEMBER 11, 2021

After the shroud rolled over the day, I remember just one dash of color in the pall, a smear of bright yellow. It was an old Schwinn steel-frame racing bicycle, and it moved like a canary in the smoke. The bike, like all bikes, was an escape, the ability to get somewhere under your own power, fast, to carve turns and pick your own lane through obstacles. But it represented something else too, that bike, as indefinably sweet as a wildflower growing in the sidewalk.

The first tower was hit at 8:46 a.m., and had I not worn the spouse's sandals and forgotten where I put them, we would have been near the foot of it. Instead, the shoe argument made us late coming back from a long weekend, and we hit heavy traffic on an expressway. We came around a curve, and I said, "What the hell are those chimneys burning?" Then my eyes adjusted to the unimaginable: the World Trade Center, smoldering. The spouse, a photographer for the *New York Times*, opened the sunroof and stood up, waist halfway out of the car, with a camera. When the first tower fell, it looked like God took his thumb and just rubbed it out of the picture. The inarticulate noises that came out of our throats were not screams exactly, just low exhalations of grieved astonishment.

On the Queensboro Bridge, thousands of pedestrians fled the other way over it, running out of Manhattan in their neckties and high heels, a sight so eerie I said something like, "It looks like a monster movie." We were on the bridge when the second tower fell. It was soundless from where we were, and then the double shroud-cloud spread over Lower Manhattan like a fast-rolling fog.

At *The Washington Post* bureau, I said, "Where do I go?" and an editor said someone was needed to cover the hospitals, so I stuck my driver's license, my press ID and a $20 bill in my running shoes and started jogging downtown. I was a runner in those days, so I ran all the way from 57th Street to St. Vincent's Hospital on West 12th without stopping. When I got there, all the nurses and docs were lined up on the sidewalk with a huge row of gurneys and lines of IV poles.

Only it was quiet. There were no ambulances pulling up. They were all just standing there.

I said to a nurse, "Where are all the victims?"

She just looked at me and said, "No one's coming in."

Down in the Financial District, people walked out of the smoke, and they were the *color* of smoke, covered with ash, as they wandered through streets overhung by blown, damaged rooftops—a steel beam stuck out of one building and quivered in the air as if Zeus had thrown a javelin, and shards of glass wavered in the wind.

A guy with a wet blanket over his shoulders, hair completely caked with ashes, said stupefied, "They were jumping out of the buildings." A construction foreman saw the second plane roar right overhead, flying at such a tilted angle that he worried the wing might hit his crane before it speared the South Tower. Smithereens of paper choked the sidewalks and gutters, and it smelled like nothing had ever smelled, a combination of burning electrical wire, wet cement and something else you couldn't even identify, acrid, hot, metallic and wet at the same time. Later it would be identified as an amalgam of glass fibers, asbestos, gypsum and lead. At Thanksgiving, I would reach up to get the roasting pan kept on top of the fridge in my Lower Manhattan apartment, and it would have silt in the bottom.

By late afternoon, the $20 bill was soaked with sweat and I had probably run six miles. Footsore, I headed to a bike shop on West 14th Street. Inside, it was deserted except for a guy at the counter. I flashed my *Washington Post* ID and said: "Hi, I'm a reporter, and I need to get back uptown. But all I've got is $20. Do you have anything I could rent for that just for today? And I'll come back tomorrow with more money?"

He said: "I don't got any rental bikes left. They took 'em all."

I said, "Listen, if you have any old junker I could use, I swear I will come back here tomorrow and buy the most expensive bike you have."

He said, "Well, if I get a bike for you, how you going to lock it up?"

I said, almost in tears, "Do you have a lock I could rent for $20?"

He said: "Hey, it's not that kind of day. I'm going to give you a bike."

He disappeared in back and after a moment returned with that creaking 1970s steel 10-speed Schwinn. It was the bright yellow of a tropical fruit, "Kool Lemon," as Schwinn advertised it in '74. It was so bright you practically had to throw a hand across your eyes to shade them. A tide of laughter rose up in my throat—in the middle of the worst day ever, I thought confusedly, how can you laugh? But that's what the color summoned.

Filmmaker Steven Spielberg once said about making "Schindler's List": "For me the symbol of life is color. That's why a film about the Holocaust has to be in black and white."

That bike was a color amid the terrible shrouded black and grayness of 9/11.

It's said that 9/11 happened to all Americans, and it did, but it happened first and foremost to New Yorkers, and I'm a lifelong New Yorker. I had watched those buildings go up as a kid in the 1970s, when I was a public schooler with a wad of Bazooka and hard little vowels in my foul little mouth. I remembered Philippe Petit walking the wire between the towers, still the single greatest athletic feat of my lifetime. I had played ballgames from crack to crack in the sidewalks, dodging a German lady with grocery bags who called me a "hoodelump." I rode a stiff wooden skateboard with clay wheels that I would brake by running it over a steel grate, which required me to make an acrobatic leap off the board and stick a landing on the soles of my Converse All Stars. Sometimes I missed and got sidewalk in my skin. One afternoon I stood before my father, stringy-haired, grime-smeared and chin-scarred. "Jesus Christ," he pronounced. "You look like a prizefighter."

That's what New Yorkers were, prizefighters, I thought, and the city was the prize. The hardpan streets had cuttingly sharp edges, but they also glinted with mica, which as a kid struck me like treasure—if you could dig it out, wouldn't it be silver dust?

The yellow Schwinn had old metal lever gearshifts on the neck and two sets of handbrakes that made a "creeeeeeeeeee" sound when you hit them, but it sailed past the roadblocks, and its thick whitewall tires seemed impervious to debris. "That's the way to travel right now," a cop called to me approvingly. My delighted bureau chief, Michael Powell, called the bike The Washington Post Emergency Escape Vehicle.

I rode it for days—because Sept. 11 did not last a day. The melting down out of a perfect blue sky lasted for months. So did the wreckage in the heart of a New Yorker, which was as deep as those black fountains that mark the footprint today. It was a seemingly endless interior hemorrhage. The posters of the missing, of the people who should not have been absent, fluttered from chain link fences and brick walls, and funeral corteges choked the streets, creating a new brand of gridlock that we bore with a solemn, silent, un-honking patience. Sometimes people just stood stock still in the streets with the tears running down their faces.

Zooming around on the bike, I tried to make some sense of the wrecked geography, the mangled tines of metal, the girder quivering in the wind stories high, and of the cold act that wrought such hot destruction, the smoldering pile that burned the boots off the feet of the first responders. In all of that, the bike was the color of a daisy chain and offered a small sense of consolation that I couldn't identify, until Stephen Jay Gould identified it for me.

Two weeks after the cataclysm, Gould, the American paleontologist and evolutionary biologist, wrote an essay that somehow stanched the interior hemorrhage. There was but a single act of evil that day, he pointed out. There were thousands upon thousands of acts of good, repeated in countless different ways all over the city. "The tragedy of human history lies in the enormous potential for destruction in rare acts of evil, not in the high frequency of evil people," he wrote in the *New York Times*. "Complex systems can only be built step by step, whereas destruction requires but an instant. Thus, in what I like to call the Great Asymmetry, every spectacular incident of evil will be balanced by 10,000 acts of kindness. … Good and kind people outnumber all others by thousands to one."

It was true. On every block, store owners and restaurant workers would offer you something, a bit of free solace—"Are you thirsty? Do you need something to eat?"—and refuse payment. Because it was not that kind of day.

"We have a duty, almost a holy responsibility, to record and honor the victorious weight of these innumerable little kindnesses, when an unprecedented act of evil so threatens to distort our perception of ordinary human behavior," Gould wrote.

So I honor the man in the bike shop who provided free-handedly a yellow Schwinn with creeeeeing brakes, gave respite to a footsore witness of the worst day ever and helped her get from the malevolent smoke into the clearer air.

It was probably 10 days before I had time to go back to the bike shop on 14th Street. I walked in there with a wad of cash and the yellow bike.

I said to the guy: "I'm really sorry it's been so long since you've seen me. You probably thought I stole it."

He just said, "Oh, I knew you'd be back."

I said, "I'm here to buy a bike." And he said, "Which one do you want?"

I said: "Honestly? I want this one." And I pointed to the yellow canary-daisy-chain bike.

He would take only a hundred dollars for it, and it became mine.

There have been so many slower-rolling catastrophes since then and with them varying cold vengeful acts and hot ugly ones. Sometimes you could wonder with a sickened heart if the victorious weight will hold or whether the proportion of evil will outweigh the good. If so, the lesson of 9/11 is that the tilt toward evil will probably not come from one huge fracturing external blow of enmity but from smaller self-inflicted hairline cracks, our own responses to each other in storms, sickness and mean political seasons.

Gould's assurance that historical evils are isolated and outnumbered is not a static truth. It does not have to remain true. If good and kind people are to "outnumber all others by thousands to one," as he wrote, then we have to free-handedly do something small and good and kind every day because, hey, it's not *that* kind of day. We have to make sure we are on the longer list. Make sure of it. That's how we will know who and where we are and find our colorful ride out of the terrible smoke.

After spending the previous decade working as a book author and as a magazine writer, **Sally Jenkins** began her second stint at *The Washington Post* in 2000. She was named the nation's top sports columnist in 2001, 2003, 2010, and 2011 by the Associated Press Sports Editors. In 2013, she won a first-place award from the AP for an investigative series co-written with Rick Maese on medical care in the NFL, titled "Do No Harm." Jenkins is the author of 12 books, four of which were *New York Times* bestsellers, most recently *Sum It Up* with legendary basketball coach Pat Summitt.

'Things Are Going to Be Different Now'

SHAKER SAMMAN

FROM *Sports Illustrated* • SEPTEMBER 10, 2021

Ibtihaj Muhammad was a sophomore at Columbia High in Maplewood, N.J., about 20 miles from Manhattan, when the World Trade Center fell. The future Olympic bronze-medalist fencer was one of only several Muslims in her community—she remembers maybe one or two other families in the area—and the only person at her school wearing a hijab.

Maplewood was a commuter town; parents sent their children to class, then boarded the Morris and Essex line into the city for work. Muhammad was in her AP English class on the morning of Sept. 11, 2001, when her teacher, like others across the country, watched through fingers as news footage captured just miles away played out across a television. First, smoke from the north tower filled the screen. Then came the panic.

After United Airlines flight 175 struck the south tower, Muhammad's principal took to the loudspeaker and instructed teachers to turn off their TVs. Parents of students at the school worked in those buildings. They didn't need to experience their panic and grief so publicly.

But the principal did something else, too: "We were called to sit in this room," remembers Muhammad, who's now 35. "My brother, this Egyptian family ... . It was like, *You just stay here.*"

They were being separated for their safety, the sequestered students were told, but Ibtihaj remembers sitting there with the few other Muslims students who were pulled from their classes. Even if their removal was well-intentioned, it ostracized them from peers. It was ghettoizing.

And Muhammad's experience wasn't unique. Muslims became a lower class of citizen in a country now fearful and filled with hatred toward them. I was one of them. I was 5—a Muslim first-grader living in rural Michigan, surrounded by folks whose image of Muslims or Arabs would come to be shaped by *24* and *NCIS*.

I don't remember the towers falling. My understanding of what happened is pieced together through videos and retellings. But I do remember September 11. I remember coming home from school to find my mother, panicked and shaken, halfway up the stairs to my bedroom. "Did they tell you in school about what happened today?" she asked. They hadn't.

She explained to me, with simplicity and caution: People had attacked the United States. People from a place near Syria, where my parents were born, long before they immigrated in 1990. Then, in a moment of clairvoyance, she sighed and looked me square in the eyes.

"Things are going to be different now."

The last 20 years of U.S. policy, at home and abroad, have borne out that truth. The world changed on a macro level, and for me, on a personal one. Wars gave way to an onslaught of Islamophobia, attacking anyone who practiced the faith or even remotely resembled those who did. Targeted harassment policies were codified and the words "Middle Eastern" and "Arab" and "Muslim" became synonymous with "terrorist."

It didn't matter that my parents were accomplished in their fields, the same way that it wouldn't matter later that Ibtihaj

Muhammad was an accomplished fencer, a medalist for the U.S. In the eyes of many, she remains a Muslim first and foremost. The lost story of September 11 is the story of September 12, the day Muslims in America woke up to a new reality. One that's continued each morning since.

BILQIS ABDUL-QAADIR REMEMBERS what it was like when she first started wearing a hijab. She was a ninth-grader at the New Leadership Charter School in Springfield, Mass., in the mid-2000s—her second year of public schooling after having been taught at home. In the eighth grade she'd made the high school basketball team, but it wasn't until a year later, as a freshman, that she covered her head, as well as her arms and legs.

Playing in a hijab wasn't easy. She didn't know many other Muslims around town; she couldn't turn to older girls for advice on how to make the garment suit an athletic activity. At the time, she wore a makeshift covering—a clunky affair made of sweatpants or T-shirts, wrapped like a turban. She couldn't use pins or needles to secure it; that would have been unsafe on the court. And the world was years away from a Dri-Fit version.

Encumbered though she may have been, she went on to be named Massachusetts's 2009 Gatorade Player of the Year, averaging more than 40 points a night. But to some opposing fans from Catholic schools in less-diverse neighboring towns, she was a target for harassment. "It made me conscious of my dress," says Abdul-Qaadir, now 30. "I was called 'Osama Bin Laden's niece.' Everytime I step on the court I'm looking at the crowds, because I see people pointing and laughing, making jokes."

In the beginning, the hecklers scared her and made her self-conscious. She noticed that the same people calling her names were often the same ones who approached her after games, impressed by her dominance, and asked about her hijab. *What is it? And why do you wear it?* They'd never met a Muslim, they'd tell her.

The unwanted spotlight followed Abdul-Qaadir to the University of Memphis, and then to Indiana State, where she transferred for her final year of eligibility. She remembers playing on the road with the Tigers against Tulsa, and how the men's players in the crowd heckled her for wearing a hijab. She remembers how students at Bradley had to be removed from the stands after they hurled hate speech at her. She remembers the game that had to be stopped temporarily, so bad had the harassment gotten. But most of all she remembers how, in many people's eyes, she was always *the Muslim basketball player*—a caricature, not a fully formed person.

With Memphis, in a game against Houston, an errant swipe from a ball-hungry opponent as she drove the lane unintentionally knocked the hijab off her head. Abdul-Qaadir dropped to the floor in a panic as her teammates huddled around her, shielding her from the crowd as she scrambled to reaffix her headwear. Years later, she remembers: At halftime, the game's TV broadcast had run a segment about her hijab and why she wore it. There seemed a degree of understanding. And yet, when the hijab fell off, the TV cameras zoomed in, invasively, trying to get a better look.

Abdul-Qaadir saw for herself a basketball life after college; she planned to play professionally in Europe. But FIBA, the international body governing the game, barred athletes from wearing hijabs. At first, Abdul-Qaadir wasn't concerned. They would see her play and realize that her hijab wasn't a safety concern, she figured. It wouldn't be a problem. But quickly she realized FIBA wouldn't budge. She had to make a choice: her sport or her faith. She admits that it wasn't always a clear one.

"I was getting ready to, honestly, take my hijab off," Abdul-Qaadir remembers. "I was questioning the hijab. I was like, *There's no way I worked this hard to reach my goal and to then have it taken away because of my hijab.*"

It was a personal crisis. For so long she'd been *the Muslim basketball player*. When the game was taken away, she says, she was just *the Muslim*. She was embarrassed that she even considered removing her headscarf; she didn't tell her family, just one close Muslim friend. Without the game, she lost the part of her life that helped her blend in and win affection from fans. If not for those fans, she might have given in.

"Young Muslim girls from across the world were learning about my story and emailing me, sending me pictures of them dressed just like me, in a basketball uniform," Abdul-Qaadir says. "This wasn't about me anymore."

Hers was a choice between faith and the sport she'd devoted her life to. And that choice ended her career. Abdul-Qaadir never played a minute of professional basketball, but she still changed the sport for those who followed her, petitioning FIBA (along with Indira Kaljo, a Bosnian Muslim at Tulane whom Abdul-Qaadir had played against) to drop the restriction. The fight took three years, but in 2017 the association rescinded its ban, paving the way for Muslim women to compete on their own terms.

Even in a sport where wearing a hijab isn't illegal, it can still complicate seemingly simple things. As Ibtihaj Muhammad climbed the ranks of fencing, all the way to the Rio Olympics, she switched from a child's hijab (tied in the back and pinched in the front, secured with a safety pin) to a georgette fabric, doubled onto itself and then pinned into place under her fencing helmet. Functionally, it was passable—it covered her hair—but the four thin layers retained sweat, creating a new problem.

"When it got wet, I couldn't hear," says Muhammad, who was at risk of losing crucial points. "My entire career, I had no idea. When the official would say, 'Start,' sometimes I couldn't hear."

It wasn't until 2017, after her fencing career ended, that Nike (with Muhammad's help) developed the Pro Hijab: a moisture-wicking Dri-Fit headscarf that made obsolete the makeshift hijabs that she and Abdul-Qaadir had worn. A singular sport product, designed for Muslim women, goes beyond making it easier for them to compete at the highest levels. It spares young girls the complexities and fears attendant of the headwear.

"For a lot of us, for a really long time, not having … a sport hijab was an excuse not to be active," Muhammad says. And that "goes against the tenets of our faith, to take care of yourself and your body. … It's given us permission to be active."

The wider acceptance of the hijab is part of what Muhammad says has been a concerted effort by Muslims to combat Islamophobia in the two decades following September 11. Younger Muslims aren't bending to a world that has harassed and villainized them. They're demanding the world bend toward them. It's part of what Muhammad calls "a wave of strength."

"As a Black Muslim, that desire to conform has never been a part of who I am," she says. "We [don't] need to look a certain way or pretend to be things we're not."

HAKEEM OLAJUWON WASN'T ALWAYS a devout Muslim. Back in Lagos, where he was raised, Islam was Olajuwon's culture more than it was his religion. He'd listen to an Imam call worshipers to prayer on the radio, fast on the holy month of Ramadan and attend the mosque on Fridays with his father. But within a few years of arriving Stateside, in 1980, he wasn't actively participating anymore. Eventually, in Houston, he was so removed from his faith that when someone asked him whether he was headed to the mosque he was shocked to hear there was one nearby. He'd never looked. Olajuwon was skeptical at first—he didn't know what to expect until a familiar sound swallowed the silence.

"It was the first time I heard the call to prayer in about two years," Olajuwon says. "And I couldn't stop crying."

Thereafter, if the Rockets, say, played in Phoenix, he'd ask the bellman at the team hotel to book him a ride to the closest mosque. Wherever Houston traveled, the same thing. At first, it was just a way for Olajuwon to connect with his God. Soon, it gave him a family.

In time, members of the communities he visited started to recognize him each time he came back through town. Local leaders introduced themselves. Others invited him over for dinner, or offered to drive him to and from the airport. Across the country, Muslims knew: If the Rockets are in town tomorrow, you can expect to see Hakeem at the Isha prayer tonight.

"When we travel, you don't know anybody," Olajuwon says. "Then all of a sudden ... the community [knew me]. So, life on the road, for a Muslim—I've never felt like I'm on the road. I'm always at home."

As Olajuwon became more comfortable expressing his faith, he practiced it more openly. Early in his career, he fasted during Ramadan, with the exception of game days. Muslims, according to Islam's teachings, can skip fasting during the holy month if they have good reason, such as illness or old age or pregnancy. But the texts don't cite "backing down David Robinson" as a reason to break fast, and so when Ramadan fell in February in 1995, Olajuwon concluded that he ought to fast, even on game days.

Some of his teammates and coaches expressed concern— *Think of the energy expended by even the most static of NBA big men!*—but Olajuwon quickly mollified their fears. Fueled by the spare dates and the few sips of water that he consumed at halftime, after the sun had set, Olajuwon would come out of the locker room roaring in the second half. In his first game fasting, he scored 41 points on Karl Malone; he outdueled Charles Barkley, Patrick Ewing and Robinson in the coming days.

Fasting, he says, made him sharper, lighter and more disciplined. Halftime dates were his own version of Michael's Secret Stuff. The dried fruits—the same as the Prophet Muhammad ate to break fast centuries earlier—propelled him. He ended that February as the league's Player of the Month. He'd fully reclaimed his faith. He was home.

Fast forward six years, to 2001, when he was traded to the Raptors, and Olajuwon was in unfamiliar territory, outside of Houston for the first time in more than 20 years. Then, a month after he arrived, the towers fell. Suddenly, Olajuwon was forced to play defense off the court.

"Islam had been looked at from a positive light all my career, until 9/11," says Olajuwon, who's now 58. "Then all this negativity started, which is totally the opposite of what Islam teaches."

The burden fell on Olajuwon and his fellow Muslims, the former NBA MVP says, to explain to those who might wish them harm: *Your vision of Islam is a distortion of reality*. And while Olajuwon admits that Islam is too big for any one person to represent, he acknowledges the role he's had to play in defending his faith. "You feel like you have to convince the people, *That's not Islam*," Olajuwon says. "You have to justify your position as a Muslim, being, all of a sudden, the enemy."

Pushing back is a role he's embraced. "I'll take the opportunity," he says, "to shape the perception of what Islam really is."

Still, those perceptions weigh heavily on many others. Husain and Hamza Abdullah—Los Angeles–born siblings and former NFL defensive backs—were raised in a small but devout Muslim community made up of immigrants from across the Middle East. For them, religion started at home and with sporadic trips to the mosque in the big city. They had fellow Muslims to lean on, and they had each other.

As they progressed through their college careers, both at Washington State and then as professionals in the NFL, they stayed devoted to their faith. Still, it tested them. Islam follows the lunar calendar, which is 11 days shorter than the Gregorian calendar used in the U.S.; thus, Ramadan comes earlier each year. Husain, the younger of the two brothers, was a senior in high school a year after the towers fell, when he first fasted during a football season. It was difficult, he remembers, running drills in practice, staying disciplined in games, all without a sip of water or a bite of food. And harder still, doing it in secret.

It wasn't until Husain's third year in the NFL, in 2010 with the Vikings, that he first let on to teammates and coaches that he was fasting. The brothers didn't want special treatment. But, more than that, as players always living on a roster's fringe, they were worried that fasting would be used as a reason to cut them.

"Nobody's gonna come out and say that, but behind closed doors, fasting may be a conversation," says Husain, who entered the league as an undrafted free agent. "And so we used to always say, 'Don't give them a reason to cut you.'"

By 2010, Husain was a frequent starter, and his Vikings training staff built him a meal plan to help get him the nutrients he needed while fasting—a far cry from what Olajuwon had experienced, back when teammates watched with concern. The support was a boon for Husain, but his fears continued. Without Olajuwon's MVP pedigree, and in a conservative league that punishes deviation from the norm, it seemed reasonable for the brothers to wonder whether their fasting would cost them their careers.

In time they'd find the limits of the league's tolerance. The practice of Islam is built on five pillars: profession of faith, prayer, charity, fasting during Ramadan and Hajj, the pilgrimage to holy sites in Mecca and Medina, where millions of Muslims travel each year. Each Muslim is to complete the trip once in their life. And in 2012, the Abdullahs felt their calling.

As soon as the brothers stepped away from the NFL they were criticized for abandoning their teams. Husain knows the choice might have looked confusing—*Why not wait a few years, until after your playing days are over?*—but as he tells it, it wasn't a decision so much as a duty.

"How do we know we're gonna be alive tomorrow?" Abdullah remembers thinking. "Allah says: 'If you walk towards me, I will run towards you.' And Hamza and I were like, 'O.K., well, *Bismillah.* [In the name of Allah.]'"

For Husain, that pilgrimage cost him a year of football, but he played three more seasons with the Chiefs. For Hamza, the cost was higher. He waited by his phone and eventually fell out of touch with his agent. "My faith shouldn't be a burden," he told The Undefeated in 2018. "It's an asset."

Even as Husain's career continued, though, he faced unfair scrutiny. During a home game in 2014 against the Patriots he tracked an errant Tom Brady pass over the middle and sprinted 39 yards through tacklers for a touchdown. Afterward, he slid through the endzone on his knees in celebration before dropping his head down in prayer. Everyday stuff. Only, when he looked up, he'd been assessed an unsportsmanlike conduct penalty.

Broadly speaking, church and the NFL are synonymous. It's not quite a joke to say that they share the sabbath. Tim Tebow, among others, made a brand for himself by falling to a knee in prayer. In Kansas City, Husain spoke with the referee after the call, and the league admitted the next day that it was a mistake to penalize him for praying. Seven years later, he says he doesn't remember what reasoning the official gave; he can't say for sure why he was flagged.

Says Abdullah: "I'm not the judge of men's hearts."

I OFTEN WONDER about the role that September 11 played in my own life. I had lived in a post-9/11 world for just under a decade when I decided that I didn't believe in God, and it wasn't long after that I shared my lack of faith with my parents. It was difficult. They were hurt—not because I'd betrayed them, but because I'd declined a part of the life that they'd bestowed upon me.

I think about how things might've been different if I hadn't grown up where I did, in a particularly Muslim-spooked part of the Midwest; if there had been other Muslims at my school; or if I'd been a few years older, or a few years younger, on 9/11. My sister was just two years behind me in school. We shared carpools and teachers and after-school clubs—in so many ways, the same experience. But she was too young to process the immediate wave of vitriol that followed the attacks. I had cousins my age who were still in their formative years when the towers fell. But they lived in Pasadena, and they went to school with friends with names like Osman and Osama. They stayed devout.

In middle school I walked from class to class expecting to be called a terrorist with frequency. I don't know whether things would have been different if I were raised alongside peers who learned more than two verses of the Quran (which is about all I can still recite from memory), or in whom I could have confided my anxieties and fears. Maybe I'd still be practicing. Or maybe 9/11 was a catalyst for something that would always, eventually, happen inside me.

I was able to escape the sort of torment that continues to befall Muslims because I don't *look* Muslim or *sound* Muslim. Back home in Michigan, I can blend into a crowd in my predominantly white community, a skill I worked hard for.

I didn't *want* to be like my Christian classmates. This was not a metamorphosis conceived of jealousy. It was a subconscious choice between being someone who would face overwhelming scrutiny for a lifetime and someone who wouldn't. But thanks to Muslims like Muhammad, Abdul-Qaadir and the Abdullah brothers, and those who followed in their footsteps, that's not a decision the next generation necessarily has to make.

"This is who we are," Muhammad says. "We're not going to change parts of who we are to make ourselves more palatable for anyone."

Shaker Samman is a writer in Los Angeles. His work has appeared in *Sports Illustrated*, *The Guardian*, Baseball Prospectus, Slate, The Classical, the *Tampa Bay Times*, and The Ringer, where he worked for more than three years. His mom doesn't know what this book is, but will likely cry when a copy arrives at her doorstep in Michigan.

In Mavericks' Dream Surf Season, 51-Year-Old Peter Mel Making Big-Wave History

BRUCE JENKINS

FROM the *San Francisco Chronicle* • JANUARY 17, 2021

In the fantasy world of big-wave surfers, the waves never stop. Giant swells arrive one after another, in perfect weather. Even the hardiest athletes take a day or two off to preserve their stamina, for there's so much more to come.

That dreamy scenario is the reality of January at Mavericks. Through Saturday, 21 of the 23 days produced legitimate big-wave size, ranging from 20 to 60 feet and beyond. The performance level makes an exponential rise. And when the proper perspective is drawn, a single name stands above the rest.

The master. Peter Mel. As a very old friendship, man and wave, blossoms as never before.

You've heard the expression "old guys rule," and it's no joke here. The Santa Cruz-based surfer is 51, with a devotion to Mavericks dating to 1991, and he's always been one of the best out there. But something happened over a three-day stretch this month, something that left Mel wondering, "Where do I go from here?"

As longtime Northern California standout Steve Dwyer put it, "Pete put himself into two Mavericks clubs—Biggest Barrel and Biggest Wave—that have only one member. Him."

On Jan. 8, the water a pristine blue-green and brushed to perfection by offshore winds, Mel paddled into a 50-foot drop that redefined the art of Mavericks "tube" riding. On that very unforgiving stretch of reef, a spot beyond the normal takeoff area that surfers attempted to conquer for years, he pulled into a gigantic cavern on his 9-foot-10-inch Merrick and came out the other side, arms raised, looking almost stunned by the accomplishment. There were shouts of amazement from watercraft in the channel, and when Mavericks pioneer Jeff Clark got a look at the video, he proclaimed it "the most technical job we've ever seen from a paddle-in surfer."

Dwyer said it connects directly to experience, "something Pete's been searching three decades to accomplish. It's a matter of 'backdooring' that bowl (the standard takeoff area), taking off behind the peak, and he's been pushing those boundaries since the late '90s. This wave was super high-risk. He had to navigate four ledges on the face, and if he falls on that last one, he's in for the beating of his life. People watching from the lineup would be like, 'Uh-oh, he could die.'

"Even making it down into the flats doesn't guarantee the barrel isn't going to clamshell on him," Dwyer said, "but it stayed open, and he made history. That comes from 30 years of studying that lineup, seeing the opportunity, then having the king-size balls to go."

"One in a million," said photographer/rescue safety operator Frank Quirarte. "I think anyone else would have been obliterated."

"Like surgery," said San Francisco big-wave surfer Grant Washburn.

Mel said he'd "never seen anybody paddle in and do that, to be honest. It was the wave I've been trying to get my whole career. And then I'm thinking, now what?"

He got the answer two days after his historic ride, last Sunday.

As a new, giant swell began to take shape that morning, paddle-surfing seemed a catastrophic proposition. "Nobody questioned that there were 70-foot waves," said Washburn, meticulous in his documentation of every swell. "A lot bigger, in my mind. There's never been anything like it. We've had days that big, but not just pure and clean the entire time. It was the first time in about 20 years where I really wondered if an 80-foot wave would come and get us all."

Bay Area meteorologist Mark Sponsler, for years the most reliable source for local wave forecasts, said "the jet stream has been raging since late December with 200-knot winds providing piles of fuel to support storm development. And a beauty of a storm developed, producing 80-knot winds and 60-foot seas aimed right at Half Moon Bay. It moved to within 1,500 miles of the coast, then veered off to the northeast, resulting in massive waves, but with light winds and relatively clear skies. It was the biggest clean-and-groomed day I think Mavericks has ever seen."

There were valiant attempts at paddle-in surfing that day, but "it was really hard to catch something," said El Granada's Luca Padua, 19, who has taken the lead among young local surfers charging Mavericks. "The playing field was so big, you're paddling 50 yards out, then maybe 100 yards over, just really hard to track down. Tons of waves came through the bowl, but almost none of them were approachable."

"There was a period around noon when it was just macking and no one could go near it," said Mel. "Way, way outside—like 300 yards outside the pack—some giant waves were coming through. The outer realm, we've always called it. That's when I told John (his 21-year-old son), let's go out there and just whip into one if we can. Tow-surfing was the only way to go."

Towed behind a Jet Ski at breakneck speed, with the aid of footstraps and a slingshot release from the rope, surfers are able to ride downsized boards with the luxury of placing themselves exactly where they want to be as the wave begins to break. Mel had a worthy companion in his son, an able driver who is coming into his own as a big-wave surfer, and the result was spectacular. Cascading endlessly down a wave of inconceivable height (judge by yourself from the photos) on a 5-foot-10-inch board he's had in his quiver for 20 years, Mel stylishly navigated the beast without a hitch.

"You have no idea how big it is when you're on it," Mel said. "You're just racing for the channel with no idea what's happening behind you. I was kinda surprised when I saw Frank's photo. I was like, what the heck? I was just so glad I didn't make a mistake. And then John came and picked me up on the inside. So cool."

Last Sunday proved to be a harrowing experience for 28-year-old Kai Lenny, the most advanced big-wave surfer in the world and someone who has dominated Mavericks in past sessions. "I learned that day that the consequences out there are as heavy as any place I've ever surfed," he said. "Looking for that really big one, a few of us were sitting out beyond that green buoy way out to sea—and we still got caught inside. It was a freak wave, breaking in such deep water it was more like an avalanche." At least 70 feet, by Washburn's estimation.

"That wave dragged me almost into the bowl, just hundreds of yards underwater—like being swept by a river, to a place where no safety vest could bring you up," Lenny said. "Where I ended up was really bad, like the worst place anyone's ever been. The next wave backed off enough where I could barely paddle over it. Otherwise, I'm not sure what I would have done. I wouldn't say it rattled me, but it made me feel like my younger self, just trying to figure out what's going on. That rarely happens."

Perusing his records, Washburn said, "Young surfers are fortunate to be able to test themselves day after day, and not just this month. We had 16 quality days in December. I spoke to Peter in the water the other day, and we agreed this is the best Mavericks season we've ever seen—even if it stops now."

Mel spent his youth immersed in Santa Cruz surf culture. He was born the same year (1969) his father, John, opened the Freeline Surf Shop that remains a thriving enterprise near

Pleasure Point. "The shop was our home, our shaping, manu-
facturing and retail under one roof, and it just grew from there,"
he said. Peter and his wife, Tara, have been married 22 years,
raising the younger John and her child, Anthony, to whom Peter
has been a stepdad since toddlerhood.

Always known for his courage and distinctly elegant surfing,
Mel became one of the most respected California surfers ever to
grace Oahu's North Shore, earning an invitation to the prestigious
Eddie Aikau contest (at Waimea Bay) for 20 consecutive years. He
was a three-time finalist in the now-defunct Mavericks contest
before winning it in 2013, and he won the Big Wave World Tour
overall championship in 2012.

"I remember Pete and Jeff Clark tow-surfing a giant October
swell, and when we went out to dinner that night, John was just
10 days old," said Quirarte. "Now, 21 years later, that kid towed
Pete into a bomb. That's so cool, and I think Pete's family is a big
reason he's lasted so long in surfing. It's hard to make any money
in big-wave surfing. Almost none at all, really. But he's always
been engaged in the sport."

Mel served as commissioner of the World Surf League
from 2015–17 and parlayed his breezy, upbeat manner into an
announcer's role in the water, analyzing contest performances
and interviewing surfers right on the spot. "That's all changed
now, with the pandemic and the tour shut down," he said, "but
I've enjoyed turning the focus toward family, not having to travel
so much.

"I've been inspired to keep surfing big waves lately, and a lot
of it's because of John, just being out there with my son, pushing
each other and having fun. I know that over time, that flame
will dim a little bit. My stamina's like an old battery in a phone.
Charges well, doesn't last as long. I've had people telling me 'walk
away!' after those great waves I had, but you know, I still have a
good time out there. I think as soon as I truly stop enjoying it,
that's when I'll be done."

Lenny could only laugh in admiration when asked about Mel's legacy. "He's letting all of us know that you don't have to stop, that you can be getting the waves of your life in your fifties," he said. "Other surfers have done that, but on this level? I'm not sure. He's always been one of the greats, but now his name is heavily into that conversation. The stone is set. It's solidified."

Just as importantly, Mel doesn't wear that "I'm so heavy" vibe that radiates through self-absorbed athletes. "He's the 100% opposite of that," said Padua, marveling at Mel's effervescent nature. "He's someone you can study, learn from, and when he comes out of the water after a session that could have cost him his life, you can see he's extremely grateful. Every time. That matters. And Mavericks takes care of him."

Bruce Jenkins began writing for the *San Francisco Chronicle* in 1973 and in 1989 became a sports columnist. He has covered 27 World Series, 19 Wimbledons, and many other major events, including the Super Bowl, World Cup soccer, NBA Finals, four major golf tournaments, and U.S. Open tennis championships. He graduated from Santa Monica High School in 1966 and UC Berkeley with a B.A. in journalistic studies in 1971.

Canelo Álvarez and the Mystical Man Behind His Quest for Immortality

ROBERTO JOSÉ ANDRADE FRANCO

FROM ESPN • NOVEMBER 5, 2021

Eddy Reynoso IS carrying Saúl "Canelo" Álvarez on his shoulders. It's Cinco de Mayo weekend, one of the most important days in boxing. And the two, Reynoso as trainer, Álvarez as his boxer, are celebrating another win surrounded by the largest indoor crowd to ever watch a boxing match in the United States. Just seconds before, inside AT&T Stadium in Arlington, Texas, with 73,126 people in attendance, Billy Joe Saunders, or his corner—whichever version of the story you believe—said they'd had enough.

It wasn't illogical to think Saunders would be Álvarez's most formidable opponent in years. He was an undefeated world champion, a slick southpaw from England who'd frustrated opponents confident they could hurt him. But, perhaps most importantly, Saunders is a natural antagonist. His personality often crosses the line between confidence and arrogance, someone who relished fighting in a stadium with enough people to rival the population of a mid-sized Texas town, of which only about a dozen wanted to see him win.

"You've never been in the ring with someone like me," Saunders warned Canelo before the fight. Once the fight started, and the crowd yelled so loud it made your ears ring and your chest pound, Álvarez handled him with relative ease. For good measure, he broke the right side of Saunders's face.

"I felt it when I hit him," Álvarez says now, in Spanish, of the right uppercut that damaged Saunders. When you punch people for a living, you can feel and hear when your fists have cracked bones. "I saw all this caved in," Álvarez says, pointing at his cheekbone, slowly dragging his finger under his right eye. He explains how he broke Saunders—with the casualness of someone talking about the weather.

"I saw this other part raised," Álvarez continues, pointing beside his eye by his temple. "That's why I started urging the crowd to get loud. I knew once the round was over, he wasn't going to fight anymore. He'd be risking his life."

To put it as plainly as possible, Álvarez put a beating on Saunders that made him, or his corner, or all of them, say he didn't want anymore. Instead of fighting, he'd rather go home.

That's why once the fight ended after the 8th round, Reynoso carried Álvarez around the ring on his shoulders in victory. Not far from a waving Mexican flag and a disfigured Saunders, who minutes later would sit inside a lonesome ambulance with a pulsing pain from a right orbital bone broken in three separate places, Reynoso screamed with excitement. Álvarez, sitting atop of his shoulders, sitting atop of the world, pounded his chest and flexed his muscles.

At that moment, just like they recognize it now, Reynoso and Álvarez know that no one in the world can beat them. Not anyone at 160 or 168 or 175 pounds. Not Saunders.

Not Caleb Plant, who they fight on Saturday for four-belt unification.

Álvarez and Reynoso have gotten to the point where they are reaching for history—to become an undisputed champion, and with that, to do what no one else from Mexico has done before.

The Plant fight and beyond isn't about a payday or win for the boxer and trainer team. They are fighting for Álvarez to ascend as the greatest Mexican boxer that ever lived.

ÁLVAREZ IS LISTENING TO REYNOSO. He's sitting on the ring apron in their boxing gym in San Diego. It's a small gym in an industrial warehouse area, which, from the outside, doesn't have a single sign that the world's best boxer trains there. In fact, with closed vertical blinds, black poster boards taped on the dark tinted windows, and a door that's locked as soon as Álvarez enters, they don't want you to know.

That's where Álvarez sits. He passively listens as Reynoso, about 20 feet away, struggles to cut a promo for a Spanish language television station that just interviewed him.

"*El seis de noviembre, no se pierdan la pelea...,*" Reynoso says, staring into the camera before it sounds like his mouth stopped working.

"*No se pierdan la pelea este seis de noviembre...*" His words trip again despite the rearrangement. He tries again, then fails one more time.

While attempting to tell viewers to tune in on Nov. 6, his words just don't come out right. The producer tries to guide him. With an escalating frustration in his voice, Reynoso says he has it.

After another stumble, Álvarez, who has stared at his phone this entire time, smiling and giggling at what he calls, "*memes y mama---s*"—memes and bull------—stands up and yells. "*No que muy fácil?*" He reminds them how everyone makes fun of him when he struggles to do the same. How everyone thinks it's so easy, but it's not. Everyone laughs, even Reynoso, who has a subdued personality. The kind that tells a writer they're wasting his time if he thinks they're asking dumb questions.

At last, Reynoso gets through the promo. Álvarez shows his phone to Munir Somoya, the strength and conditioning coach, and they both laugh. It's a relaxed atmosphere before anyone gets in the ring. So much so that when Álvarez, still sitting on the ring apron, receives a phone call from a friend, he immediately puts them on speaker so all can help decipher what the fast-talking voice is saying. *"No se te entiende ni madres,"* Álvarez laughs while saying he understands nothing. *"Habla despacito."* Talk slowly.

If you don't see how they interact, you might think Álvarez and Reynoso are quiet, often giving simple answers to the questions they're asked—at least in English. If you don't speak Spanish, you might not understand that there's always something lost in translation. You might not know the relationship between Álvarez and Reynoso is many things. Somewhere in the middle of a Venn diagram, Reynoso is trainer, manager, older brother and sometimes more.

"I've known him since he was a boy," Reynoso, who turns 45 on the day of the fight, says, in Spanish, of Álvarez, 31. He has a tattoo of Álvarez's face and frame on the outer part of his left forearm. He got it about 10 months ago after they defeated Englishman Callum Smith, a boxer they completely dominated even though he was an undefeated world champion, tall, had a long reach, was a good technical boxer and moved well. Immediately after that fight, in the locker room, Álvarez told Reynoso that he'd never fail him. And that, to prove it, he was willing to die in the ring.

The relationship between Álvarez and Reynoso is special, in part, because, ever since Álvarez's older brother, Rigoberto, first brought him to his gym in Guadalajara, Mexico, the trainer has helped mature the young boy to a world champion. Today, Álvarez is more than that; he's more than just a superstar in boxing. He's one of the world's most marketable male athletes. The clear example is that boxing isn't dead in the United States— as the common trope argues—it's just become a Latino, largely Mexican, sport. For his part, Álvarez says Reynoso is the best trainer in the world and that there's no team better than his.

"We've always been together," Reynoso says. Regardless of the relationship label, he says his job is to protect Álvarez. To make sure, inside the ring, he's well prepared. To make sure, outside the ring, he's doing things right.

"I worried a lot about him," Reynoso says of Álvarez, using the past tense as if he's talking about the 13-year-old he helped raise. The boy who had six older brothers who also boxed and a sister who helped him along his boxing path. Álvarez was the youngest and had a genius for fighting. He imagined winning world titles but couldn't possibly visualize he'd become this big. "I still worry," Reynoso adds, suddenly speaking in the present. Boxing is a tumultuous ocean where the most treacherous sharks wear suits and tuxedos.

"Lots of negatives, lots of greed," Álvarez says when asked about the dark side of the boxing business. "But it's part of the deal. It comes with the territory, and you just have to know how to navigate it."

When that's the world you live in, you can't ever put your guard down. Those you keep the closest are the ones you trust with your life.

And so, around Álvarez and Reynoso is a team that's been together for years. It's their small world that's only gotten tighter as Álvarez's star has gotten larger. Reynoso, who demands hard work, says they're all friends. Canelo, who demands loyalty, says they're all family. They all understand they're here now, to help Álvarez become the first Mexican, and Latino, undisputed world champion. Those who can't help, are let go. Sparring partners who don't push Álvarez enough are sent home with broken ribs and crooked noses.

"That was Eddy's idea," Álvarez says of fighting to win all four major title belts, becoming just the sixth male boxer to ever do it. "It occurred to him last year."

The Plant fight is important for Álvarez, but if you talk to them enough, you get the sense it might be more critical for Reynoso. Besides his other shifting titles, he's a boxing historian.

The one whose life has revolved around boxing since the bug first bit him. Reynoso was just eight years old when his father—Don Chepo—took him to boxing gyms around Guadalajara, in the western Mexican state of Jalisco.

He never left those gyms that all smell of stale sweat. It's the kind of stench that, at best, cleaning supplies can only temporarily mask. Reynoso, who wears cologne to the gym, is the one who—about 15 years ago when hardly anyone knew Álvarez's name, when if you knew him, you more than likely called him Saúl—came up with what became their mantra: *No Boxing, No Life.*

Reynoso is the one who understands better than all that any claim Álvarez may have at being Mexico's greatest boxer rests on him becoming an undisputed champion. "He'd be categorized as the best in Mexican boxing history, no matter what others say," Reynoso says.

"To be the best, you need to have the wins, and Saúl will have that," Reynoso continues. "No Mexican will have accomplished what Saúl has done."

IF SOCCER REMAINS MEXICO'S most popular sport, boxing, especially among the working class, is the county's Freudian id. Where boxers, even those who don't become world champions, can still become national heroes. Those who win titles become folk heroes, living forever in songs, movies and telenovelas.

There's no analog in the United States for what boxing means in Mexican culture. Perhaps the closest example comes from over a century ago when baseball symbolized democracy and morality. With that, the expanding American empire introduced its national game everywhere it spread, including Mexico. Back then, as America told it, playing and watching baseball—instead of fighting—was a way of becoming civilized.

Boxing is almost of existential importance within Mexican culture, whether in Mexico or the United States with Mexican Americans. Because if what Mexican novelist Carlos Fuentes said is true, claiming the country's history is one of crushing defeat compared to America's grandeur, then boxing remained one of the few places where victories have been plentiful.

Those victories on the nights when, surrounded by family and friends, boxers like Julio César Chávez affirmed that though others couldn't see them, it never meant Mexican people were invisible. A Mexican national hero on both sides of the border, called El Gran Campeón Mexicano, and largely considered the country's greatest boxer, Chávez never spoke English. Every time he won and spoke Spanish, it became clear that even if others couldn't understand him, what he had to say was no less important.

It's why on the late January night in 1994 when the great Chávez lost to the now departed American Frankie Randall—his first defeat after 91 fights—Reynoso felt like boxing, the sport he loved, had broken his heart. Decades later, his voice still gets low as he talks about that loss and how it hurt.

Whenever Álvarez fights, it sounds like an entire stadium in the United States is singing the Mexican national anthem. Fans— from the ones sitting in the nosebleed sections to the Mexican and Mexican Americans with enough money to sit as close to the ring as possible—will then chant Álvarez's name. And even if, for some, distance has strained that connection, they'll also chant the name of their spiritual home. "ME-XI-CO! ME-XI-CO!"

Countless people gather across two countries, in homes, restaurants, bars or any place with a television to watch him fight.

When he holds media workouts in fancy resort hotels, the guests may not know who Álvarez is, but those who clean the rooms, make the food, cut the grass and park the cars, often do.

Even if metaphorically, there's dignity in taking a beating today then returning tomorrow to likely get punched in the face again. That even if you lose, there's something heroic in not backing down. It's part of that basic philosophy of the Mexican working class. Even if the task is Sisyphean, it must get done because there's no way around it.

Imagine if this is you and you find someone on the other side. Someone inflicting that damage and not taking it. Someone that comes from where you do, speaks the way you do, laughs at the same *memes y mama---s* that you do. Little wonder why someone like Chávez, or Álvarez—who used to sell popsicles on the streets, then disobeyed his father when he stopped going to school in the 8th grade so he could work and fight—get treated like they have the power to make their people feel a little less alienated. It's why the two most important boxing days in the United States are held on weekends that commemorate important dates in Mexican history.

"I feel that fanaticism," Álvarez says of the fans of Mexican heritage across two countries. Because of that zealotry, whenever Álvarez fights, he seemingly becomes the center of Mexican culture. Grandmothers will light candles, asking God to protect him. Against Saunders, in Mexico, over half the people who had their television on, watched Álvarez. "Whatever day I fight," Álvarez explains, "that's for all Mexicans and for all of Mexico."

REYNOSO USES A GRAY TOWEL to wipe the sweat from Álvarez's face. It's in between rounds of shadow boxing, where Álvarez moves effortlessly across the ring. It looks like he's gliding. He then mimics punching to the body, a shot to the liver. That's the cruelest punch in all of boxing and a cornerstone in the Mexican style of fighting.

Cruel because if you get knocked unconscious, you might not feel a thing. Sometimes, boxers awake from a punch and must get told their fight is over. But get hit hard enough with a body shot, and you feel the excruciating pain that makes you want to quit. It makes you wonder if a major organ's been ruptured. A handful of honest seconds that feel like minutes which make you think you might be dying.

"*Se lo metes,*" Reynoso tells Álvarez as he watches him practice those punches. Put it in him.

In this case, *him* is Caleb Plant. He's the boxer from Tennessee who holds the last belt—IBF super-middleweight (168 pounds) title—needed to complete the undisputed puzzle that Álvarez and Reynoso have been solving since early in the pandemic.

Álvarez and Reynoso have zero doubt that they'll do it. It's more than the usual boxing bravado. It's something deeper. It's that Mexican fatalism that convinces us there's no stopping whatever's meant to pass. It's not Plant that's keeping Álvarez, Reynoso and the rest of their team, from their post-fight, in-ring celebratory photo. It's that Nov. 6 has yet to come. But once it comes, and they beat Plant, they'll take that photo, have it framed, then hang it along with the many others inside their San Diego gym.

On those walls, you can see the arc of Álvarez's career. A fight poster against California-native Josesito López when Álvarez was just 22 and baby-faced. Back then, in 2012, during Mexican Independence Day weekend, some influential voices wondered if Álvarez's popularity came because he was good or because he, often portrayed as some sort of fighting heartthrob, was perfectly marketed. So loud were those questions that, on that same Las Vegas night, Julio César Chávez, Jr.—the son of the Mexican national hero with the golden name—fought less than two miles down the road.

Though they fought different opponents, that night, Álvarez and Chávez Jr. were fighting to see who'd become the next great Mexican boxer. They eventually met in the ring. Álvarez won easily. That fight poster also hangs in the gym where, from the outside, the only sign of what's happening inside is when Álvarez hits the heavy bags, and it sounds like a gunshot. There's also a framed photograph of that fight. It's Álvarez punching Chávez Jr.'s body. That punch made Chávez Jr. shrink in pain. It may not have been the blow that hurt most, but instead, Álvarez beating him out of his birthright. That was the last time any person said "next great Mexican boxer" and Chávez Jr. in the same sentence.

"The people have gotten on board," Álvarez says of the Mexican and Mexican American fans that had once questioned how good he was. "For as much as they didn't want to, they've started admiring what I do and have become fans."

He also knows there will always be a few who question some part of his career. But this side of his lone loss to Floyd Mayweather Jr., where he fought one of the best boxers of his generation at just 23 in 2013, this side of his two hard-fought battles against Gennadiy Golovkin in 2017 and 2018—a draw and a close win respectively—Álvarez has become the world's best boxer. The few that still have doubts will likely never be convinced. Even if—or when, if you're as convinced as Álvarez and Reynoso—he becomes undisputed, and there's no one in the division left to beat.

"At the end of the day, to be the best, you don't need people to love you," Reynoso says, a defiant tone in his voice. As he talks, he stands close to those fight posters and photos inside their gym that are monuments to Álvarez's accomplishments. And because the two are interconnected, those same posters and photos are a testament to Reynoso's achievements, too.

They're tangible proof that their tree of sacrifices has given fruit. "When we started, there was no one there," Reynoso remembers. Even today, the months away from family, months away from home, is easier to stomach because they, together, are doing what they love.

They understand the responsibility that comes with becoming the best Mexican boxer. The symbolism of fighting in the very places that were once part of Mexico, places with a history of anti-Mexican violence. So, they might all laugh and play around for a bit, but once the actual work begins there's no room for bulls------g.

Once that bell rings, after Reynoso has wiped the sweat from Álvarez's face and given him water and it's time to work again, it's a complete focus.

Back to shadowboxing, Álvarez punches at an opponent that only he can see. Beads of sweat fly from his arms, staining the canvas. There's a seriousness that's invaded Álvarez's face. Like some part of that respectful person who shakes hands with everyone as he enters the gym has left. Like he's forgotten how, not long before then, he told me he's always been a quiet person. How he plays golf every day because it breaks the training camp loneliness and monotony while helping him stay calm inside the ring.

In his place, is the boxer who before each fight tells his family—including his wife and four children—he loves them because he knows either him or his opponent may, in the literal sense, be fighting for their lives. He tells them that if something were to happen to him inside that ring, that at least it happened while doing something he loves.

Álvarez, inside that ring, where he's his truest self, has stopped singing and laughing, dancing and joking. The muscles around his jaw become tense. The veins from the sides of his muscular neck are suddenly awake.

"*LE VOY A DAR LA P----A DE SU VIDA!*" Álvarez breaks his silence, yelling what's heard throughout the entire gym and even outside. He says he's going to give him the beating of his life.

Again, *him* is Caleb Plant.

Soon after Álvarez makes his proclamation, Reynoso, with a gray towel hanging over his shoulder, standing outside the corner of the ring, looks at how Álvarez practices his brutal trade. "Move your waist," he tells him. "Protect yourself with your arms," he adds before showing him.

"*Así, así*"—like this, like this—Reynoso, with his fists near his ears, says as he bends his waist side to side and back to front. Álvarez nods then follows instructions.

"*Bien m'ijo,*" Reynoso says.

Good, my son.

REYNOSO IS HOLDING BACK ÁLVAREZ. The press conference between Plant and Álvarez, about six weeks before their fight, just got physical. Not in the way that boxers sometimes fake beef to help sell their fight. Physical in a *Plant might have landed the first shot but now he's bleeding from under his eye after Álvarez landed three* sort of way.

Before they were face to face, Plant had called Álvarez a drug cheat after the Mexican boxer tested positive for trace amounts of clenbuterol in 2018. Álvarez said it was the result of eating contaminated Mexican beef. The same state athletic commission that suspended him for six months, later said a hair follicle test didn't detect any banned substance. That gave Álvarez's tainted beef theory some credence. Plant, who isn't alone in his skepticism, didn't buy it.

Once in front of him, Plant—who says the Mexican boxer has never been in the ring with someone like him—called Álvarez a motherf---er. That's when their face-off turned violent.

Because it's what sometimes happens when you speak in a tongue that isn't your own, Álvarez took the insult as literal. Parts of Mexican culture are full of machismo and in those spaces— boxing being one—every macho has a mother that can't be disrespected.

"YOU'RE THE MOTHERF---ER!" Álvarez responded after pushing Plant away. Often, because it's useful in moments like these, cursing is the first thing you want to learn in a new language. They then threw hands and were separated.

Even before that all happened, through no real fault of his own, Plant represented the nemesis in the historical tension between the United States and Mexico. Plant didn't need to say a single word for Álvarez's camp to naturally see him as their adversary. But once he started talking, he became more than that. He offended some part of Álvarez and Reynoso's Mexican sensibilities.

"Why talk?" Álvarez asks rhetorically. "At the end, we're going to find out inside the ring. There, words are useless. I don't see a need to talk. The things I say, I say them because I feel them in my heart."

Álvarez and Reynoso say Plant talks too much. They say they'll have little problem beating him. They know his strengths—he's an undefeated world champion, tall, has a long reach, is a good technical boxer, and moves well—and they also know his weaknesses. They've studied his fights. They know which rounds he's most dangerous, throwing more punches, applying more pressure. They also know when he tires. But more important than any of that, they know Plant isn't Álvarez.

"Saúl will beat him any way he wants," Reynoso says of Plant. "Why? Because he's at his peak. He's beaten better boxers than Plant. He has more experience. He's young. He's strong. And more than anything else, he stays in the gym."

Hard work and discipline. That's Álvarez's greatest strength, according to Reynoso, who'll sometimes rant about boxers pretending to work hard by posting things on social media. He says Álvarez has that because it's what he learned as a young boxer. Without putting it into words, Reynoso is saying Álvarez is that way because that's how he taught him.

Asked about Plant's chances of winning, Álvarez says, "Right now, I don't see anyone who can beat me."

WATCH ENOUGH BOXING and you'll almost inevitably hear the young stars talk about how they want to retire before their bodies begin to fail them. How they want to make their money and get out. How their career will be unlike the stereotypical boxer that ends up broke, physically and economically. Fighting, only because that's the best way they know how to make money.

That's no criticism against young boxers. Boxing is a painful, horrible business that can drown you, and, if they can, they should think of a way to get out as soon as possible.

Álvarez, however, says he loves fighting. Even when he isn't preparing for a fight, he's still training in the gym. Though he says he fights for the Mexican people, wherever they might live, he says he's reached a point where he no longer feels any pressure. That there's no adrenaline to match knocking out an opponent. Or even better, making them quit.

"*Nada, nada, nada,*" he says. Nothing. "It's something different," Álvarez tries to explain the surge of electricity he feels when seeing another opponent—who has been training for months to hurt him just the same—can no longer fight.

Imagine that. To not just dominate the best of the best within this cut-throat sport but make them, the hardest of men, no longer want to fight. Imagine the beating that someone who trains to ignore pain, must take before their instinct for self-preservation takes over. If their pride would let them, they'd admit what their body's already confessed. An admission that could wreck their identity. If the body could put into words what it's saying, it'd be something like, *I was convinced there was no one in the world who could beat me, but then I fought you.*

It's a bit unnerving when Álvarez sometimes practices his violent gift while listening to Mexican ballads and love songs. How, from this idyllic coast he perfects his methods to break the will of men. Instead of trying to intimidate opponents, Álvarez is the opposite. He's disturbingly calm.

There's something unsettling about a man who doesn't need to fight, at least for economic reasons, but does it because he loves it. Álvarez almost shuns the boxing gods, ignoring the sport's most real proverb saying it's hard for a boxer to wake up and train when they sleep in silk sheets. Álvarez does more than that. On the days before he fights, he wears little else besides silk pajamas. "It's more comfortable for me," he says, as a way of explanation.

That's just the kind of thing you do when you're convinced no one can beat you. When you plan to fight another seven years, including again in Mexico—something he hasn't done in a decade—against the toughest competition, and then just leave. Maybe to play golf. Maybe to tend to his businesses. Both would seemingly help him fulfill that competitive drive that's brought him here. Maybe to ride his horses. Maybe something else. Anything that would be the opposite of a life spent fighting. Álvarez can do whatever he wants, but for now, he fights. And when he does, he says Reynoso worries too much.

Reynoso worries because, as the trainer, the loss that's hurt him the most wasn't against Mayweather. It was when Óscar Larios, well past his prime, lost to Jorge Linares, who was barely entering his. "That's the one that's stung the most," Reynoso says of the 2007 fight that left Larios with a bleeding brain.

As the historian, he knows a boxer, today, may beat every man walking the earth, but tomorrow, they'll never beat time. That's the one thing Reynoso will never be able to protect Álvarez from. He knows it better than anyone else.

"Ánimo cab--n, póngase listo," Reynoso will tell Álvarez each time before the bell rings and the fights that count start. Before he fights Plant, Reynoso will tell him the same thing. And like always, Álvarez's response will be a confident nod.

At this point, Álvarez and Reynoso are fighting for titles, yes, but also for pride, country, respect and all the things that come with that. Days after *Día de los Muertos*—the Day of the Dead, an early November holiday where those of Mexican heritage remember the lives of those who have died—Álvarez and Reynoso are fighting for a sense of immortality. So that after Álvarez has stopped fighting, he'll be remembered as the greatest boxer from Mexico, surpassing even Julio César Chávez, as blasphemous as that sounds. That maybe, one day, they'll be songs and movies and *telenovelas* made about Álvarez. And since their accomplishments are as intertwined as their lives, if that happens, Reynoso will get remembered as the one who helped him live forever, even if not physically.

Right now, when a sense of inevitability surrounds him, maybe the only tension that remains in Álvarez's career is if he can get out before it's too late. He's been fighting for money since he was 15, and Reynoso has been with him every step of the way. If Álvarez can get out and stay away, Reynoso can stop worrying, maybe move on to fret about someone else. If he can get out and never come back, Álvarez will be the only one who has reached this height—hearing his name and that of his country chanted while carried on shoulders—who then didn't risk his life trying to feel it again.

———————

Roberto José Andrade Franco is a feature writer at ESPN. He's been a finalist for the National Magazine Award and the Dan Jenkins Medal for Excellence in Sportswriting. He lives in the El Paso–Juárez borderland.

The Luckiest Two Women in the WNBA

MIKE PIELLUCCI

FROM *D Magazine* • SEPTEMBER 23, 2021

Arike Ogunbowale and Marina Mabrey celebrated winning the 2018 Women's NCAA Tournament—the defining moment of their basketball partnership to date, if not their friendship—exactly the way you would, too, given the circumstances.

There was no partying on a team road trip, so barhopping was out. Besides, it was late, and they were exhausted. Their Notre Dame team was so injury-ravaged that only six players suited up; Ogunbowale and Mabrey, the Fighting Irish's only healthy guards, each played 39 out of a possible 40 minutes. So after the confetti poured down and the net was cut and the trophy got raised, they plopped down in their hotel room and flipped on the TV—to *SportsCenter*, where they watched highlights of their win, punctuated by Ogunbowale's title-winning three-pointer rainbowing into the basket with 0.1 seconds left on the clock. The shot became instantly iconic. It would soon propel Ogunbowale to a run on *Dancing With the Stars* and an appearance on *The Ellen Show*, where she would be surprised by her hero, Kobe Bryant—and so over and over her game-winning shot played. The two of them kept watching their exploits and laughing, one word on their minds. "Woowwww," they say in unison outside a

Starbucks on UTA's campus, where the Wings play their games, before laughing some more.

That night was everything they'd imagined when they'd enrolled three years earlier. They'd barely crossed paths until then, the go-with-the-flow girl from Milwaukee and the high-strung trash talker from New Jersey, but already their vision of the future was in lockstep. "We could have gone to other schools and been two people that won again like everybody else," says Ogunbowale, referencing traditional powerhouses like UConn and Tennessee. "But we really wanted to be marked in history." By the time they did that, they were best friends—sisters, they say—and they'd won by doing things their way: loose but never lax; focused but never uptight.

When they graduated a year later, "Marike" (a moniker their Notre Dame coaches gave them) had a new vision. Some way, somehow, they would reunite in the WNBA. And wherever they did, they would win another championship. Two best friends sharing the same backcourt, conquering college and the pros together.

It took less than two years for Ogunbowale and Mabrey to find their way back to one another in Dallas. Now, as the Wings prepare for their first playoff game since 2018, the women will once again be looking for that rainbow.

BEFORE WE GO FURTHER, a disclaimer: nothing you read in this story can encapsulate Marike. Nothing in any story does, because you have to see their friendship to appreciate it, and even when you do, there are elements—such as a well-documented and self-professed tendency to get on each other's nerves—that, as their teammate and close friend Satou Sabally says, "those two have been together so long that it's something so normal that you wouldn't understand it as an outsider."

Marike is side eyes and deadpan deliveries. It is "Are you SERIOUS?" and "Don't start ..." and "This Girl!" It is exaggerated stares that precipitate even bigger crackups. It is Ogunbowale declaring that her favorite breakfast to cook is scrambled eggs before Mabrey, in a sing-songy voice fit for a caffeinated waitress working the morning shift, elaborates: eggs with fruit and a piece of toast, possibly some peanut butter—"Right," Ogunbowale chimes in—but not too much.

It is Ogunbowale's spirited self-defense—"It was the academic adviser just lying!"—recounting the time Mabrey went ballistic after she mistakenly heard Ogunbowale got someone else into a class Mabrey was hoping to take, but not her.

It is Mabrey getting so fed up with Ogunbowale's snoring in hotel rooms at road games that she threw a pillow at her and banged on a dresser, but then declaring, "I would have brought earmuffs, earplugs, headpiece, just not to switch my roommate." And it is Ogunbowale thinking aloud about the day, deep into the future, well after their playing careers have ended, when she and Mabrey can sit down and fully take stock of all they accomplished together.

Not bad for two players former Notre Dame head coach Muffet McGraw once was scared to put around each other.

McGraw, who retired last year after 34 seasons and two national championships, can chuckle about it now. She always took great care to build recruiting classes with chemistry in mind as much as talent, which is why she worried about what could happen if two players she deemed so different encountered each other in a high school AAU tournament. There was Ogunbowale, so even keeled and armed with the capacity to internalize critiques without taking them personally, whose teammates joke about how liable she is to drift to sleep on the couch at any hour. Then there was Mabrey, the Type A ball of sarcasm whose energy and intensity agitate the opposition. Whenever McGraw knew her two star recruits in the class of 2015 were both at an event, the same fear entered her mind: "Oh, my God, I hope they don't guard each other. That could be a disaster."

McGraw, to her pleasant surprise, was wrong. Ogunbowale and Mabrey hit it off well enough during their first year in South Bend—familiar, friendly, but rarely around one another away from the team. Their circumstances were their greatest commonality: bit players buried behind a collection of all-business upperclassmen who didn't understand how they could be so carefree in their attitudes and so trigger-happy with the ball. "Our seniors, they thought we were just the dumbest things walking," Ogunbowale says with a snicker. "We just didn't care about the same things," Mabrey adds.

Then came the offseason. Ogunbowale needed a workout partner, and she knew that Mabrey, who racked up overuse injuries at Notre Dame from rarely taking days off, was always game for more time in the gym. The Irish graduated four seniors, and both were driven to pick up the slack. In that gym, they pushed one another with a seriousness that the outside world—and their teammates—rarely saw. Those hours forged respect into friendship, and when they combined for 45 points in an Elite Eight loss to Stanford the following spring, they began to understand what their coaches were telling them: Notre Dame would only win if they brought the best out of each other every night.

Living together wasn't part of the plan. Ogunbowale had a place off campus and needed a roommate; Mabrey, just prior to the start of their junior year, decided she'd rather not live on campus. That's how they wound up together at University Edge, a complex seven minutes from Notre Dame, in a two-bedroom apartment with a kitchen and a living room. Mabrey did most of the cooking. Grilled chicken on a George Foreman grill was a staple, as was a concoction of egg noodles and cheese that Ogunbowale insists "was fire." Ogunbowale handled the dishes. They slogged through homework for their shared major, business management, and they attempted to binge watch shows like Starz' *Power*, a good idea inevitably derailed by Ogunbowale falling asleep before the end credits rolled. "We watched a lot of partial shows, let's just say," Mabrey says wryly. They'd hit karaoke night at Salsa's Mexican Grill and help orchestrate ice cream cake parties for teammates on their birthdays. They were now more like family than just friends, two women with a sisterly knack for fighting hard and loving harder. "Fire and fire," Wings head coach Vickie Johnson calls them.

"Which is weird," the coach is quick to note, but it works. Notre Dame had gone 17 years between national championships until the 2018 team, and while that title was an ensemble effort—four of the six healthy rotation players would be selected in the 2019 WNBA Draft, including top overall pick Jackie Young—Ogunbowale and Mabrey set the tone. They'd grown up by then, learned to let go of their flightier moments and ride the freshmen just as the upperclassmen had once ridden them. But they still refused to take any moment too seriously, which made no moment too great to overcome. They jacked up shots and dribbled full bore, and if it didn't work out on one possession, it probably would the next. Everybody just relax.

In that way, the depleted roster almost worked in their favor. McGraw says, "Marina told me her favorite part of the year [was] ... turning the ball over and looking over at you shaking your head, looking down the bench, and realizing you couldn't take me out.'" Notre Dame had no choice but to play the Marike way, and the Marike way got things done. Which is why, three years after the fact, Ogunbowale and Mabrey still relish the reaction of their all-too-serious former teammates when they ended the nearly 20-year-long title drought after so many teams before them had failed.

"They were so proud of us," Mabrey says, but also, "They're all like, 'I can't believe you two won it.'"

LOOKING BACK, OGUNBOWALE AND MABREY recognize that spending the first year of their WNBA careers apart was for the best. The time away from one another helped them develop as individuals—Ogunbowale in Dallas after she was the fifth pick of the WNBA Draft; Mabrey in Los Angeles, where she was selected 19th by the Sparks.

That doesn't mean they enjoyed it. They FaceTimed constantly and carved out time for dinner or an apartment visit whenever one was in the other's city on a road trip. During one Wings road trip out West, the two of them were so excited to see one another that they stayed up late into the evening before their game zipping around downtown Los Angeles on scooters. "Rookies," Ogunbowale says with a shrug and a laugh, by way of explanation.

So when Mabrey got dealt to Dallas prior to the 2020 season, they could resume the work they'd begun in South Bend well ahead of schedule. Privately, they assumed they wouldn't get a chance to reunite until one or both reached free agency, years down the line into their WNBA careers. Doing it at 23 years old allowed them to lay down the foundation more methodically.

"We can get a culture and a core going at a young age, so hopefully we'll be able to develop everybody around us and ourselves and get a championship rather than have to put it all together at 29, 30, 31," Mabrey says.

They say they were back to being Marike within one practice, although those around them believe their games have broadened since their Notre Dame days, from Mabrey's offensive repertoire to Ogunbowale's defensive chops. That fine-tuning has, in their third professional season, carried them to new heights, with Ogunbowale making her first All-Star team while Mabrey has become one of the league's premier sixth women after moving out of the starting lineup to boost the second unit.

But the things they do on the court are just byproducts of how they play, and how they play remains unaltered. There is, they insist, a larger point behind their loose attitude on the floor, one that informs that culture they want to instill in a roster that ranks among the league's youngest.

"I feel like if you have two leaders who are always kind of carefree but competitive and playing hard the whole time—those two things combined with it, I think it instills confidence in everyone else," Mabrey says. "So even if it's not exactly your game, if you're not just super loose or whatever, it might help you loosen up a little bit."

Already they've found a pair of similar minds in Sabally and fellow guard Ty Harris. The four of them eat together, vacation together, work out together. Ogunbowale and Mabrey lived with Sabally during last year's WNBA bubble season in Florida, and Mabrey and Harris carpool together to practices now that the team is back in Arlington. All of them are between 23 and 25 years old, and they can't help but dream big about how high they can soar and what they can do for a franchise that last experienced genuine success two cities and one nickname ago, as the Detroit Shock.

Their first chance to realize those ambitions comes on Thursday, when Dallas plays its first postseason game since 2018. The Wings are light on experience; collectively, the roster has competed in 10 playoff games, none of which involved Ogunbowale or Mabrey. But in a sense, this is exactly what they are used to. Once again, they are underdogs walking into unfamiliar territory in a single-elimination setting, with little certainty beyond their own skills and each other. The surroundings have changed, the competition heightened, but they are still the first to push one another, to tweak one another, to support one another. It is still Marike interpreting one another in a way no one else could. "Some stuff somebody else might not be able to say to Arike or Marina, they tell each other," Harris says. "They depend on each other a lot."

For Dallas, Thursday night is the beginning of something. For Ogunbowale and Mabrey, it is the continuation. They'll amp each other up like they always do because, as Sabally notes, "sometimes fire is the only thing that can handle fire." No one has been able to extinguish it yet. They can't envision a world where anybody could.

Mike Piellucci is the sports editor at *D Magazine*. He is a former staffer at The Athletic and VICE Sports, and his freelance work has been featured in *Sports Illustrated*, *The New York Times*, *Los Angeles Magazine*, and The Ringer. He lives in Dallas with his wife and rescue dog.

How a Gymnast Who Lost a Friend in the Parkland Mass School Shooting Came to Iowa and Found Ways to Heal

MARK EMMERT

FROM *The Des Moines Register*
and *Iowa City Press-Citizen* • MARCH 10, 2021

Before every competition, Iowa gymnast Alex Greenwald takes a pen in her callused right hand and carefully inscribes three words of inspiration on her left thumb:

"Just Keep Swimming"

It's the title of a song from the 2003 Disney movie *Finding Nemo*. For Greenwald, it is a way to preserve the memory of a childhood friend who died in a mass murder at their Florida high school, four months before graduation and one week after he had accepted a scholarship to become a college swimmer.

Nick Dworet was 17, and always will be. The dreams that Greenwald and he had nurtured—of pursuing the sports that consumed their young lives to the highest level—were forever stalled for Dworet on Valentine's Day 2018, when an armed intruder fired four bullets into his body while he sat in his Holocaust history class at Marjory Stoneman Douglas High School in Parkland,

Florida. He was one of 17 students and faculty members who perished in the deadliest high school shooting in U.S. history.

For Greenwald, the next big stop would be Iowa City. An elite gymnast from a young age, she had committed years before to compete as a University of Iowa Hawkeye.

In the weeks that followed the shootings, Greenwald attended vigils and marched with her classmates. She saw her hometown of Coral Springs subsumed by sadness. She vowed to leave as soon as she could, thinking everything would be better once she got to Iowa City, where she felt pulled to begin living the perfect future—for Dworet and herself.

On June 3, 2018, Greenwald was one of 764 Marjory Stoneman Douglas seniors to walk across a stage to grasp their high school diplomas. TV talk show host Jimmy Fallon surprised the crowd by showing up to deliver the commencement address. Greenwald posed for photos with her parents and younger sister.

Hours later, she boarded an airplane alone.

"I was looking forward to stepping on campus ever since I committed my freshman year," Greenwald said. "I thought, 'Things are going to be so much happier in Iowa City.' I couldn't wait to get away."

Greenwald intended to leave a grieving community behind, but in retrospect was just carrying her own pain to a different place. She may not have known it then, but Greenwald came to Iowa for more than instruction on the vault or floor exercise or uneven bars, for more than a college diploma. She came to Iowa to heal.

Two gymnasts meet in Ohio; a daughter follows their path in Florida

Christine Hiler is from Pennsylvania; Mark Greenwald is a native of Florida. In 1988, they met at Kent State University in Ohio, where both were gymnasts. Hiler specialized in the uneven bars, where upper-body strength is paramount. Greenwald was an expert tumbler, showing off his powerful legs while twisting and flipping gracefully across the mat.

They married and moved to the South Florida warmth of Greenwald's youth. Alexandra was born July 11, 2000; a second daughter, Gabrielle, soon followed.

Alex took to her parents' sport immediately. By age 7, she was immersed, training 4½ hours a day, six days a week, at American Twisters Gymnastics.

"We saw that she was willing to put in the work and make the sacrifice, which is more important than the talent, actually," Mark Greenwald said.

When Alex started kindergarten, Hiler began pedaling the mile to school, Gabrielle strapped to her back while her oldest daughter tottered along the sidewalk on a bicycle of her own. Hiler noticed another blonde mother undertaking the same routine, except her children were both boys. "Mirror images," she called her family and the Dworets.

Hiler bonded with Annika Dworet during those commutes and soon discovered a mutual passion for endurance running. Annika and her husband, Mitchell Dworet, enjoyed testing themselves in local 5Ks. Mark Greenwald and Hiler had also taken up the sport as a way to fuel their competitive fire once gymnastics ended.

Alex Greenwald and Nick Dworet were the tag-alongs, entertaining themselves on a blanket in the grass while their parents ran. Alex would demonstrate her latest gymnastics routine, laughing as Nick tried to mimic it. He was already into swimming, another sport that requires hours of solo training to master. They supported each other, talking openly about their goals of getting college scholarships one day.

"That was something we bonded over, our drive for success," Alex said. "Just wanting to be the best that we could."

By high school, it was evident that it was more than just talk. Alex signed her letter of intent to compete at Iowa in November of her senior year. Nick held a small ceremony at the school

Feb. 7, committing to swim at the University of Indianapolis, his specialty the freestyle events. These were moments of pride and promise for the families, a sign that their oldest children were about to make their mark on the world together.

"He was so mature," Mark Greenwald said of Nick, apologizing for sounding as if he were writing a movie script. "He would be the kid that, if he saw some other boy sitting alone at lunch, he'd go over and make sure he wasn't by himself. He was just so unique. He was a good-hearted human being in every sense."

The following Wednesday, Nick was gone. Alex woke to that realization at 5:30 a.m. Feb. 15, googling the list of shooting victims, hoping not to recognize any of the names.

She was shocked to see "Nicholas Dworet." Shock turned to sadness, then contemplation as happy memories of her days with Nick flashed through her mind. Ice skating together at a local indoor rink. Visiting his house and goofing around with Nerf guns instead of the Barbie dolls she and her sister typically played with. Those long-ago days on the blanket while their parents ran a race.

"He was always laughing, always smiling, always in a good mood," Alex said.

At age 14, Alex Greenwald sets sights on becoming an Iowa Hawkeye
Alex was a 14-year-old high school freshman when she visited the University of Iowa, already trying to determine where she wanted to spend her college years. She had previously checked out the universities of Denver and Michigan, with her father in tow, as a prized gymnastics recruit.

Alex was looking for somewhere to pursue her goal of a career in health care, but also for a coaching staff that would make her feel comfortable. She said she felt that immediately with Hawkeye coach Larissa Libby. Libby was impressed by how mature Alex was; she asked questions as if she were on a job interview.

Alex wanted to commit to Iowa on the spot, but her parents convinced her to give her decision some more thought.

Alex canceled all other campus visits. A month later, she told Libby that she was coming to Iowa.

"Immediately when I walked on campus, I felt accepted," Alex said. "And I could tell that the coaches cared about me as a person over everything else. That was something that was really a value for me."

"The community here is so focused on 'Hawkeye this' and 'Hawkeye that.' I loved having that community support behind you."

Mark Greenwald knew better than to try to alter his daughter's thinking. It was her choice to make. Privately, he was excited for Alex because he felt like she was aiming for the same experience he had when he left Florida for four years to enjoy the embrace of a close-knit college town in Ohio.

Alex snapped up all the Hawkeye apparel she could find. Her friends at school would laugh at her for always wearing Iowa gymnastics shirts around town. She followed the competitions of her future team from afar, counting the days until she would perform in Carver-Hawkeye Arena.

On Feb. 14, 2018, Alex saw Nick as usual in their morning anatomy class.

"He was his typical goofy self," she said.

Class ended at 9:10 a.m. Nick left, telling Alex: "I'll see you tomorrow."

At 2 p.m., Alex left the school grounds as she did every day. A straight-A student, she was allowed to take her final class of the day online. She smiled and waved her thanks to security guard Aaron Feis, a 37-year-old popular with the students, as he let her out. In 25 minutes, he would be among the dead.

Alex's parents had bought her first car, a Chevy Spark, with the stipulation that she use it to ferry her sister to and from gymnastics lessons. Alex also picked up two girls from another middle school to bring to American Twisters, a 20-minute carpool route that got everybody to the gym in plenty of time for the 2:30 p.m. training.

When Alex arrived at the gym that day, word had just gotten out about some sort of shooting at the high school. There was no initial indication that anyone had been injured. The gymnasts got to work. So did Hiler, who is a sports psychologist at the facility, with appointments in 30-minute blocks.

In between, Hiler kept monitoring the news from the high school. By midway through that day's practice session, it was known that there were fatalities. By the time it was over at 7 p.m., the tally of 17 dead had been made public, although the names weren't known.

The family drove home and turned on the TV. Nick's picture appeared as one of the students unaccounted for. There was confusion because Alex Dworet, his brother, was among the 17 people wounded in the attack. The freshman was in a classroom across the hall from Nick. A bullet grazed the back of his head.

Hiler had heard that Alex Dworet was in the hospital but was expected to recover. Maybe the TV news crew had mixed up the brothers?

That's what Alex wanted to believe as she finally fell asleep at 2 a.m.

"I felt like it was such a big school, and I don't think you're able to comprehend the severity of something like that," she said. "Your brain tries to protect you and tell you, 'No, everything's fine.'"

Hours later, she learned the truth. Nick Dworet was among those slain when former Marjory Stoneman Douglas student Nikolas Cruz came to the campus armed with a semi-automatic rifle and multiple magazines. (His trial has still not started, meaning the school has been considered a crime scene for three years, even as classes have resumed amid the yellow tape.)

Alex attended a vigil for the victims Feb. 15. She went to a gathering at the home of an English teacher who wanted to give students an opportunity to see one another and sort through their feelings. At another gathering, she heard a survivor of the 1999 shooting at Columbine High School in Colorado speak about that experience.

CNN came to town for a show devoted to the Parkland shooting. Alex was there. She marched with her fellow students in an effort "to turn our frustration and anger into something good." She wrote a letter about America's gun laws to Florida U.S. Sen. Marco Rubio, and got no response.

Alex paid her respects at Nick's funeral the week after the shooting. It was delayed so that his relatives from Sweden could fly over. It was a draining experience for her, seeing so many people she didn't know, mourners surrounded by television cameras, and, ultimately, coming face to face with her friend's mortality.

"It was open casket, so that's obviously as real as it can get. You see him and he's not smiling, not breathing," Alex said. "Everyone was speaking so highly of him, but also so upset about the event. I felt like there was so much sadness and so much pain on that day."

Alex did not feel the need to take advantage of the free counseling that was, and still is, offered by the school. She felt like she could sort through her emotions on her own.

Gymnastics helped.

Three days after the shooting, Alex competed in the Magical Classic in Altamonte Springs, Florida. There were 2,146 gymnasts; she finished 23rd.

"I was so grateful to have some sense of normalcy back in my life," she said.

Added Hiler: "Alex kept her practice routine as well. She could let the aggression out by vaulting, or just forget about it for a while. Gymnastics was a godsend."

Alex's last competition before coming to Iowa was the Junior Olympics in Indianapolis in May 2018. She finished second in the nation on the uneven bars.

In Iowa, Alex Greenwald finds a confidante in coach Larissa Libby

Larissa Libby has been the head gymnastics coach at Iowa for 17 seasons. She competed in the sport for her native Canada in the 1988 Olympics. She is 48 years old, with two daughters of her own. She does not mince words.

In the aftermath of the shooting, it was Libby that Alex chose to confide in. Libby said she was so nervous about Alex's phone calls that she consulted with psychologists on the Hawkeye staff first, fearful that she might otherwise deliver the wrong message to her future athlete.

Libby was so dedicated to her role that she slept with her phone under her pillow, wanting to be available whenever Alex might call in search of a friendly voice.

"My God, no child should see that," Libby said of the trauma Alex was coping with at age 17. "A lot of the time, I just let her talk. She would be quiet at first, but that's her nature. Maybe I was an 'out' for her where she felt safe saying, 'I don't want to do anything. I don't want to get out of bed.'"

The phone calls often lasted an hour. Alex's parents would watch her retreat to her bedroom, never asking what she and Libby discussed.

"I could tell by the way (Alex) was when she rejoined the family that she was in a better place," Hiler said. "Whatever Larissa did, even if it was just listening, it seemed to help."

Libby encouraged Alex to participate in as many events as possible with her classmates, just to be around people. She gently tried to dissuade her from coming to Iowa immediately after graduation. But Alex would not relent on that point.

"The one thing that bothered me about that was it felt like she was running away from it," Libby said. "I was worried that being here would keep her removed enough that she would never heal."

Libby is accustomed to dealing with athletes that are broken in some way. Gymnastics is a constant strain on young sinews and psyches. The physical toll is enormous, but the mental strength required to excel may be even greater. Each event begins with perfection (a score of 10) and punishes the competitor with deductions for every slight mistake.

But Libby had never inherited a gymnast who was damaged in the way Alex was. She arrived on campus "blocked off" to everybody but Libby. It frustrated her new teammates and the other coaches. Libby advised them to give the newest Hawkeye some time.

"This was bigger than gymnastics, and I committed to helping her through this, knowing she may never do gymnastics because of this," Libby said. "But that's not her fault. She didn't ask for that."

Libby saw the scars Alex was carrying firsthand that Fourth of July when the noise of the fireworks bothered her. Alex tried to conceal her tears. Libby took note.

She wasn't the same gymnast that Libby had recruited, either; she struggled to keep up as a freshman. The only event Alex was able to compete in that year was the vault, where Iowa had the greatest need. That had historically been her worst apparatus. During one childhood competition, her daughter even got a zero on it, Hiler remembers.

But at least it was something.

By the end of the season, Libby believed she needed to take a firmer stance with Alex. She believed their relationship was strong enough that Alex wouldn't resent it when she told her: "You are not valuing Nick's life and your friendship with him by hanging on to all those negative feelings. He would be pissed if he knew you were not living your own life."

Alex realized it, too. She went home that summer and returned to Iowa a more confident gymnast. She worked her way into the rotation on the floor exercise, her leg muscles developing the way her father's had.

She tried to back off from the obligation she felt to live out Nick's dream and her own simultaneously.

The first meet of the season, in January 2020, was moved from Mexico to Orlando, Florida, as the COVID-19 pandemic first started making headlines. That meant Annika and Mitchell Dworet could drive up to watch Alex compete for the first time since Nick's death.

Alex had remained close with Nick's parents. But Hiler felt the occasion was a breakthrough for her daughter in easing some of the "survivor's guilt" she was carrying.

Alex knows she's not alone among her high school classmates in wondering: "These (victims) were all such good people. So why did this happen to them and not me?"

She knows that unanswerable question will likely be with her forever:

"But I also understand that I should be grateful for the opportunity that I have," Alex said.

The two families gathered and smiled for photos after the competition like old times.

"I think for Alex, knowing that (the Dworets) were there and they were just so proud of her, I hope in some way unlocked that a little bit for her," Hiler said. "Because there was no pressure, nothing but love from them. She performed very well that day. Maybe that was the beginning of knowing that, 'It's OK now. Just go out and do your gymnastics.'"

The pandemic cut Iowa's season short last year. There were no Big Ten Conference championships, NCAA regionals or nationals.

But this season has been the Hawkeyes' most promising yet. And Alex has been in the middle of that surge.

Alex joins in the fun on "obnoxious" Hawkeye team, attacks uneven bars

Libby refers to her current group of Hawkeye gymnasts as "obnoxious." She means that as a compliment.

They dance and joke and make sure their presence is felt at every competition. Along the way, Iowa earned its first Big Ten championship and was ranked as high as seventh nationally, its best showing ever.

"They don't care if people think that they're loud or if people think that they laugh too much," Libby said.

Alex is allowing herself to be part of the silliness, a member of the "volleyball squad" that stages an impromptu game before each meet, convinced that their performance in that sport will predict the scores they receive when the gymnastics begins. It is not a natural part of her personality, and Libby is thrilled to see it emerging.

"I'll always be connected to her in this way," Libby said of the three years she's spent helping Alex become a better gymnast while also trying to move on from unspeakable tragedy. "I worry about her, as a mom would worry. I think she's strong enough, but you always worry."

Alex said it's the moments of camaraderie that she'll remember when she thinks back about her time as a Hawkeye gymnast.

"The stupid things in between the gymnastics competitions or the dancing and singing that we do. The hours spent on buses or waiting in airports," she said. "We definitely build off each other's energy and are always laughing and having a good time."

Hiler sees the change in Alex in her posture, the way she stands straighter at the beginning of her floor routine, as if commanding the room.

"She doesn't do a cheerleader, smiley-type routine," Mark Greenwald noted with approval.

"I get chills," Hiler said. "I can see the things that she's been through and her inner strength. It's as if she's saying, 'I'm going to survive. Nothing's going to hold me down.'

"She did come to Iowa to heal. It's always going to be part of her."

Alex is posting her best scores on the floor exercise this season, including a 9.925 in a Feb. 13 home meet against Minnesota and Maryland.

Libby realizes that Alex's struggles may be subsiding but have not disappeared. Alex still won't commit to wearing headphones over both ears, for example, always wanting to keep one ear uncovered so she can be in tune with her surroundings.

"Sometimes, she doesn't need people to talk to her. She needs to sit on your couch for four hours," Libby said. "Just let her do her homework and feel safe."

The day after the Minnesota and Maryland meet was the third anniversary of the shooting.

"Valentine's Day was tough for her," Libby said. "I had to tell her, 'You cannot stop living because it's Valentine's Day, and something bad happened on that day.'"

Alex's favorite event has always been the uneven bars. It's the most difficult gymnastics discipline to teach, Mark Greenwald said, because its foremost requirement is the proper genetics.

Alex got those from Hiler: Powerful shoulder muscles. Hands so strong that her father usually turns to her for help when he needs a jar opened.

As a freshman at Iowa, Alex found herself failing on the bars for the first time in her life. She was unable to crack the Hawkeye rotation.

She went back to work. This season, she has added the bars to the vault and floor, competing routinely in three events.

On Saturday, when the Hawkeyes defeated Illinois in their final home meet of the season, Alex earned a 9.750 on the vault, 9.775 on the bars, 9.875 on the floor. Iowa is ranked second in the nation on the floor heading into the last meet of the regular season this weekend at Nebraska.

Alex writes the "Just keep swimming" motto on her left thumb with a Sharpie so that the ink can withstand the sweat and strain of the bars competition. She wants the words, like her friend's legacy, to be indelible.

"I get this opportunity, and he doesn't," Alex said. "I feel like I'm getting to maybe help him live on and continue spreading his story and his name, and everything that was so great about him."

Excellence on the uneven bars requires a natural ability to swing gracefully, to time your maneuvers perfectly, to achieve the maximum amplitude so you can hit your handstands at the proper angle. There can be no hesitation, or the routine is doomed. Hours of practice leave competitors with callused hands and aching muscles.

The bars are made of fiberglass with a wood coating, placed 6 feet apart, with a 2½-foot difference in elevation. Elite gymnasts like Alex report the sensation of flying when gliding between them.

Grip is everything. In the course of 45 seconds, Alex's hands go from supporting her weight upright to preventing the tug of gravity from sending her to the mat below. Over and over.

Just keep swimming. Just keep swinging.

As her routine ends, Alex's thumbs burrow into the bar for one final second.

And then it's time to let go.

Mark Emmert, a Minnesota native, has been a newspaper reporter and editor for 34 years, at publications ranging from North Dakota to Maine. He covered the University of Iowa athletic department for *The Des Moines Register* from 2016 to 2021. He is currently the editor of the *Iowa City Press-Citizen* and the *(Burlington) Hawk Eye*.

Charlotte's First and Forgotten Sports Star: Life, Death and His Season in the Sun

SCOTT FOWLER

FROM the *Charlotte Observer* • DECEMBER 6, 2021

Forty years ago, before Major League Soccer, the Charlotte Hornets or the Carolina Panthers ever existed, Charlotte witnessed the birth of its first soccer superstar.

His name was Tony Suarez, and you've probably never heard of him.

He was the handsome, homegrown, ridiculously fast, out of nowhere star who led the Carolina Lightnin' to a minor-league championship in front of 20,163 fans in Charlotte's Memorial Stadium in 1981. In a few short months, the 25-year-old rose to regional fame. His joyous smile beamed from the city's two newspapers. His goals were replayed on local TV stations. The home crowd would chant "Ton-eee!! Ton-eee!!" when No. 18 found the back of the net yet again.

It was a spectacular season, the kind Charlotte's new group of MLS players can only hope to achieve.

Tony Suarez's backstory—from the team's bus driver to its leading scorer—was a fairy tale.

When he first attempted to make the Carolina Lightnin' at an open tryout in 1981, Suarez failed.

But he talked team officials into letting him become an unpaid member of the practice squad and also volunteered to drive the team bus. After several injuries, he got his chance to play. From there, Suarez morphed into an overnight wonder and the league's rookie of the year.

"When Tony got on the field... he became famous, you know?" said Ana Suarez Fleming, Tony's youngest sister. "Locally famous. He was good looking. Girls loved him. And I really think he helped get people to games."

What was Suarez like then?

Said Rodney Marsh, the Lightnin's coach at the time: "A lovely, naive boy. Trusted everybody. Laughed all the time. Just wanted to play soccer."

True fairy tales, though, don't always end happily.

And Suarez's story was not a Disney-fied tale, but a Grimm one.

"TONY WAS SO USED TO BEING NO. 1"

After that glorious season and his eventual retirement, Suarez searched for something that could duplicate the rush of scoring a goal in front of a screaming crowd. Sometimes he found it. Mostly he didn't. His life was a cautionary tale, intertwined with moments of delight.

Suarez eventually found himself in a North Carolina prison for two years. He had trouble staying married or keeping a steady job. Once he took off his light blue and gold jersey for good, Suarez's carefree personality got trampled by the world.

"Tony was so used to being No. 1," said Carlos Suarez, Tony's brother. "And that meant that anything after his playing years was hard."

As for the fact that Tony Suarez died in 2007, at age 51?

That still haunts everyone who knew him.

But during "Tony's season in the sun," as former teammate Hugh O'Neill describes the year 1981, Suarez was a comet. He streaked across the Charlotte sky when the city was looking for a sports identity and, for one sweet summer, found one in the Lightnin'.

Charlotte was often confused with Charleston, S.C., or Charlottesville, Va., back then. The city had no NFL team, no NBA team, no MLS team and no uptown nightlife. It was a time when entertainment options were limited, when more than 20,000 people would pack a stadium for a minor-league soccer team's championship game on a Friday night, even when a lot of them didn't know a corner kick from a cornerback.

On the morning after the Carolina Lightnin' won its championship in 1981, *Charlotte Observer* sports columnist Bob Quincy wrote: "There hasn't been a night like it in Charlotte sports history."

Tony Suarez was that team's unquestioned star. For one year, he was as big locally as the showboating grapplers in Charlotte's then-thriving pro wrestling scene, or NASCAR drivers Dale Earnhardt Sr. and Richard Petty.

"Tony was one of the early sports stars of Charlotte," Carolina Lightnin' teammate Dave Pierce said. "And our team? We took the headlines away from everyone, even pro wrestling. Even Ric Flair was probably getting pissed off. Tony was a local boy made good in a huge way. And then … things happened."

Yes, things happened. And on the eve of an MLS expansion team beginning play in Charlotte in early 2022, Tony Suarez's improbable journey is a long-forgotten story worth telling.

CASTRO, CUBA AND THE SUAREZES

Roberto Suarez was the patriarch of the Suarez family and the reason Tony came to Charlotte. A member of a well-respected Cuban family, Roberto had gone to a private high school in Cuba. Fidel Castro was a classmate and friend at the time.

Castro was one year older than Suarez, and the two played together on the school's basketball and baseball teams. They both were mentored and coached by the school's athletic director, Otilio "Cappy" Campuzano, a Cuban sports legend who starred in multiple sports and was inducted into the country's sports hall of fame.

"My father was really the Jim Thorpe of Cuba," said Miriam Campuzano Suarez, 89, who was Coach Campuzano's daughter and eventually became Roberto's wife and Tony's mother. "Fidel would come over to our house all the time when I was a girl. But it was Roberto who I knew I would marry, even at age 9."

The couple wed in 1950 and had 12 children in 14 years. Tony was child No. 4. Packing school lunches, Miriam Suarez said, was like preparing to feed an army five days a week. And it was rare that all the children were trouble-free at the same time.

"Now everybody's an adult," Miriam Suarez said. "But it used to be when the phone rang, I would say, 'What happened?' even before 'How are you?'"

Roberto Suarez went to America for college and graduated from Villanova in 1949. He returned to Havana in the 1950s, believing Castro's plan to overthrow dictator Fulgencio Batista and install a more democratic government sounded promising.

Suarez helped Castro in his 1959 Cuban revolution, believing his former classmate's new government would be much fairer to the Cuban people. After Castro took power, he placed Suarez as the leader of the country's most powerful bank.

But Suarez quickly grew disillusioned with Castro, whose government turned out to be even worse than the one it replaced. "It made the Batista regime look like boy scouts," Suarez wrote in his unpublished memoir.

Remembered Rolfe Neill, the *Charlotte Observer*'s publisher from 1975–97 and a longtime friend of Suarez's: "It didn't take Bob very long to say 'Hey, this man Castro is a communist!' He was stunned to find what Castro's political beliefs really were."

Suarez would always regret siding with Castro initially and switched course, working against Castro's dictatorial government as part of a resistance movement. The work was dangerous. At one point, Suarez was part of an underground group that planned but couldn't pull off an assassination of Castro.

Roberto and Miriam Suarez already had eight children at the time, and he sent his wife and children to Miami in 1960 for safety's sake. Tony, who had been born in Havana, was 4 years old when he got to America. Eight months later, fearing for his life and worried about his family, Roberto Suarez wangled his way onto a plane and sneaked out of Cuba. He had $5 in his pocket—all you were allowed to take out of the country—and was able to join his family in Miami as a Cuban refugee.

COMING TO CHARLOTTE

For most of the next decade, the Suarezes lived in Miami. Roberto began work in the mailroom of the *Miami Herald*. His finance degree from Villanova made him over-qualified for the job, but at the time it was all the work he could get.

"Miami had these stainless steel chutes that the papers theoretically tumbled down in bundles," Neill said. "But they would get jammed. Bob was sometimes used as the human bomb, sliding down the chutes, to break up the bundle jam."

Suarez rose through the newspaper's business ranks and eventually got offered a new job in Charlotte in 1972 on the business side—both newspapers were owned by the same Knight Ridder company at the time. The family found Charlotte on a map and took off for North Carolina. Roberto Suarez eventually became the *Charlotte Observer*'s president, running the company's thriving business side and cooking paella once a year for the entire staff. He worked for the *Observer* from 1972–87 before leaving for another big promotion in Miami.

Tony Suarez was 16 when the family moved to Charlotte, and he lived in the city for most of the next 35 years. He attended Myers Park High, where he became a star on the soccer team. Although Tony was the best soccer player in the family, most of the Suarezes played soccer at least at the high school level.

"Every year when the *Observer* would publish the all-county soccer teams, it seemed like about half the team was named Suarez," Neill said.

The family often spoke Spanish in the home, and Tony was nicknamed "Flaco"—the Spanish adjective for skinny—by his family. At 5-foot-11 and 150 pounds, he went to Appalachian State to play college soccer.

"But he kind of flunked out there," said Ana Suarez Fleming, his sister. Suarez transferred to Belmont Abbey, where he kept playing soccer in the late 1970s.

"For Tony, it was all about soccer," said Pierce, Suarez's teammate at Belmont Abbey and then later with the Carolina Lightnin'. "School really wasn't his thing. He did what he needed to get by."

After college, Suarez was at loose ends. He hadn't graduated. He worked some odd jobs while playing on a high-level amateur soccer team in Charlotte and dreaming of getting paid to play the sport he loved.

When he heard about the Carolina Lightnin's open tryout in early 1981, he knew it was his chance.

THE BUS DRIVER
Ed Young has long been a key figure in N.C. soccer, as well as a fine goalkeeper for some local teams. Young and Suarez had played together for an amateur soccer team sponsored by The Press Box, a Charlotte restaurant, and Young had been astonished by Suarez's speed. When Young made a save, he'd do the same thing every time.

"I would punt the ball as far as I could and Tony would just outrun everybody," Young said. "It was like a Hail Mary. Half the time it seemed like he'd get a one-on-one with the goalkeeper and he'd score. I got a few assists that way."

In 1981, local Charlotte sports entrepreneur Bob Benson decided to bring a minor-league soccer team to Charlotte. It would be called the Carolina Lightnin' and play one rung below the major-league North American Soccer League, with a talent level analogous to Triple-A baseball.

Young was tabbed as the team's director of operations and Marsh, a former English soccer star, as the coach. For the team's open tryout, Young seeded the field with some of the best players from the Press Box amateur team, including Suarez.

Marsh wasn't impressed, and it was he who got to pick the team. He didn't like Suarez's technical skills.

"Tony had a poor first touch," Marsh said. "One of the things you look at, as a forward, is you've got to be able to control the ball and take a shot. He would stumble. The ball would get away from him. It wasn't technically good enough."

Thus, the bus.

"Tony didn't make it, but he was very persistent," Young said. "I said, 'Tony, do you want to drive the bus?' And he did."

The bus-driving gig allowed Suarez to practice with the team, too. He was on the minor-league soccer version of an NFL practice squad, if that practice squadder also flew the team plane.

"He was a great player already, I thought," Young said of Suarez. "And so driving the bus—that could be demoralizing for some people. He never felt that way."

TONY SUAREZ'S BIG BREAK

Suarez got his shot when a couple of the forwards got hurt early in the season. Marsh moved Suarez to the active roster and, suddenly, it became clear that the coach had made a mistake from the beginning.

"Tony got on the field and he was just dynamite," Marsh said. "So quick. So good at putting the ball in the back of the net. Now, he still didn't have a good first touch. That never changed."

It was how fast Suarez was, though, that was the game-changer.

Said teammate Santiago Formoso, who would later become one of Suarez's roommates in Charlotte: "Tony had the one thing they can't teach: Raw, unadulterated speed."

Suarez scored nine goals in his first 12 games. Marsh began calling him "Tony the Tiger" in interviews. Suarez was the Most Valuable Player of the league's all-star game. He began getting asked to come on local TV and describe his storybook rise.

"I'm starting to feel natural on the field," he told WBTV's Paul Cameron at the time. "At first, I was scared and nervous. But so now, every game, I learn a little bit more and I'm just relaxing more."

Said Ana Suarez Fleming, who at the time was 15 years old and going to her brother's games with her family: "Can you imagine being 25 and out of nowhere, you're just living a dream?"

Cameron, who had just gotten to WBTV in 1981 himself, quickly latched onto the Lightnin' story and interviewed Suarez numerous times.

"Charlotte was so hungry for something it could call its own back then," Cameron said. "You could feel it. We traveled all over the place at the station to cover things, but that's the thing—we had to travel. Then suddenly here was this pro soccer team in Charlotte, and this young local guy scoring goals, and people coming to see him. When he ran, he had this flowing mane of long hair. Everyone seemed to love him. Tony was the kind of guy who seemed invincible. And I'm sure he felt he was."

Suarez didn't score in the championship game that the Lightnin' won 2–1 over New York United on Sept. 18, 1981, generating front-page coverage in both of the city's newspapers. The other team's defense paid so much attention to Suarez in the game, though, that it allowed other players better goal chances.

"Tony was on fire that whole season," said O'Neill, one of Suarez's roommates in 1981 and the player who scored the winning goal in the championship. "He was passionate. He was local. It was Tony's season in the sun."

Cameron once interviewed Roberto Suarez in the stands while the father watched his son play soccer.

"He's on Cloud Nine right now," Roberto Suarez said of Tony, "and he hasn't come down. He'll come down sometime soon."

He did.

THE END OF PRO SOCCER

Suarez had dreams of making it to the NASL, which was the top level of U.S. soccer and had employed such players as the legendary Pelé in the 1970s. His next step was to sign with an indoor pro soccer team called the Cleveland Force in late 1981. But in Cleveland Suarez sustained his first serious knee injury, at a time when operations on knee ligaments were in their infancy.

"That was the beginning of the end," Suarez Fleming, his sister, said. "Things were never really the same, because they couldn't repair knees the way they can now."

Suarez appeared on one of Cameron's sports shows in January 1982, wearing an enormous cast on his leg and saying: "By June, I'll be able to run."

And Suarez was able to play again, for three more years in Charlotte: Two with the Lightnin' and, after that team folded because of financial difficulties, one with the Charlotte Gold.

There were some nice moments in those three years. In 1984, whenever Suarez scored at home, the P.A. would always blare a song from the new movie *Footloose* called "Let's Hear It for the Boy."

But Suarez tore up his other knee during that period. And those Charlotte teams—although ahead of their time with promotions such as a postgame Beach Boys concert and an airplane giveaway—never won a league championship and didn't draw nearly as many fans.

By the end of 1984, Suarez was just an average minor-league player, hanging onto the threads of a dream. Soccer—at least at a high level—was done for him, even though he wasn't done with soccer.

"It took Tony until he was 25 or 26 to really get there," O'Neill said. "And by age 28, it was over. And for every athlete that comes to the end of their career, there's a void."

A COCAINE CONVICTION

As soccer ended, Suarez needed to find something else to do. His brother, Carlos, was on the verge of opening the successful Suarez Bakery in Park Road Shopping Center, a business that has now been a mainstay in Charlotte for 29 years.

But Tony Suarez wasn't interested in the bakery. He started working at Whispers, a local nightclub where he had hung out frequently as a player. He had a difficult time handling regular life.

"He had gotten so much attention," Carlos Suarez said, "that I think it probably got to him a little bit. Your picture is in the paper, you're on TV—and then that's not there anymore."

Said Suarez Fleming, Tony's sister: "He wasn't really good about sharing emotion. But I can only imagine he was kind of devastated at having to come back to reality and be a normal person."

Suarez's first marriage, to his college sweetheart, had ended after only a year. His second marriage produced a daughter, Autumn, in early 1990. But it was around that time that Suarez was using cocaine frequently enough that he also started dealing it to make enough money to support his drug habit.

By the end of 1990, Suarez had been arrested for conspiracy to possess cocaine with intent to distribute. He was a small-time player in a big-time drug sting, one called Operation Avalanche. Authorities said they had thwarted a $240 million cocaine smuggling operation, according to a *Charlotte Observer* report at the time, and arrested dozens of people in both North and South Carolina.

"Tony should never have done it," Suarez Fleming said. "It was completely wrong. But he also never made millions of dollars dealing drugs, either. He made enough to, say, buy a nice couch."

Suarez pleaded guilty, cooperated with authorities and eventually went before a local judge named Robert Potter in late 1990. The judge's nickname was "Maximum Bob," and he was known for handing out longer sentences than average. In 1989, Potter had sentenced the disgraced televangelist Jim Bakker to 45 years in prison for defrauding his followers, although that sentence was later dismissed on appeal.

Suarez's attorney argued that community service, in the form of soccer clinics for youth, would be a better punishment than prison for Suarez. Said Suarez at the sentencing: "I want to give back to the community something I owe it. I'm very sorry for what I got involved in."

Potter was unmoved. "I have to remember the victims of these drugs," Potter said. The judge sentenced Suarez to four years in prison.

NEW MARRIAGE, NEW BABY

In prison in the early 1990s, Suarez would sometimes write letters to his sister, Ana, describing his various athletic exploits behind bars. He had never lacked for confidence in his ability on any sports field.

"He could be kind of arrogant," Ana said.

"I've been playing basketball in the prison league," Suarez wrote in one letter. "I'm known as the great white hope. I'm too much for this group. ... I run everybody ragged."

But in a letter to another friend, Suarez sounded more down, writing: "Life here is still miserable. ... I feel really good physically. Mentally, I ride a roller coaster, up and down."

With good behavior, Suarez ended up serving about 22 months in prison. He also completed his college degree from Belmont Abbey while incarcerated, and the prison let him out for a day to go to his graduation ceremony.

Shortly after he got out of prison, Suarez's second marriage crumbled. He would be an inconsistent presence in his daughter's life after that.

In the meantime, he worked in the *Charlotte Observer* mailroom and returned to playing soccer in some local amateur soccer leagues. He also met his third and final wife. She was 12 years younger than Suarez and had gone to some of his Carolina Lightnin' games as a middle schooler. Their families had long known each other, with both involved in the Catholic faith and attending some of the same churches and schools. They married in 1997.

"When I met Tony, he had just gotten out of prison," Marianne Suarez said. "He was full of life. He sweetly wooed me. Then we got married. ... Tony was a great guy. He just wasn't a good husband."

When there were disagreements, the couple didn't really argue, Marianne said. "When we'd get in a fight, he'd walk out of the room," she said. "We never talked through anything…. It was more like he'd get in the car and leave, and then we wouldn't talk for 3-5 days."

Sometimes, the two would be on the way to a Carolina Panthers game and argue in the car so much that Marianne would sell her ticket on the way into the game to another fan, leaving Tony to sit with whatever random stranger happened to buy the seat.

There were many good times, too. In 2006, Marianne got pregnant after years of hoping for a baby. They decided to name the baby for Tony and for the baby's maternal great-grandfather— Antonio "Capy" Suarez. When the baby was born, in October 2006, they called him Capy.

But two months before Capy's birth, in August 2006, Tony lost his job at the *Observer* in a dispute. He tried to start a new career, selling boats and working at a marina on Lake Norman.

Marianne and Tony continued to have marital problems. They briefly split up several times. On April 17, 2007, the two were in the Suarez Bakery, getting something to eat and visiting Carlos, Tony's brother.

"Tony had brought the baby," Carlos Suarez said. "He and his wife were arguing. And at one point he turned to me and said, 'Man, I'm done with this, you know? I'm just done.' I was thinking he meant he was done with his third marriage, because he and his wife were having issues. But that's not what he meant."

THE VESPA

Decades before scooters whizzed all over big cities around America, Tony Suarez had a Vespa. He had seen them in Europe and decided he wanted one, and he frequently used it to zip between his office and the couple's townhome near uptown Charlotte. Once again, he was moving fast.

Marianne Suarez was staying at her mother's house on the night after the argument in the bakery. But Tony asked her to come over to their house and bring the baby, Capy, who was then 6 months old.

They argued again, and at one point Suarez took the baby into another room by himself. Marianne worried about what might happen. "I screamed: 'You need to give me the baby right now!'" she said. "I didn't know it at the time, but he was saying goodbye."

Marianne left a few minutes later with the baby.

At some point later that night, Tony Suarez grabbed a blanket and pillow and went into his small garage. He closed all the doors to the garage, but didn't lock them. He turned on the Vespa's gasoline-powered motor and laid down on the floor.

At 11 a.m. the next day, Marianne stopped by the townhome, which the couple was preparing to sell. Tony was already supposed to be at work at the marina, but his truck was still in the parking lot outside. Marianne had a bad feeling.

"I knew the truck wasn't supposed to be there," she said, "and I thought: 'I can't enter this place by myself.'"

She called a friend, who came over so they could go in together. Marianne walked inside to the smell of gas and went straight to the kitchen, thinking something had been left on. There was nothing amiss there. She kept checking rooms. Nothing, nothing, nothing.

Then she checked the garage.

Her husband was on the floor. The Vespa was still running.

Marianne flung open the garage door and called 911, but it was too late.

Tony Suarez was dead from carbon monoxide poisoning. He was 51 years old.

"HE NEVER DISAPPOINTED US"

Tony Suarez, Charlotte's first real soccer star, died by suicide on that day in 2007. He left three separate suicide notes—one for his daughter, one for his wife and one for his family. The common theme was disappointment. He wrote that he believed he had disappointed people for too long. He asked to be remembered for the happy-go-lucky man he once had been, the one who loved sports and just about everyone he met.

In retrospect, Suarez's family and friends believe that Tony was clinically depressed. But the idea that he disappointed them, as his suicide notes read—they don't buy that.

"Tony had his ups and his downs," Ana said, choking back tears. "He wasn't perfect. I just want people to know that he was a really, really good person who made mistakes like all of us did. But he never, ever disappointed us. And I think that's what he thought, and that's the hardest part to take."

Suarez Fleming has established a charity called "Inspire To Live" that is focused on suicide prevention.

"I want to get more awareness out there about depression and mental health," she said. "I want to break the stigma and want people to know that it's OK to talk about it. And that life is worth it."

It's a cause close to her heart. She had another brother, Armando, who fought mental health issues for most of his life, according to several family members.

Armando Suarez went to Tony Suarez's funeral and told some family members: "That should have been me." Then he died by suicide in Florida four weeks later. The remaining 10 Suarez siblings are still living. Family patriarch Roberto Suarez died in 2010 at age 82 from Alzheimer's disease complications, with his death notable enough to warrant coverage in *The New York Times*.

The year 2007, when two brothers died by suicide in four weeks, scarred the family permanently.

Tony's death echoed in his own small family. "I wish things would have worked out better for us," Marianne Suarez said of her marriage to Tony. "I hate that it ended how it did, because he's missing out on two wonderful kids and three beautiful grandkids (Autumn, Tony's daughter, is now 31. She lives in Pennsylvania with her husband and their three children). The first eight years after it happened, I was angry. But now I just have a sadness. And I miss him."

Most Carolina Lightnin' teammates still gather for reunions to celebrate their 1981 championship season. They did so again in September for their 40 year anniversary, a full weekend that included being honored at a Charlotte Independence game. They spoke lovingly of Tony one night at a local bar, wishing they could have helped him more.

"I'm getting a little emotional," O'Neill said, remembering Suarez. "I miss him terribly. I'm sorry. It's just, after all these years, it still hurts so bad."

The stigma associated with admitting to depression or mental health issues was also a part of Suarez's death, those close to him believe.

"Now people don't hide depression as much," said Young, the Lightnin' official who first helped Suarez get a tryout. "But 15-20 years ago, people still hid it. It was a sign of weakness that you couldn't deal with things, where people would say if you complained: 'Hey, strap on your boots. Don't be a whiner.' Now we know a lot more. Then, it was more taboo."

"Tony was our candle in the wind," Marsh, the coach, said. "I have nothing but affection for him. I think we all feel that way."

CAPY PICKS A NUMBER

Stories from those Carolina Lightnin' reunions serve as a tangible reminder to Suarez's impact and stardom 40 years after his magical summer and 14 years after his death.

At nearby Hough High in Cornelius, there's another reminder, too.

He's a 15-year-old freshman, a very fast soccer player with dark hair. He's skinny, as his father was, although his hair is cut a bit shorter. He plays forward. He led his JV team with seven goals in 14 games this fall.

He wants to play soccer in college and already has attracted some recruiting interest. Who knows? If he keeps improving, maybe one day he can play professionally for Charlotte's MLS team.

Capy Suarez was 6 months old when his father died by suicide in 2007. He only knows Tony Suarez through stories and photos. But his mother sees an uncanny resemblance.

"In Capy, I see a strong young boy who is very focused on what he cares about," Marianne Saurez said. "He definitely has his father's eyes. And he has his soccer skills."

Capy shares one more thing with Tony, too. On Hough's JV team, forward Antonio "Capy" Suarez proudly wears the No. 18 on his black and silver jersey.

It's a tribute to Suarez, his father, Charlotte's first real soccer superstar and a man whose legacy still shines brightly, 40 years after his season in the sun.

Editor's note: If you need help, the National Suicide Prevention Lifeline has a 24-hour crisis hotline at 1-800-273-8255. Confidential online chat is also available at SuicidePreventionLifeline.org.

Ana Suarez Fleming, Tony's sister, has launched a charity that aims to save lives by raising awareness and eliminating the stigma associated with death by suicide. Go to Inspire-to-live.com for details.

Sports columnist **Scott Fowler** has written for the *Charlotte Observer* since 1994. He has authored or co-authored eight books, including four about the Carolina Panthers. Fowler has won the Thomas Wolfe award for outstanding newspaper writing and has earned 18 national APSE awards. He also hosted the *Observer*'s eight-part podcast "Carruth," which *Sports Illustrated* named 2018's "Podcast of the Year."

The Resurgent Appeal of Guinness World Records

TOVE K. DANOVICH

FROM The Ringer • JULY 20, 2021

While some people spent time baking, gardening, or raising poultry in 2020, Laura D'Asaro was on her hands and knees crawling around a track near her San Francisco home. Twice a week for three months, D'Asaro would don a mask as well as some more unorthodox gear. She put adhesive bandages on her palms, then covered those with bicycle gloves to keep from getting blisters. She wrapped her knees in bubble wrap, then added hard knee pads on top. She even put extra knee pads over the front ends of her shoes so they wouldn't get rubbed away from friction. "It was pretty comfortable," she says.

D'Asaro often crawled on Wednesdays, when a San Francisco marathon training team ran at the same track. "At first I got some weird looks," D'Asaro says. "Then finally someone on the team stopped me and asked what I was doing."

The answer? Training to break the Guinness world record for the fastest time to crawl a mile.

Last year wasn't the first time D'Asaro, 30, had tried to break this record. She first attempted it when she was 17 as a way to raise money for cancer research and honor her grandmother who'd recently died from the disease. Training was different back then. "My mom would ask me to take the dog for a walk after school, but instead of walking, I would crawl," D'Asaro laughs. She crawled around her neighborhood and on beaches and trails while wearing a sign that said "World Record in Progress" so strangers would stop asking her questions. Everyone at school knew her as the crawling girl. She even got a write-up in the local paper. "When you're 17, you haven't found a place in the world," D'Asaro says. "This was something uniquely mine."

When it finally came time for the attempt, family members and kids from her high school showed up to watch and support her. She crawled four times around the inside of a track and thought she'd beaten the record. But there was a snag. "I didn't realize at the time that four times around the inside of a track is only 99 percent of a mile," D'Asaro says. "I submitted the record, and it didn't get approved."

Getting 99 percent of the way there wasn't enough for D'Asaro. So each January for the last 10 years, D'Asaro added "breaking the record" to her list of New Year's resolutions. She'd train a little in January, maybe even February, and then life would get in the way. "I felt really embarrassed," D'Asaro says. She always felt like it was "one extra box that didn't get checked."

Then the pandemic happened.

Suddenly, no one was inviting her to restaurants or parties. The biggest event on her social calendar was when people opened their windows to cheer for health care workers and first responders at 8 p.m. And most of all, training gave her a purpose—something she could control during an otherwise uncertain and scary time. "For the first time ever, there was nothing standing in my way," D'Asaro says.

So she started crawling in earnest, and on June 24, 2020, she made her official attempt. Some friends came to watch, and her grandmother, parents, and other people who had seen her first attempt watched through livestreams. This time, D'Asaro crawled a mile in 21 minutes and 36 seconds to get the women's record. (The men's record, set in 2007, is 23 minutes and 45 seconds.)

D'Asaro started graduate school a few months later, and when she got her official certificate from Guinness World Records, she framed it and put it on a shelf above her computer in her dorm room. "I'm proud of it," she says. "In some ways it doesn't matter at all—it's a stupid paper certificate for crawling around for a mile. But in other ways, it means a ton."

Since the organization that's come to be known as Guinness World Records made its first book of superlatives in 1955, it's grown to occupy a strange space in global culture. Guinness, which has not been connected to the beer brand since 2001, commemorates the newsworthy superlatives—like the longest aggregate time spent in space by a single person, or the deepest dive by a crewed vessel—as well as the ones that are hard to categorize and even harder to forget. (Remember the photos of people who hold records for the most body modifications or juggling the most samurai swords?) At its core, though, the Guinness series is a love letter to the superlative nature of humans. It stretches people's imaginations of what's possible, for individuals and society alike. "With the pandemic," D'Asaro says, "it forced us to think about who we want to be. And how we want to show up in this one life we have."

In a year that often felt like treading water, many saw breaking a world record as a chance to feel part of something good, to stand out, and even to connect with others. Guinness World Records saw a 10 percent increase in record applications between April and December 2020; in North America alone, time-related records like "most in a minute" or "fastest time to" went up notably, according to the company. "Our fear was that we'd never have enough records to fill the book," Craig Glenday, the editor of Guinness World Records, says of the early days of the pandemic. But they had thousands more than he could ever fit in the 2020 edition.

SIR HUGH BEAVER, managing director of the Guinness brewery, was on a hunting trip when he got into an argument about what the fastest game bird in Europe was. He and his cohort debated and debated, but no one seemed to know the answer: the golden plover. It was exactly the type of arbitrary question that humans still fight about at parties—what's the bestselling record ever? Can a human outrun a horse? What is a caper, anyway?—only now we have the internet to get us the answers. Back in the 1950s, though, Sir Beaver was on his own. So he hired twins Norris and Ross McWhirter to publish a book of superlatives that he could give to pubs as a marketing tool.

Within 16 weeks, the McWhirters "extracted -ests from the -ists," as they famously said, contacting everyone from archeologists to geologists to mycologists to collect whatever superlatives existed in these fields. And the book was born.

Copies of *The Guinness Book of Records*, as the 1955 edition was known, were given away to pubs throughout the U.K. Complete with waterproof covers to protect against spills, they were an instant hit. There was so much demand for this first book that a bound print edition came out for purchase that fall. It was a U.K. bestseller by the end of the year. Then, in 1956, Superlatives Inc. put together a new edition and decided to sell it in the United States.

The original U.S. edition included just 15 pages of black-and-white photos; the rest was text. The types of human records listed were more staid than what you'd find in an edition today: tallest, fastest, oldest, along with some world records for sports. The book didn't have the immediate success in the U.S. that it had enjoyed in the U.K. But soon the bookmaker realized people didn't just want to read the collection of records—they wanted to be in it. As Larry Olmsted writes in his 2008 book *Getting Into Guinness*, the first person to get into the book for a bizarre human achievement was Jim Rogers, who marathon-drummed for 80 hours, 35 minutes, and 14 seconds in 1956. From there, all hell broke loose. "At first, records were merely a way of finding one's statistical bearings," wrote Jerry Kirshenbaum in a 1979 article about record breaking. "But they soon became ends in themselves as fans, athletes and sportswriters got caught up in the giddy allure of somebody 'going for the record.'"

And, according to Guinness World Records, no country breaks more records than the United States.

"We have the Protestant mindset that you should always be engaging in something productive, and anything you do should be to prove yourself," says Francesco Duina, author of *Winning: Reflections on an American Obsession*. In the U.S., the idea of winners and losers has gone beyond business deals and the courtroom to saturate popular culture. Reality television exploded as a genre once competition was brought into it. Shows like *America's Next Top Model* and *American Idol* gave contestants a chance at celebrity and the possibility of a career in a difficult but glamorous industry. Even dating shows learned early on that love could be a game to be won or lost.

Having a Guinness world record is a paradoxical achievement because it's a claim to fame that doesn't actually make most record holders famous. "No one typically knows outside of friends and family," Olmsted says. Yet in modern society, standing out for *something* has become so important that people have gone to great lengths to do it.

Shridhar Chillal started growing the nails on his left hand when he was 14 and didn't stop until he was 82. He eventually set the record for longest fingernails on a single hand, but for his troubles got permanent disfiguration in his hand from carrying so much weight, and constant pain. Yet he doesn't regret it. "What does man not do for fame? He jumps from boats, dives from planes and does stunts on motorcycles," Chillal told *The Guardian* in 2000. "Were I to have another life, I would do it again."

Ashrita Furman, who lives in New York City, broke his first world record in 1979. Since then, he has broken more than 700 records and is the current holder of 200. Furman follows the teachings of a man named Sri Chinmoy, who believed extreme physical challenges were the key to spiritual growth. Training to break so many records—like the longest distance jumped on a pogo stick, which he set by hopping up Japan's Mount Fuji, and beating his own record for most consecutive somersaults by rolling the length of Paul Revere's midnight ride—takes up an enormous amount of time and can be physically grueling. But the process of outdoing what he previously thought was possible is important to him.

How could something as seemingly insignificant as a paper certificate saying "World Record" or, best-case scenario, having your photo featured in a *Guinness World Records* book, be worth all this? It's a chance for people to define themselves, Duina says, and a way to gain the internal satisfaction of knowing they can be the best in the world at something, no matter how strange or small.

One of the beauties of the *Guinness* books is the way they present the records as equal. The planet Mars gets a two-page spread in the 2021 book for its various superlatives, but so do write-ups for most things done in a minute, biggest fruits and vegetables, and backyard inventors. It divvies up information about the world in a way that most people wouldn't think of: the desert that gets the most rainfall, the highest clouds. For adults who tend to take the world around them for granted, paging through a book is a brief reminder of what it was like to be a child: questioning everything and constantly being astonished by what's possible. Highlighting the amazing things people do every year is life affirming, Glenday says, adding, "By definition, everything [in the book] is amazing."

ZAILA AVANT-GARDE, 14, knew she wanted a world record as soon as she got a copy of the book for her eighth birthday. Children, of course, are the books' primary audience. "[The book] puts it out there that things that might seem kind of impossible are doable with a bit of practice," she says.

Avant-garde didn't know which record she'd go after when she got the book, but a few years later she got an idea. Avant-garde, who has been playing basketball since she was about 5, honed her skills over the years. "I started dribbling two or three balls at a time to help with hand-eye coordination, so dribbling one ball would be easy," she says. Ahead of her 12th birthday, she decided that her present to herself would be breaking her first world record. Instead, she broke two: most bounce juggles in a minute with three basketballs, and most bounces in 30 seconds using four balls.

Avant-garde, who also became the first African American winner of the Scripps National Spelling Bee in July 2021, wasn't surprised to win. "When I go for my records it's not too stressful," she says. She wouldn't try for a record if she weren't positive she could get it.

Some time after she broke her first record, Guinness World Records called Avant-garde and asked whether there was anything else she wanted to break. This isn't uncommon. While many people apply for records, the company notes achievements by people who are already famous in their own right: Jane Goodall for "longest running wild primate study"; BTS for breaking five world records with their song "Dynamite," including most viewed YouTube video in 24 hours; and Greta Thunberg for being the youngest *Time* Person of the Year. Likewise, people who upload videos of themselves doing unusual things to the internet might find themselves getting a phone call, nudging them toward making it "officially amazing," as the company says.

Avant-garde took her previous record, added another ball to the routine, and in November 2020 set another record for doing 255 bounce juggles in a minute with four basketballs—this time while she and her family were evacuated from their home in New Orleans because of Category 2 Hurricane Zeta. She could have postponed her attempt, but they'd already set a date and gotten cameras (each attempt requires video from multiple angles to ensure that the video wasn't manipulated) and witnesses. "It was a welcome chance to get out of the hotel room," she says of going out to practice, as Avant-garde, her parents, and three siblings all shared one room. "I like doing things that put a little pressure on you."

Randy DeGregorio feels similarly. The 23-year-old lives in New Jersey, and before the pandemic he worked as an intern at Madison Square Garden. "Because of COVID, they delayed the process of rehiring," DeGregorio says, so he went to work as a pizza delivery driver. Quickly, though, he realized his job could offer an opportunity to break a record. For DeGregorio it wasn't just a way to set a personal accomplishment, but to show future employers he wasn't "slacking off" during the pandemic.

It all started with folding pizza boxes. That's part of the job—a chore that pizzeria employees have to do before clocking out for the night—and DeGregorio was always better at it than his coworkers. During a bout of boredom at home, he looked up the record for box folding and saw that it was only 14 boxes in a minute. He knew he could do better, so he worked through the pandemic, spending an hour every other night for months— sometimes three or four hours—folding pizza boxes at home. He even asked his boss for extras he could practice with. During his official attempt in October, which took place at the pizzeria where he works, DeGregorio folded 18 boxes in a minute and easily took the world record. For the honor, he got to create a pizza named after him; he did not get a raise.

"As soon as I did the record, every pizzeria in my area was attempting it," DeGregorio says. He's not worried about local competition—a friend told him that employees at another area spot were only able to fold eight boxes in a minute. But it's only a matter of time until someone—maybe the person from Italy from whom DeGregorio took the record—beats him. "I check the website every once in a while to make sure [my title] is still there," DeGregorio says.

Even if someone else gets the title one day, DeGregorio will always be able to say he broke it once upon a time. For however long it lasts, DeGregorio has proof that he could do something better than anyone else in the world. "My dad always said that there's something special about saying you're the best at something."

PEOPLE MAKE FUN OF THE MORE FRIVOLOUS records listed in *Guinness*, like running a marathon in a nurse's uniform or the fastest time to put together a particular Lego set. Some think it's odd that a book that lists the first people to row across the Atlantic or skydive into a jet stream would also showcase people with big feet or a preternatural skill for stacking Jenga blocks. But are these records really so arbitrary?

"We cover the spectrum of 'Everests,'" Glenday says, "whether it's climbing the actual mountain or putting together a Mr. Potato Head. Why not accept that everything is amazing if you do it in an amazing way?"

When Pam Onnen, a teacher in her 50s, talks to herself, it's usually backward. She spells words backward and says words backward even when no one is around. "I find my fingers are trying to type things backwards," Onnen says. There's a video of her reciting the alphabet backward *backward*, flipping the phonetics of each letter, which sounds like something from *Twin Peaks* if it had been made for elementary school students.

It's been this way since middle school. "It was just a weird thing I didn't tell anybody about," she says. She eventually shared her strange skill with her husband, and when her children were young, she'd talk to them backward sometimes just to watch them double over laughing. But then she got the record for spelling the most words backward in a minute in July 2020, and now she talks about it all the time. "The only reason it's cool is because it's a world record," she says.

Onnen is a mom and a substitute teacher. For years, she says, she's been focused on doing things for everybody else. This was something just for her. When asked how the record compared to her life accomplishments, Onnen said, "I can't say number one, because I'm married with kids," then laughed. But she noted that if somebody were to go to her house and look at the walls, they'd see her certificate has the largest frame in the house.

"The overview effect" describes how astronauts feel when they go into space for the first time and see Earth looking as small as a ball they could grasp in their hands. In many people, the experience produces a strange euphoria and a sense of interconnectedness that lingers long after the astronauts return to Earth. Getting a copy of a *Guinness World Records* book may not be as special as going into outer space, but it's still a unique snapshot of life on earth—disasters and triumphs and people who do strange things with their bodies that make you squirm. Each new edition of the book acts as a snapshot of the world at that time, and serves as proof that the benchmarks keep moving.

"The 2022 edition, which we're working on now, will be an interesting time capsule of what life was like during the pandemic," says Glenday. Mass participation events like "loudest scream by a crowd" or "largest gathering of people dressed like Superman" went from a third of Guinness World Records' events to single digits. The book mostly features lots of people wearing masks, and plenty of images captured via Zoom. "There was lots of online record-breaking," Glenday says. But some were still able to gather together to break records and share in the experience.

"IF YOU'RE LYING ON YOUR DEATHBED and look back at your life, what did you do?" says Chris Shields, 60, when asked about the appeal of a world record. He and nine friends set the record for the longest wiffle ball game in March 2020, just before lockdown. It wasn't his first record—he caught a softball dropped out of a plane 250 feet in the air in 2013 after his daughter suggested he try it. But his friends were always curious about his record, and this was something they could do together. People flew to Illinois from Washington and Florida for the marathon game. Breaking a world record was an excuse to see one another. They played for 27 hours straight, roughly 426 innings.

While there were more individual records set than usual during the pandemic, group records are a popular category and continued in virtual form during lockdown. In August 2020, a life insurance company set a record for the "largest online video chain of people doing the arm wave" with 359 videos from employees all over the world. The London Marathon had a shocking number of participants last year, as 37,966 people signed up to run remotely, setting a record for "most users to run a remote marathon in 24 hours." (This year, the London Marathon is planning to hold both in-person and virtual events.) People feel like they're part of a long tradition when they break an individual world record, but there's something extra special about doing it as a team.

Shields says that his wiffle ball team formed a deeper bond through their marathon game. "We're getting on in age now," Shields says, but this is something they can always look back on. Officially, the group got the world record, but between the time of their attempt and when their certificates arrived months later, another team tried for the same record and broke it. "We had the record for four months," Shields says. He consoled his friends by telling them they were "kings of the world" for those four months.

Shields is an electrician and he's planning to retire in a few years. "I don't want to hit the couch and do nothing," he says. He's thinking of what record he could break next.

Tove K. Danovich lives in Portland, Oregon, where she writes about food, culture, crime, chickens, and curious things.

Can a Boxer Return to the Ring After Killing?

JACOB STERN

FROM *The Atlantic* • NOVEMBER 18, 2021

It's the tenth and final round, and Patrick Day is fading. He's still circling the ring in search of an opening, but his punches have lost the switchblade quickness they had in the early rounds. If he doesn't do something dramatic, he is going to lose this fight.

He had once looked like a star: No. 1 amateur welterweight, Olympic alternate, undefeated in his first 10 professional fights. But boxing is unforgiving. One bad loss to a weak fighter, and the glow was gone. Now not even a comeback can restore it. Just a few months ago, he was overwhelmed by a Dominican prospect who called himself "El Caballo Bronco." On this October night in 2019, at the Wintrust Arena, in Chicago, there is a sense that the 27-year-old Day is fighting for a good deal more than the mid-tier title belt officially under dispute. If this bout does not go well, Day's career could be over.

And it is not going well: Day went down in the fourth round and again in the eighth, and he's way behind on points. "You got no choice," his coach told him before the final round began. Either he scores a knockout in the next three minutes or he loses.

So he presses. He jabs, then hooks, then jabs again, but his blows all deflect off Charles Conwell. At 21 years old, Conwell is everything Day once was and more: an 11-time national champion, a 2016 Olympian, a perfect 10–0 since he went pro. He is a defensive virtuoso, but he hits hard enough to crumple a body like cardboard, and even as he repels Day's blows, he stalks forward in a spring-loaded crouch, peering over the tops of his gloves with a kind of predatory patience.

Conwell knows that he can wait this round out. The fight is already his. But he also knows, as all boxers do, that people don't pay to see a 10-round decision. They pay to see a knockout. Sometimes, before fights, Conwell will write himself a short note to hang above his bed. Before this one he wrote I WILL KO MY NEXT OPPONENT AND DOMINATE.

Conwell throws a straight right and an uppercut left, and another right and another left, the punches flowing together in quicksilver combinations, and all Day can do is bear-hug him. But Conwell will not have it. He shoves Day off. Day tries to wheel away, as he has done all night, but this time his legs fail him, and Conwell is ready for the maneuver. As Day retreats, Conwell stuns him with an overhand right. Day staggers. His guard falls away. Another overhand right whistles by his cheek, but a big left hook hits him square on the chin and he collapses onto the canvas.

The referee doesn't even bother with the 10-count. It is clear that this fight is over. The crowd is roaring, and Conwell is pounding his chest. He vaults onto the ropes and flexes his biceps, then leaps down and flashes an electric smile.

A man shoves his way into the ring. His voice is sharp with panic. "Get away! Get—get away from him!" Only now does Conwell turn and see that Day has not moved. EMTs climb through the ropes. Day's chest heaves and heaves, but he does not blink, just stares glassy-eyed into the floodlights. The crowd has gone quiet. The house music plays on.

Charles Conwell stands in the neutral corner, rocking from one foot to the other. He blinks a lot. Someone points a camera in his face. He looks out at the crowd and up toward the lights and anywhere but into the lens. He looks across the ring, where physicians are crowding around Day. One checks his watch.

Conwell looks the way fighters sometimes do after suffering a big knockout, as they struggle to stand, desperate and uncomprehending. He has never felt this way before. He has never been knocked out, and while he has knocked out many opponents, he has never, until this fight, knocked one out cold. He looks at the body convulsing on the mat. And for the first time in his career, he is afraid.

WHEN PATRICK DAY'S HEAD hit the canvas, it bounced once, then again, then settled and was still. A blood vessel had burst in the thin space between his brain and its protective covering beneath the skull, and now this space was filling with blood, compressing the brain. Oxygen flow weakened. Neurons began to blink out.

The ringside physicians stabilized Day's spine and held an oxygen mask to his mouth, then the EMTs loaded him onto a stretcher and passed it carefully through the ropes. On the way to the ambulance, he had a seizure. The EMTs tried to intubate him but could not insert the breathing tube. This unsettled the doctors at the hospital. Even five minutes without oxygen can do the brain permanent, catastrophic harm; nearly half an hour had passed before Day was finally intubated.

Conwell had a cut above his right eye stitched and then made his way to the locker room, where he changed into street clothes. When he heard about Day's condition, he broke down in tears.

At the hospital, doctors removed part of Day's skull to alleviate pressure on his brain. His camp prayed in the waiting room. Joe Higgins, his coach and manager, wore the red-and-blue silken robe that Day had entered the ring in. The next morning, his parents and one brother arrived. Then his other brothers, his friends, and other fighters. They sat in the waiting room and took turns visiting him. "It was very, very surreal," Higgins says. "Being in there with him and feeling his hands and his muscles—they're all still there. But he wasn't. We sat there for two days and prayed for a miracle."

Conwell flew back to his training camp in Toledo, Ohio, and drove home to Cleveland the next day. His girlfriend was waiting to greet him. When she started to unpack his black gloves and bloodstained uniform, he asked her to take them away. He said they scared him.

He kept his phone on silent and hardly left the house. He couldn't sleep. When he tried to watch a fight on TV, his heart started racing, and his hands started sweating. He felt like he was having a panic attack. He turned it off and told his girlfriend he didn't like boxing anymore. He said he was done.

Two days after the fight, he wrote Patrick Day a letter. He didn't know how to reach Day's family, so he posted it to Instagram in the hope that it would make its way to them. He cried as he wrote.

Dear Patrick Day,

I never meant for this to happen to you … I replay the fight over and over in my head thinking what if this never happened and why did it happen to you … I see you everywhere I go and all I hear is wonderful things about you. I thought about quitting boxing but I know that's not what you would want. I know that you were a fighter at heart so I decided not to but to fight and win a world title because that's what you wanted … With Compassion, Charles Conwell

Two days later his girlfriend called to tell him she was pregnant, and for the first time since the fight, he felt happy. That evening, the two of them were at the mall when his phone rang again. Patrick Day had died.

PATRICK DAY'S FATHER WAS A DOCTOR. His mother was a multilingual secretary at the United Nations. Most boxers come from poverty. Day did not.

His parents were Haitian immigrants who settled in Freeport, Long Island, in a pleasant little burgundy-and-yellow ranch house so close to Baldwin Bay that, some evenings, you could feel the salt breeze blowing off the water. They had four sons and named the youngest Patrick. Then they divorced, and Patrick's father moved out, but Patrick never did. He lived all 27 years of his life in that house by the bay, made honor roll there and earned his college degree there.

On a summer day in 2006, at the age of 14, he walked into a neighbor's open garage and started hitting an old Everlast heavy bag. He was a quiet freshman, a *Dragon Ball Z* fanatic who sometimes got picked on at school.

He'd never boxed before, but his father used to buy Mike Tyson fights on pay-per-view. And one of his older brothers had started training at a nearby gym. As Day hit the bag, his neighbor appeared in the doorway. Joe Higgins was a former New York City firefighter who could still remember how the air at Ground Zero had tasted like metal and sparkled at night. He'd lost a brother there, and he figured he might die soon, because so many of his crewmates were getting sick. Since 1992, he'd run the Freeport Police Athletic League Boxing Club. He showed Day how to jab and throw a simple one-two and told him, "Don't do nothing more than this, and you do it 150,000 times." Day stayed all afternoon, then returned the next day, and the day after that.

Higgins wanted to bring Day to the gym, but first he would have to speak with Day's mother, a Christian who did not tolerate violence. She told Higgins that she did not want her son to box. She worried he would be injured. "I understand, Mrs. Day," he told her. "He's just gonna come and work out." By the end of the year, he was entering tournaments, and winning them. Six years later, he went pro. His gym-mates idolized him. "He could be working on something by himself, and it would still seem like the light was on him," one said. And then he'd come talk to you, and you'd feel like the light was on you, and for a moment you were at the center of the world.

His mother refused to watch him fight. When other family members tried to talk to him about the risks of head injuries, he got annoyed—not because he denied the risks but because he'd already taken them into account. Once, after his brother Jean-philippe voiced concern about brain injuries, they didn't speak for a week. "He wasn't ignorant about that," his girlfriend, MaryEllen Dankenbrink, says. "He knew there were consequences." But he never thought about them in the ring. That was part of what he loved about fighting. In the heat of combat, he told her, everything else fell away.

Day understood that he was not like other boxers. He said as much at the press conference before his fight with Conwell: "People look at me, look at my demeanor, and they're like, 'Oh, you're such a nice guy, well spoken, why do you choose to box?' But, you know, it's about what's in your heart, internally, and I have a fighter's soul, a fighter's spirit, and I love this sport … Hopefully you guys enjoy the show that me and Charles are going to put on. It's going to be an entertaining fight. You don't want to miss it."

Day was confident. Young boxers with stainless records didn't faze him. He knew they could be beaten, because he'd been one of them and he'd been beaten. Coming out of the amateur ranks, he'd been the top fighter in his weight class. He was undefeated in his first 10 professional bouts. When he lost his 11th in a close decision to an exceptionally tall super middleweight with an elastic reach and a near-perfect record, that was all right—an off night, a bad break. But three fights later, when a journeyman with fewer wins than losses beat him in just 79 seconds, that was different. His promoter quickly dropped him. In the locker room after the fight, he rushed to Dankenbrink to explain what had happened. They'd just started dating, and this was the first time she'd seen him fight. "He thought I would leave him because he lost," she says.

For the first time in his career, it seemed like boxing just might not work out. He'd always been a good student—his gym-mates called him "Straight-A Day"—so he enrolled at an online university and earned a bachelor's degree in health and wellness. He wanted to have a backup plan. The prospect of having to use it terrified him. "That was his nightmare," Dankenbrink says. Boxing was his identity. He loved it, he once told his brother, "because it tells you exactly who you are."

But the golden-boy days were over. Now he was a B-side fighter, an opponent, the guy promoters brought in to give their top prospects a good workout and a résumé boost. He hoped to resurrect his career, and over the next three years, he won six straight fights, all against highly regarded prospects who by rights should have beaten him. "I love humbling these undefeated guys with the big egos who think they're invincible," he told a reporter. "In life, nobody is invincible."

His streak ended in June 2019 against "El Caballo Bronco," the Dominican fighter, who looked more like a heavyweight than a super welterweight. Next came Conwell. From the opening bell, he was landing big punches. This unnerved Day, an elusive fighter unaccustomed to getting knocked around. In the fourth round, Conwell floored him with a straight right to the chin, but Day hopped up immediately. It was only a flash knockdown. In the eighth, though, a hard one-two left him sprawled against the ropes and sent his mouthpiece spinning into the crowd.

It was at this moment that Higgins thought, *No more. I should stop this fight.* But at the end of the round, Day jogged back to the corner. His eyes looked clear, and his legs looked good. Higgins decided not to throw in the towel. *Keep your stance angled and your guard tight, and tie him up when you need to.* Day did all of this, and fought the ninth round to a stalemate.

In the corner before the tenth, Higgins knew a win was unlikely—Day would need a knockout. *But if he can give me a round in the tenth round like the ninth round*, Higgins thought, *he goes out with respectability.* Day would win the round, and on the plane home Higgins would suggest that he retire. With his degree and his title belts and his raw charisma, Day could get a job as a health-and-wellness instructor, maybe at a school. The kids would think he was so cool.

Day rose from his corner for the beginning of the tenth round. Higgins laid a black-gloved hand on his neck, tenderly. "You good?" he asked in a low voice.

"Yeah," Day answered.

He looked Higgins in the eye. Higgins touched his cheek. The bell rang.

CONWELL WEPT AT THE NEWS of Day's death. He had conceived a child and killed a man and learned of both on the same day, hours apart. At first, he thought maybe it was reincarnation, but later he decided it was only chance, because the baby turned out to be a girl, and anyway he was not a particularly religious man.

His phone rang all the way back from the mall and kept ringing when he got home. It was his mom, his dad, his brothers, his coaches. He shouldn't blame himself, they said. He was just doing his job. It was just boxing. But he kept thinking, *Did I really do that?*

He'd never liked telling people that he was a fighter, and now when strangers stopped him to ask, "Hey, are you that guy who boxes?," he'd say, "Nah, that's not me, I don't box," and for a moment they'd stare, but then they'd leave him alone. One time, he'd noticed a man eyeing him from across the barbershop. Eventually the man asked if he boxed, and this time he couldn't deny it—everyone else at the shop already knew. The man didn't say anything more. *He must know what I've done*, Conwell thought.

Several major news outlets had covered his open letter to Day, and since then hundreds of people had commented on it. Most were supportive. Some were cruel. He knew he shouldn't read their comments, but he did: "Go retire before you kill more people"; "U need to be in prison for murder"; "I hope u go to jail and get raped for killing someone"; "Bro you killed him"; "You killed Patrick"; "You killer"; "Killer."

On a bright September afternoon in 1842, the Englishman Chris Lilly and the Irishman Tom McCoy met in a makeshift arena on the eastern bank of the Hudson River for a bare-knuckle boxing match. Two thousand spectators looked on. McCoy had not wanted to fight, but when he'd rebuffed the challenge weeks earlier, Lilly had punched him in the face, and so here they were. That morning, McCoy had vowed "to win or die."

For a time, it seemed like he might win. He knocked Lilly down early. But by the 30th round—which, back then, meant the 30th knockdown—it was all Lilly. Forty rounds later, McCoy staggered and gasped and spat blood, and some in the crowd cried, "For God's sake, take him away!," but the doctor did nothing, and McCoy's second snapped back, "He ain't half licked yet!" So the fight went on. McCoy wouldn't quit. In the 120th round, he fell on his back and did not get up. The first casualty of the American prize ring drowned in his own blood.

More than 2,000 fighters have since died in the ring. They have died in backroom brawls and at intercollegiate competitions and, occasionally, after fights viewed on live television. Several rule changes have made the sport safer now than it once was, but it is not safe: Most professional fighters suffer brain injuries. About nine or 10 still die each year.

There has long been a sense, on account of this carnage, that boxing is merely the vulgar vestige of a less enlightened time, destined to go the way of bloodletting and cockfighting. After the Lilly-McCoy bout it seemed as though it might: 18 men faced manslaughter charges, including Lilly, the seconds, and the ringside physician. The jury deliberated for three hours before convicting all of them, and for a time boxing virtually disappeared in America. Within five years it was back—it has always come back.

By the 1920s, it had made its way from the seedy peripheries of American culture to the roaring center. When Gene Tunney fought Jack Dempsey for the heavyweight title in 1926, *The New York Times* ran a banner headline and six front-page stories about the match. By the 1950s, boxing was one of the most watched sports on television, and by the 1970s, Muhammad Ali was the most famous athlete in the world.

Over the years, boxing's demise has been prophesied again and again, but each time the sport has come back. In 1965, the *New York Times* editorial board forecast that "a sport as sick as this one surely cannot survive much longer." More than half a century later, the members of that editorial board are dead, and boxing has survived.

But it is not what it once was. Today, few people can name the heavyweight champion. Fights have retreated to pay-per-view. And the ones that generate the most hype usually involve aging titans necromanced out of retirement or B-list celebrities clamoring for attention—sometimes both. These are not so much fights as circus acts.

Boxing no longer faces any real risk of extinction on account of its brutality. Now the threat comes from the opposite flank. Why watch boxing when you could watch mixed martial arts? Why settle for mere punching when fighters elbow and kick and choke each other into submission? Boxing, once both celebrated and reviled as the most primal of all sports, has been made to look a little prudish, a little repressed.

In a way, it always has been. It has always felt the need to justify itself by appealing to something loftier, to be more than violence for violence's sake. It is the sweet science. It is the manly art. It is, as David Belasco, the famous theater producer, once put it, "show business with blood." For years, each big fight was a parable; an allegory; a morality play staged, quite literally, on canvas. Such grandiose pretensions have come to sound a little silly, but the pageantry persists. Just look at the referee, in his starched shirt and bow tie. What boxing promises spectators is the chance to indulge their appetite for violence without offending their self-image as good people. For the most part, it delivers on this promise. Except, that is, on those rare occasions when something goes very, very wrong.

CHARLES CONWELL SR. wanted desperately to be a fighter, but he didn't have the stuff. He trained and sparred in the basement of the local Salvation Army with a coach everyone called "The Godfather," but he never fought a single bout. He always had the desire to box, but he had neither the discipline to work at it consistently, nor a disciplinarian to make him. His own father wasn't around much.

Conwell Sr. became a brick mason. He bought a house in Cleveland Heights, Ohio, and he hung a heavy bag in the living room and another in the basement, and when he had children, he taught them to punch, same as he taught them to walk and read. The neighborhood kids came by too. They'd try on the gloves, and he'd show them the right way to hit the bag. They started calling him "Coach Chuck," then just "Coach." By the time Charles Jr. was born, people he'd known for years couldn't have told you his real name.

His first four children all tried their hand at boxing, but none of them took to it. The next two, Charles and his half brother Isaiah, started competing when they were 11 and 7 years old, respectively. Charles's earliest memory is play-boxing with his older brothers with cheap gloves from Walmart—and losing badly. He and Isaiah would hit the bags that hung around the house with the gloves they got each year for Christmas. When they were older, their father asked if they'd like to box for real, and they said they would. The one condition, he said, was that if they started, they couldn't quit until they were 18. They agreed.

Charles hated it at first. He wasn't used to the hard work, and training sessions made his whole body hurt. He wanted to quit, but his father wouldn't let him. In the backyard, Chuck hung lights and a third heavy bag from a tree so that the boys could train after dark. Some nights, at 3 or 4 a.m., he would wake them and make them run laps around a nearby graveyard in the headlights of his pickup truck. Other nights he would dream of some new combination, and when he awoke in the middle of the night, the vision still ablaze in his mind, he would rouse Charles and Isaiah so the sons could lace up their gloves and animate the father's dreams.

Charles got good. He started winning fights, and he kept winning fights, and in time he came to love it—whether the winning or the fighting, it's hard to say. All boxers have nick-names, and his, at first, was "The Body Snatcher." Then one day he was pounding some hapless opponent, and his father started shouting, "Bad News! You got 'em, Bad News!" and he kept shout-ing it at the next fight and the one after that too, until his son became Charles "Bad News" Conwell.

By ninth grade, Charles had begun telling his classmates he wasn't going to college. He spent most of high school on the road for tournaments and rarely went with his friends to parties or basketball games. Mostly this did not bother him. He does not drink or smoke, and he has always been reserved. He is, in his words, "the Kawhi Leonard of the boxing game." But even so, he occasionally chafed in high school at the strictures of his voca-tion and wondered, *Why can't I just do normal-people stuff?* "I don't think he knows how to have regular fun," his mother says, "because all he's ever done was box."

He was in Miami, he was in Morocco, he was on the news, and then he was walking in the opening ceremony at the Rio Olympics, just two months after he walked at his graduation. The school still displays his photo and one of his title belts in a trophy case.

Chuck was at every fight, even after Charles moved to Toledo to train with Otha Jones Jr., an elite coach, at his gym. After one bout, the three of them convened in their casino hotel room for a midnight film session among unfolded clothes and grease-stained pizza boxes. Charles had fought well enough—he'd commanded the ring from the bell and finished his opponent in the ninth round with a nose-breaking uppercut. But for stretches, the fight had looked like a stalemate. It was not a dominant performance, and did not make for good TV. This bothered Chuck: "The fuck is you doing, man!?" He turned to Jones. "You gotta cattle-prod him, man. I'm sorry, man, you gotta light a fire under this motherfucker's ass!" Charles said nothing.

After they watched the video replay, Chuck turned back to Jones. "He's mad at you now, but he'll love you later," he said, laughing. "If he wins, he'll love you later."

A DEFENSIVE POSTURE, THE PASTOR THOUGHT. It was Sunday morning, an hour before the service started, and Bible school was still in session. The church halls were quiet. The pastor sat behind his desk, and Conwell sat on a couch across from him, hunched over a little, elbows on his knees. *He's only a child*, the pastor thought, *young enough to be my son*. They made small talk.

Conwell hadn't been to church in years, but his mother, his father, and his grandmother had all suggested he seek spiritual counsel. "You're going to be facing a lot of demons in your life," they'd told him. And he was. He sometimes felt as though he should never fight again. He could not bear the thought of hurting anyone else. At random moments, he would think of Patrick Day and wonder, *Is he looking down at me? Is he in the room?*

"Your grandmother kind of explained to me what was going on," the pastor said. "But tell me how you feel. What's going on in your mind?" Conwell's eyes started to well up. What he needed to know, he said, was whether he was going to hell. He had killed a man, and he was afraid that God would not forgive him.

The pastor assured him that God would. He spoke of grace and mercy and redemptive love. He said that if Conwell requested forgiveness, he would receive it. But even then, he said, Conwell must also forgive himself. "It was not in your heart to kill him. You're a man who was doing your job."

But Conwell wanted to be certain: Was the pastor sure he would not go to hell? Was he sure God would forgive him? The pastor reassured Conwell that he was, then rose and laid a hand on his shoulder. He closed his eyes and asked God to protect this fighter and grant him "peace as he moved on with his career." He invited Conwell to come back anytime, and Conwell said he would. When he left the church, he felt lighter. He was ready to box again.

His promoters wanted to take things slow, so they scheduled a fight on a small card in Hammond, Indiana. The competition would be tame, the crowd small, the TV cameras absent—a perfect comeback bout. Conwell understood his promoters' concerns. Some fighters came back fine after a killing; others could never hit the way they once had.

When he returned to the gym he looked tentative, and Jones said, "You ain't look like you was … You gotta come on, B! You gotta go back to how you used to be!" Conwell wasn't trying to hold back. He felt like he was hitting hard. He kept at it.

Every so often, the pastor would text him messages of encouragement, which he appreciated. But he couldn't imagine returning to the church. "Maybe I should," he says. "It's hard, though. I just don't want to feel—I know he's not judging me, but it's just hard to look at somebody. I feel like—I don't know. I just—I don't know."

He's never gone back.

GOD MAY HAVE FORGIVEN CHARLES CONWELL, but Jean-philippe Day has not. He has not forgiven him for the way he stood over Patrick in the moments after the knockout, or for the way his camp talked about his brother's death as an obstacle to be overcome rather than a loss to be grieved. Nor has he forgiven Lou DiBella, Patrick's promoter and Conwell's too, for the way he profited at Patrick's expense. Most of all, he has not forgiven Joe Higgins for taking the Conwell fight so soon after Patrick's last loss, or for failing to stop the fight after the second knockdown, or for trying, since that night, Jean-philippe says, to cast himself as a victim, even a tragic hero.

Sometimes, Jean-philippe struggles to forgive himself. He had a bad feeling about the fight from the moment his brother mentioned it. "I just wish I could have been there that night, so I could have said something, or jumped into the ring and stopped the fight, or been there to catch his head when he fell," he says. "But instead I was sitting in front of the TV like a fucking sap."

His mother, his father, and his two other surviving brothers try not to think about all of this. Two years have passed, and they do not want to talk about the fight anymore, do not want to be drawn back into the emotional riptide. They are exhausted. Jean-philippe understands this, though he does not feel the same. He intends to talk about what happened "until I take my last breath."

For the past two years he has been turning over in his mind the circumstances of Patrick's death. He has come up with theories; he has questioned the cosmos; he has always run up, in the end, against the blank senselessness of what happened. In these moments, he wishes that his brother had died pushing his mother out of the way of oncoming traffic. That way at least his death would have meant something. But boxing matches, he knows, are not parables or allegories or morality plays. "To die in the ring," he says, "means nothing."

It was snowing when Conwell and his camp drove into Indiana. Fight night was three days away. The boxers all stayed at a truck-stop hotel where the concierge was always pissed off and someone had carved the words BEST FUCK EVER into the elevator doors and the quilts had little black-singed holes where guests had put out their cigarettes. The only store within walking distance was an old liquor shop across the iced-over parking lot. A sign out front advertised CARRY-OUT JACK. Conwell understood why he was here. But he sure as hell wasn't fighting on another card like this ever again.

At the weigh-in he got his first look at his opponent. The guy he was originally supposed to fight had bailed at the last minute, and word around the camp, maybe apocryphal, was that he got scared when he heard about the Day fight. No matter—the promoters had lined up a replacement, a journeyman from Mexico named Ramses Agaton who'd lost 10 of his previous 15 fights. They'd called him up on Wednesday, flown him in from Mexico City on Thursday, and here he was on Friday. That morning, Conwell had watched one of Agaton's old fights and said, "I can't lose to this guy."

Agaton evidently had not studied Conwell's old fights, because he knew almost nothing about him, and the little he thought he knew—"he moves fast and he doesn't punch hard"—was wrong. No one, it seemed, had thought it worth mentioning that the fighter he was about to face actually punched quite hard—hard enough to kill. Conwell had been training for a couple of months; Agaton appeared to have hardly trained at all. He had a visible paunch and was over the weight limit, but Conwell's camp told the officials to let it slide.

After the weigh-in, Conwell and his team ate lunch at a Red Lobster—lobster rolls, shrimp platters, biscuits—and then had nothing to do but wait. Conwell ran on a treadmill and threw punches in the hotel gym, but mostly he lay on his unmade bed chewing gum and watching reality TV.

He would be all right tomorrow, he told himself. He would go in there and fight like he always did. Lead with the jab, break down the body, finish strong. In his mind he envisioned ending the fight with a heavy blow to the body—but he knew the crowd would not like that. *You just can't win in boxing*, he thought. You go for the knockout—you must go for the knockout—and yet you have feelings. You strike your opponent down, and yet you wish him no harm. *It must get easier with time*, he thought.

Conwell wasn't worried much about getting hurt himself. He trusted his defense. And later in his career, after he'd won all there was to win and made all the money he could ever want to make, if he started taking damage, he'd quit. He'd go into real estate, flip houses maybe—nothing to do with boxing. Unless his kids boxed, that is, but he'd much prefer that they didn't. He doesn't think any boxer would want their kids to fight. When asked whether his own parents should have let him, he pauses, then says, "At this point ..." then trails off.

By nightfall, Conwell's girlfriend and mother had joined him in his hotel room. The TV played softly. Conwell and his girlfriend sat side by side on the bed, and she ran one hand through his hair, and he held her other hand in his, and they murmured to each other in the low light. He sat up and shadowboxed a little. Then, to no one in particular, he said, "One fight can change your life." Everyone was quiet. The TV filled the silence.

To step into a boxing ring, a fighter must convince himself that several things he knows to be true are, in fact, false. He must convince himself that the blows he sustains to his brain will not do irreparable damage and that the accretion of these blows will not, eventually, destroy him, as it has so many others. He must convince himself that his opponent is not altogether human, because otherwise how do you strike someone toward whom you bear no ill will, and strike him not just for show but savagely, to hurt him? Above all, he must convince himself that what goes on inside the ring and what goes on outside it are separate matters entirely, that the one has no relation to the other. And he can have no doubt, because doubt breeds hesitation, and in the ring, hesitation can be deadly.

Charles Conwell has never had much trouble with any of this. He always found it easy, he says, to "turn the switch on and off." But that was before the Day fight. Now he has knocked out a boxer in the ring, and a human being has died in the hospital. The wall between the boxing ring and the real world has come down. Having been made to see in the worst way that all those things a boxer convinces himself are false are in fact true, he must again convince himself that they are false. He has killed a man with his fists, and now he must get back in the ring and punch another man in just the same way.

So he does the only thing he can do. He tells himself what he needs to believe, and the people around him do too: "Maybe there were some prior issues going on with the man." "I've seen fighters get knocked out and take a harder punch than that and get right up." "We really think it was something that happened prior to this. It didn't have anything to do with us."

Conwell has his own version: "I've fought hundreds and hundreds of fights before, and it never happened. What makes this fight different from any other fight? I just try to think about it like that. Maybe there was something wrong with him rather than what I did to him."

These stories may or may not be true. What matters, when the lights come on and the bell sounds and he meets the gaze of his opponent, is that he believes them.

THE NERVES BEGIN WITH THE HISS of the tape winding around his wrists. The locker room smells of leather and sweat. The chords of the national anthem echo through the hazy halls. A door opens. "Charles," someone says, "it's time."

He skips down the hall with his entourage, throwing one-twos at phantom foes. He bounds up the steps two at a time and into a dim backstage corridor, where EMTs wait with stretchers. He removes his hood and stamps his feet. His shoes squeak on the linoleum. He wears red, white, and blue, as he often does, to remind the crowd that this isn't just anyone they're watching— this is an Olympian. Sewn onto his trunks is a red-and-white patch that says ALL DAY PAT DAY—his idea. Earlier that evening, as he dressed in the locker room, he had paused for a moment to look at it. On the ride over, he'd gotten a text from Joe Higgins, Patrick's coach and manager, wishing him luck. "Pat is watching over you," it said.

The ring announcer bellows his name and the speakers blare Kanye West's "All of the Lights" and he bursts through the curtains and into the smoky glare of the arena. The arena is not much of an arena at all. It's a New Deal–era gymnasium with rickety bleachers. Conwell's coaches strip off his shirt and Vaseline his face until it shines. They massage his shoulders and review the plan one last time. Now the nerves are gone. "Ain't no point in being nervous," he will later say. "Now you're here."

The bell clangs. Conwell has always been, by his own admission and to his coaches' chagrin, a slow starter. He almost never throws the first punch of a fight. Agaton opens with a series of jabs, then tries a one-two. He doesn't get anywhere near Conwell. His punches have no pop. When Conwell fires back with a jab of his own, there's no comparison. The punch doesn't connect, but it goes off like a warning shot. He begins to stalk Agaton, working him into the corner until Agaton, unable to escape, tries to tie him up, but before he can, Conwell catches him with a pair of hard left hooks to the ribs. The crowd loves it.

No one seems to notice the man at ringside with tears in his eyes. He is a cutman, the person who treats a boxer's wounds during a fight, and as such has an intimate familiarity with the damage the sport can inflict. He has worked some of Conwell's fights before, but at this one he is only a spectator; he is here for another fighter. He has not worked a corner since October, when he watched the live broadcast of Day's fatal bout with Conwell. Day was one of his fighters. They were both from Long Island, and the cutman had known him since he was an amateur. After Day's death, the cutman thought about quitting boxing altogether, but he reconsidered, because he thought that Day would have wanted him to continue on. Tonight, as he watches Conwell pound Agaton, he can't help but see Conwell pounding Day, and he can't take it anymore. At the end of the first round, he walks out.

In the next two rounds Conwell's body blows seem to almost literally deflate Agaton. Early on he had tried to match Conwell punch for punch, but now he simply leans on him. When, in the fourth round, Conwell breaks Agaton's guard and lands a powerful shot to the head, Conwell does not flinch. "In the moment," he will say after, "it's just boxing."

Nothing extraordinary happens. If some subterranean psychodrama is playing out deep within Charles Conwell, the surface registers no tremors. At the end of the fourth round, as he leans against the turnbuckle and drapes his arms over the ropes, he looks at ease. One of his coaches wipes his brow. Jones pours ice water over his chest. And then, all of a sudden, the referee is waving his arms. Agaton will not come out for the fifth round. The fight is over.

There will be no brutal knockout, no paralyzing flashback, no moment of reckoning. Just two human beings fighting for some money, and a thousand more intoxicated by the spectacle, and an empty folding chair at ringside, where not long ago the cutman sat, until he couldn't watch anymore.

Jacob Stern is an assistant editor at *The Atlantic*.

I've Covered Nine Olympics. Nothing Prepared Me for Seeing My Daughter Win a Medal

PAT FORDE

FROM *Sports Illustrated* • AUGUST 5, 2021

"Is Pat Forde in here?"

I was indeed there—there being the Tokyo Aquatics Center, specifically the final press conference of the Olympic swimming competition. Caeleb Dressel was the speaker. I was in the media contingent, preparing to write this story about him. I was not prepared to be called out from the dais.

Dressel and three American teammates had won the men's medley relay in spectacular fashion, setting a world record from an outside lane and keeping intact the United States' streak of never losing that event in the Olympics. It was the perfect way to end a week of wild ups and a few downs for the Americans. It was Dressel's fifth gold medal, finalizing his stature as the biggest global star in his sport.

And in response to a question about team bonding, Dressel had an anecdote to share that he wanted me to hear—bringing the sweetly surreal duality of my media/parent role here to its conclusion. His anecdote involved my daughter, Brooke—Dressel's U.S. swimming teammate—and a failed strategy.

"We [some of the men's swimmers] taught some of the girls on the team how to play poker," Dressel explained. "This is one of my highlights and shows some of the uniqueness of USA Swimming. ... We were, I guess, the coaches, and I've got to come clean. I had Brooke go in on king-6, which is my favorite hand, and I said, 'Hey, shove all-in.' And she busted. So I apologize.

"Moments like that, it's so much fun. And they all clapped for each other on every hand, it's the craziest thing. But moments like that, and moments at [training] camp, are where we become Team USA. ... The stupid little moments—it's not the big moments that are caught on camera. It's the moments you don't see."

This was the second time this summer that the phrase "little moments" made me realize—they actually are the big moments. At the end of June, friend Scott Van Pelt from ESPN texted me a picture of his young daughter's swim meet. "Road game. Nervous. Won her heat. She was beaming. ... Just enjoying the little moments."

No such thing, SVP. The little moments are the DNA of everything profound—every great relationship, every great accomplishment, everything that lasts and matters and lingers in our memories as we age. Specific to this story, Brooke's Olympic experience sits at the top of an athletic pyramid built upon little moments.

The neighborhood pool races where winning a heat ribbon was a triumph. The jump up with her older brothers Mitchell and Clayton to the year-round team, and the excitement of overnight trips from home in Louisville to exotic locations like Indianapolis and Nashville. The advancement to two-a-day practices and 4:20 a.m. wake-ups, where breakfast with teammates was the reward before heading off to school. Earning a black national team swim cap as a member of the Lakeside Seahawks club team—a true stamp of arrival. Then the bigger meets all over the country, and eventually the chance to represent the United States internationally in Singapore, Europe, Taiwan, Hong Kong, Japan and South Korea. A scholarship to Stanford, and the unmatched fun and camaraderie of a college team environment. All of the doubt and stress that went into the 16-month final leg to making the Olympic team, which melted away in an unforgettable experience in Omaha in June.

Now this. All of this. A place on Team USA, an anchor spot for the 800-meter freestyle relay preliminaries, a silver medal. All of a sudden, the little brown-eyed girl who used to sit on my lap in the stands at age-group meets is taking pictures with Kevin Durant and playing poker with Caeleb Dressel.

(Despite busting that king-6 hand, Brooke gives the male star of these Olympics credit for being a good poker coach. She says she went on to win more than she lost in matches with her teammates. No money changed hands, though in one game nuts were used as currency—cashews, almonds and macadamias.)

As Brooke reached the top of the pyramid, the reflections on all the building that got her to this point kept coming for me. The overwhelming realization that this was actually happening—we are in Tokyo for the Olympics, and I'm just about the only non-coach-parent on the planet with this opportunity—had to be processed in increments. One of the sayings I've often used with Brooke when she felt she was facing an impossible task—academically or athletically—was this: "How do you eat an elephant? One bite at a time."

So it was for me, seeing something dreamed about for so many years take tangible shape in front of me. Pictures from the Olympic Village—wow, this is real. The sight of her on the Olympic pool deck—are you kidding me? That's really my kid? We are acquaintances with the parents of Will Smith, the Los Angeles Dodgers catcher and a Louisville homeboy, and his mom articulated it well when we saw her over Fourth of July weekend: "I still don't believe it. I'll be driving on the Watterson Expressway and suddenly it hits me: *Will won the World Series.*"

This is my ninth Olympics, so I know what they're supposed to look and feel like. It's not this, with quiet venues and limited movement and such extreme caution when it comes to human interaction. I felt bad for what the athletes were missing: the fellowship with their peers from around the world, the immersion in a melting pot of cultures and sports, the feeling of all being in this extraordinary event of a lifetime together.

Despite what was not present, there was no squelching the athletes' excitement. That was palpable from the opening ceremony onward. After coming so close to not having these Games happen, every athlete was so happy to be here and acutely appreciative of the opportunity.

My situation was more complicated. With a child on the team and friendships with many of the athletes and their parents, I would have loved to slip into the Team Dad role—but the lockdown prohibited that, so there would be no orange slices or juice boxes or food deliveries from me to them. Also, I had to work roughly 12-16 hours a day, factoring in bus time to and from Tokyo Aquatics Center. Most awkward of all, I had to attempt to objectively (and at times critically) cover the U.S. swimmers and their coaches while trying not to put my daughter in a difficult position.

This was by far the best assignment of my life. It also was by far the strangest assignment of my life.

The day before they lit the torch, I got my first chance to see Brooke in person. I was at the aquatic venue for a media session with the U.S. coaches; she was there for practice. We got 5-10 minutes to talk in a back hallway. I wanted to hug her, of course, but safe social distancing had been the team mantra for a month—don't mess it up now, on the cusp of the Games. At least I was there, in her presence for the first time since Omaha for Olympic trials in mid-June; I had empathy for all the athlete parents who couldn't get closer than FaceTime to their children.

She looked great, sounded upbeat—all systems go for her event six days away. When the competition began on July 24, you could see how fired up the American team was to swim—they were easily the loudest cheering team in the venue. From my vantage point in the press tribune on the other side of the pool, it was a joy to see Brooke as engaged as anyone in the U.S. team section. Americans storming to six medals on the first full day of swimming may have happened without that team spirit, but I'd like to think there was some correlation.

Three days out from her event, there was a hiccup. (Because there always is a hiccup with this child.) She swam a time trial for her coach, Greg Meehan, and her time was very slow, well off what she recorded in Omaha to make the team. Being the relay anchor created some stress; now this added to it. Despite the knowledge that the U.S. did not have to be spectacular to make the eight-team relay final, everyone wanted to swim fast while representing their country in the Olympics.

But that was the last time any worry was voiced. When I saw her on the pool deck, she waved at me in the stands—something she was not prone to do before this trip. Text exchanges were humorous and stress-free. She seemed ready for her moment, Wednesday night in Japan and Wednesday morning in Louisville.

Back home, the support and excitement were heartwarming. Her club team put up a banner at the pool. Her high school put up a banner. Local media all ran stories. And a breakfast watch party was organized for family and about 50 people with ties to our original neighborhood team. All she had to do was step up and swim against the world's best.

One of the restorative, stress-releasing rituals I've undertaken before my kids' biggest swims is to find some quiet alone time to consciously express appreciation for the moment. When Brooke and her brother Clayton were competing at the U.S. Nationals in Irvine, Calif., in 2018—when both had the best 400-meter individual medleys of their life—the quiet time came after I dropped my wife and mother-in-law off at the front gate, then parked and walked around the facility to the pool. Every afternoon I had the same conscious thought, "What a gift to be here. How fortunate we are."

In Omaha earlier this summer, that time was the 20-minute walk from the hotel to the arena. It was harder here to find any solitude, however brief. But before the night session started I walked around the side of the venue and found the setting sun shining on my face. Eyes closed. Inhale. Exhale. Gratitude activated. I was about to watch my daughter swim in the Olympics.

Relieved of work duty for the night and able to watch as a father, I asked my friend and colleague Michael Rosenberg to get video of the race on his phone. I watched Brooke and her relay teammates be introduced, and there was another wave of realization—this is going to happen, right in front of me.

Before the start, I did in fact cheer in the press box—I've yelled, "Go, Brookie!" before every race she's ever swum, and I wasn't going to stop at the Olympics. Fortunately nobody objected.

The race unfolded pretty much perfectly. Bella Sims swam a solid leadoff leg, then Paige Madden put the U.S. in front, then Katie McLaughlin increased the lead. When Brooke went in, she had a solid lead over the Chinese. When she finished, exactly one minute and 57 seconds later—the fastest time of her life—the lead was maintained and the American relay had advanced to the finals as the No. 2 seed. She had put in the work, and she performed when called upon.

What happened next was my moment of the Olympics. After touching the wall, being congratulated by her relay mates and checking the scoreboard, Brooke looked up and found me in the stands. The look on her face wasn't clearly visible from where I stood in the arena, but the slow-motion TV replay made my heart grow three sizes that day. Her countenance radiated joy, satisfaction and relief.

And with that, I was running. I had to get down seven flights of stairs to get to the media mixed zone, where I could meet up with Brooke for my favorite postrace interview of my career. McLaughlin, a California Golden Bear, threw some shade at my Stanford swimming shirt (same one I wore when Brooke made the Olympic team, this was no time to mess with the mojo). I'm not sure I actually even asked her anything, but it was a moment to cherish.

The next morning, it was up to her teammates to bring it home. Allison Schmitt subbed in for Sims, and Katie Ledecky subbed in for Brooke—two of the most decorated swimmers in U.S. history. What followed was one of the best races in Olympic history.

With China blazing in lane 3 and Australia following in lane 4, the United States was playing catch-up in lane 5. Ledecky gave a furious chase in the anchor leg, splitting the fastest 200 of anyone in the race by a wide margin. She passed the Aussies and nearly caught the Chinese. All I knew at that point was that my kid had an Olympic medal; later on I figured out that all three teams broke the world record.

Brooke Forde, Olympian, was now Brooke Forde, silver medalist. Like, for real. All the work, all the so-called small moments, had yielded this moment too big to dare believe it could happen. She sent a picture later of her wearing Ledecky's borrowed silver (she wouldn't get hers until the end of the meet), which brought it home even more.

Congratulations poured in via text, email and other methods. It was gratifying to see all the excitement from people who knew her. Next thing I know, she's on the *Today* show with five of her teammates and Michael Phelps. I got to be together with Brooke one more time in Japan, when we met for a CBS interview in the

Main Press Center (no hugging, and masks on). Other than that, it was just a few more waves from across the venue.

On the final day, Caeleb Dressel dropped his poker anecdote—the last of the surreal moments in Tokyo for me as a parent-journalist. I checked the story with my closest source on the team. She confirmed.

The little moments. They have added up to something grand beyond measure.

Pat Forde is a national columnist and senior college sports writer for *Sports Illustrated*. He previously worked for ESPN, *The Courier-Journal* in Louisville, Kentucky, and Yahoo! Sports.

'His Name Is Sang. He Is a Pitcher.' A Family's American Dream, Their Unbearable Loss

STEPHEN J. NESBITT

FROM The Athletic • SEPTEMBER 22, 2021

Salisbury, MD—The week he arrived in America, Seong Han Baek left his shift at the poultry factory each evening and bicycled the streets of Salisbury, searching for baseball fields. He spoke little English, but he had a map and purpose. Pedaling from stop sign to stop sign, he rehearsed a line.

Can my son play on your team? His name is Sang. He is a pitcher.

It was the end of April in 2014 when the family of four immigrated from Seoul to Salisbury. Youth baseball rosters were full. When the father biked back to the family's apartment after sunset, the son would be waiting for him. No, the father would tell the son, he hadn't found a team yet. He'd try again tomorrow.

They'd come to this city of 30,000 at the center of the Delmarva Peninsula, between Chesapeake Bay and the Atlantic Ocean, to write a new chapter. Salisbury was nothing like Seoul, and their new life nothing like their old one. The family found Salisbury charming and spacious, with a small but bustling downtown and leafy parks—a rural, small-town feel within a growing city.

But it wasn't the East Coast that initially drew the family to the United States. When the father was in his 20s, he had flown to California to visit cousins and thought, I'd like to live here one day. Later, he married En Young Lee and honeymooned out West, seeing the Grand Canyon and Las Vegas and Los Angeles. She hoped to live there one day, too.

They waited for a door to open. None did. They had a good life and made a good living in South Korea. Seong Han worked as a fire inspector, and En Young was a classically trained opera singer teaching voice and piano lessons.

Then came the children—the son, Sang Ho Baek, in 2001, and the daughter, Sun Ho "Sunny" Baek, in 2003—who stoked the parents' American dream. The father and mother say they wanted their children to have better educational and economic opportunities. They saved as much money as they could, and when Sang and Sunny were toddlers, the father filed paperwork for a work visa and started looking for jobs in the United States.

Ten years passed.

Meanwhile, the son loved baseball. He was 8 when he first played, and for the rest of his baseball life he'd always ask to wear jersey No. 8. After work, the father would crouch and catch for the son. The son grew, and his fastball pounded the father's mitt harder and harder. The son's Little League coach, Kim Gun-Woo—a former pitcher who was once Korea Baseball Organization's rookie of the year—told the father that his son had a strong right shoulder, a sign he'd grow into a great pitcher.

In 2014, the father found work at the poultry factory in Salisbury.

"I gave up everything there," he says now, "to come here for my kids."

Leaving Seoul, however, was heartbreaking for the son. He asked his father, "Can I still play baseball in America?" The father promised to find him a team.

So the family's first purchase in Salisbury was a beat-up black bicycle. As darkness fell one night that April, the father found a baseball field south of Salisbury, and asked a coach if there was room for one more. His name is Sang. He is a pitcher. The coach looked around and saw a field full of players. But he also saw a bicycle and a father's love. Yes, he said, there's room for Sang.

SANG'S DREAM WAS TO PITCH in the major leagues and buy his parents a house.

This was no secret; a child's dreams rarely are. In a video from his mother's birthday in 2012, 11-year-old Sang is seen wearing his Little League uniform, singing and dancing in their Seoul kitchen. In his birthday letter, he writes that he'll work and study hard and become a famous baseball player, then ends it by reminding his mother to wake him early for practice in the morning.

Sang wasn't a phenom, wasn't the biggest or strongest player on his team at any level, but he believed he was bound for the big leagues, and he'd let nothing stop him. And why wouldn't he believe that? Look at what his parents did. After all they sacrificed to see him succeed in the United States, why couldn't a 5-foot-9 Korean kid wearing wire-rimmed eyeglasses pitch in the majors?

"He was stubborn in the sense that he'd never stop persevering," says Josh Kwak, a friend from Salisbury. "He knew what he wanted, and he'd work toward it."

Connor Lefort, the catcher for Sang's first team in Salisbury, had never caught a pitcher like him. Though Sang had only a limited grasp of the English language, the two of them communicated like catchers and pitchers do—one finger down for fastball, two for curveball. Lefort would set up at the corner of the strike zone, and Sang hit his mitt. Sang threw smoke and buckled knees.

"His curveball made batters fall down," Lefort says, "and it'd be strike three."

Away from the ballpark, transitioning to American life was difficult for Sang and his sister. Sunny didn't speak for all of fifth grade. Sang came across as shy, but friends say once he opened up he was goofy, curious and kind.

Baseball offered Sang a fraternity and a universal language. He always wanted to talk baseball. His favorite team was the Dodgers because his favorite player, Korean left-hander Hyun Jin Ryu, pitched for them at the time. One day, during health class in seventh grade, classmate Max Taylor wore a T-shirt from the Cal Ripken World Series in Aberdeen, Md. Sang said, "I played there." He'd been on the Korean team in the 2013 Cal Ripken World Series.

"I didn't even know he played baseball," Taylor says. Later, they played each other in a tournament. "I was like, Hey, that's the guy in my health class!"

When moving to Salisbury, Seong Han had planned to work at the poultry factory for a year to receive his green card, then move the family to California. But that first year came and went, and the kids were settling in at school. Sunny had friends. Lefort had invited Sang to play on his travel ball team, the Delmarva Aces. En Young was working at a factory assembling cables and wiring. And the family had found a community at the Korean Presbyterian Church of Salisbury, halfway around the world from Seoul, that had embraced them—helped them line up their first apartment, ferried them around the city before they had a car, and eventually got Seong Han a new job installing flooring, where he works to this day. Salisbury was starting to feel like home.

"I thought, *Maybe it's not a good idea to move again*," Seong Han says. "So, we stayed."

Sang was an eager learner. He took drum lessons and joined the youth group's worship band. He'd hear slang or an unfamiliar word and immediately ask his friends to explain it. (An example: "We went through a phase of saying 'gander,'" says Jun Lee, laughing, "like, take a gander at that.")

On a church mission trip to Nicaragua, Sang, Lee and Kwak ran a Bible program for local children, sanitized houses, laid a foundation for a new building and sprayed pesticides. At night, they were teenagers. Kwak and Lee taught Sang card games. He taught them Korean wordplay games. They stayed up late and pulled harmless pranks. And then, when everyone else was asleep, they talked about the future.

One night in Nicaragua, Lee noticed the calluses on Sang's pitching hand and asked, "Yo, are you making it to the MLB?" Sang just smiled.

JESSE SERIG, THE CO-HEAD BASEBALL COACH at James M. Bennett High School, remembers first seeing Sang pitch in the seventh grade. Serig was tossing batting practice to high schoolers; Sang was throwing to his dad in the bullpen. Serig couldn't decide who impressed him more: the 13-year-old with *that* fastball, or the father with the guts to catch it without any gear.

Two years later, when Sang's name appeared on a list of freshmen interested in Bennett baseball tryouts, Serig told the other coaches to keep an eye on him.

Temperatures were around 40 degrees in the first week of March, and Sang was the only one of the 60 players in short sleeves. The day tryout results were posted, Sang didn't bother bringing baseball pants to school. Only varsity practiced that day. Taylor read the rosters first, then he tracked down Sang in a hallway and said, "Dude, we made varsity. Go get your pants!"

The varsity team that year was a rowdy bunch, but they embraced Sang. He was quiet, a little quirky, and a secret weapon on the mound.

In his first start against one of Bennett's rivals, Sang threw six scoreless innings. "It was just ridiculous," Taylor says. This was a theme over Sang's four years at Bennett: He always appeared calm and composed. He laughed when friends got nervous riding on a roller coaster. He took off his shirt and belly-flopped into a foot of freshly fallen snow without flinching to win a $5 bet. He went to a haunted house and fist-bumped the zombies and slashers trying to spook him. And he barely broke a sweat pitching in big games.

Serig started to think Sang simply didn't understand how important these games were. But when Serig mentioned that to Sang's parents, they laughed.

"(Sang) always said he was so nervous," Seong Han says, "but nobody knew."

As Bennett headed into Maryland's 3A state tournament in his junior season, in 2019, Sang was deployed as the closer so he could pitch every game. Bennett had started the season 10–0 and then stumbled down the backstretch, losing five of its last six games. Taylor remembers thinking the team would be one and done in the playoffs. But they defeated Chesapeake at home, and the dominoes started to fall: conference rival Stephen Decatur, Atholton, then defending champion Thomas Johnson. Sang, who like the rest of the team had bleached his hair blond, escaped a bases-loaded jam to send Bennett to the 3A state final against C. Milton Wright at Ripken Stadium in Aberdeen—the same complex where Sang had played with the Korean team in 2013.

Bennett led 5–3 when Sang entered for the seventh and final inning in the championship game. For the first time, his father felt no nerves as he watched.

"That night, he looked confident and happy," Seong Han says, "so I felt happy, too."

Sang hit the leadoff batter on an 0-2 pitch—just enough to raise blood pressures in the Bennett dugout—and then settled in. He got back-to-back groundouts, then pumped a fastball for strike three and the third out. Before the game, he had told his sister, "Everyone throws the glove in the air when they celebrate. I'm going to do the opposite." So, Sang spiked the glove. He raised his arms in the air. Teammates dogpiled.

THE ELBOW PAIN started last fall.

Sang was a freshman at George Mason University in Fairfax, Va. His senior season at Bennett had been canceled due to the COVID-19 pandemic—no repeat championship run; no prom; no graduation—but not before he'd gone to George Mason's prospect camp and impressed head coach Bill Brown and pitching coach Shawn Camp, a former major league pitcher. The two coaches watched as this undersized right-hander mowed down one hitter after another.

"You could see the incredible potential in him," Brown says.

So, after spending a year pitching in the backyard in Salisbury, throwing into a net 60 feet 6 inches away from a makeshift mound his father had built, Sang left for college. As he started his preseason throwing progression, his right elbow hurt. He'd been injured before, like the time in middle school when he broke a finger on his right hand sliding into a base and still pitched the rest of the game. But arm injuries were worrisome. And unlike any elbow aches he'd had in high school, this one wasn't gone in a day or two.

Sang wondered if he'd ramped up too quickly after a year without baseball. He was itching to pitch, to prove himself to the coaches as fall practices began, but he needed answers about his elbow issues. The first arm specialist he saw recommended Tommy John surgery—a repair of the ulnar collateral ligament, or UCL, which typically has a 12- to 18-month recovery. A second specialist prescribed physical therapy instead. Sang opted for the latter, for rest and rehab, hoping to recover before the spring season.

Pitcher Matt Henson transferred to George Mason mid-year and became Sang's daily throwing partner. Though the time off had helped relieve some of the pain, there still were days when Sang said his arm felt terrible. Henson encouraged him not to push it. As they played catch, Sang and Henson, who is a quarter Korean, bonded over Korean food and culture. Sang was missing his mother's cooking and his favorite dish—Gamjatang, a spicy stew with pork and potatoes.

As a freshman still finding his way away from home, on a new team and a college campus, Sang said little but had an infectious energy. Brown laughs as he remembers Sang working the bucket during batting practice. Most pitchers stand in center field waiting for teammates to throw them baseballs to collect. "The grass dies underneath them," Brown says. Not Sang. He'd race across the outfield, chasing fly balls, then book it back to the bucket.

The jitters Sang had suppressed in high school bubbled to the surface at the idea of staring down Division I hitters. Before George Mason's season opener in late February, Sang told senior pitcher Jonathan Kaiser, "Jon, I don't know what'll happen if I go in. I'm so nervous I might throw up on the mound."

Sang didn't pitch that day. He debuted against Maryland Baltimore County two weeks later, coming out of the bullpen to fire 1 1/3 scoreless innings. He wore No. 44—4 plus 4 is 8, his favorite number—and was buzzing when he bounced back to the dugout. Teammates came to expect this from Sang, the kid who once told his father he felt like a different person when he stepped on the mound. Off the field, he was innocent and gullible. On it, he was fiery.

Sang's fastball sat at 90 mph, climbing a tick or two higher when he was amped, but his bread-and-butter pitch was an eephus-like curveball.

"I remember one game, he came in and was just throwing fastballs by guys," outfielder South Trimble says. "And then he threw the eephus-style curveball. The dude swung so early and absolutely whiffed. The other team's bullpen was talking to me, saying, 'Wow, this is insane. This guy has it all.'"

"When he'd throw that curve, our guys would go crazy," says Brown, chuckling. "The hitters were absolutely, completely paralyzed by it. They'd double-clutch and could never pull the trigger on it."

Sang allowed only two runs over his first five outings, and his confidence grew with each pitch and punchout. He phoned his father after each game to fill him in.

But the elbow pain persisted, and eventually it was too much to pitch through. After Sang was hit around by Dayton and Virginia Commonwealth, the coaching staff shut him down for the rest of the season. Sang returned to the arm specialists. This time, there was consensus.

"It was getting worse," his father says.

To pitch again, Sang needed Tommy John surgery. He told teammates the surgery scared him. What if he wasn't the same pitcher when he came back?

Once Sang decided on surgery, though, he didn't waver. He sketched a rehab plan. He'd stay in shape until he could start throwing, then take private pitching lessons for the first time. When the spring semester let out and George Mason's season ended, his family says, Sang wasn't anxious. He was relieved, rejuvenated by a new thought: He wouldn't be the same pitcher when he came back. With a healthy elbow, without the pain, he'd be even better.

In the days after surgery, Sang's leg hurt worse than his arm.

This isn't entirely unexpected. Tommy John surgery is a two-part procedure in which a surgeon takes a tendon from the leg or another part of the body and uses it to replace the damaged UCL in the elbow. But Sang was in significant discomfort. He couldn't climb the stairs to his bedroom, so he temporarily moved into the downstairs bedroom, trading places with his father.

Sang phoned the Washington, D.C., medical center where he'd undergone surgery June 8 and asked if the leg pain was typical. According to Sang's family, the surgeon who had performed the procedure was not concerned.

"We just believed that it was normal," Seong Han says.

As Sang rested, his little sister kept him company. Sang and Sunny had always been close. He was her confidant. "He would just listen to me," Sunny says. "I could tell him about my problems." While Sang was attending George Mason, they spoke all the time. Sunny's friends teased her about it. Who FaceTimes their brother for hours? On one of their calls, Sunny was fretting about finding the right college. She woke up the next morning to a long text from Sang. It was so sweet and supportive, Sunny says, that she immediately accused their mother of putting Sang up to it. (En Young swears she didn't.)

The two weeks between Sang's coming home from school and having surgery have a hold on Sunny's memory now. The brother and sister flew through the first five films of the Harry Potter series. They made plans for the summer. They drove to Assateague Beach, Sang's favorite place to swim and surf, in his truck, a 1996 Toyota Tacoma. It was early June, the water chilly and the wind whipping. After a while, Sunny was tired and cold. But Sang ran back into the water again and again. Sunny snapped photos of him and laughed. He looked like a puppy running on the beach, Sunny says. He was so happy.

On a Friday, three days after surgery, Seong Han gave Sang his medications at 10 p.m., then turned off the lights. "Good night, Sang," he said. "See you tomorrow."

When Sunny stopped by the downstairs bedroom two hours later to see Sang, she found her brother unresponsive. He wasn't breathing. Sunny raced upstairs and woke her father, who phoned 9-1-1 and started CPR.

An ambulance arrived within minutes and, as paramedics tried reviving Sang, carried him down the long driveway and to Peninsula Regional Medical Center. The family car followed.

The mother, father, sister and a few family friends, helping to translate, huddled in a hospital room and watched helplessly as doctors and nurses tried saving Sang's life. At first, there was hope. But as minutes turned into hours and darkness into dawn, that hope evaporated.

At 9:12 a.m. on June 12, Sang was pronounced dead. He was 20.

In the hospital room, resuscitation attempts turned to funeral preparation. Two men in suits wheeled a gurney into the room and took Sang's body to the funeral home.

The medical examiner would later list the cause of death as a pulmonary embolism, a blood clot that resulted as a complication of the surgery. But the family is still waiting for more answers.

They say a third-party investigation is ongoing and incomplete, which is why they're choosing not to name the surgeon or the medical center at this time. The family wants to know how a surgery performed on so many baseball players had killed Sang.

SERIG, THE BENNETT BASEBALL COACH, was getting ready for the high school's graduation ceremony at the minor league Delmarva Shorebirds' stadium in Salisbury when a colleague called to tell him Sang had died. "I was stunned," he says. "Devastated." Many of the 300 students in caps and gowns knew Sang. During the ceremony, Serig's phone pinged with messages from parents asking if what they'd heard was true. Serig couldn't confirm anything yet. He sat there lost in thought, his mind replaying old memories. Sang had pitched at that ballpark, which was almost a mirror image of Ripken Stadium in Aberdeen where he'd thrown the last pitch of the championship game two years earlier.

Serig was glad the ceremony was outdoors, so he could wear sunglasses.

"I was crying the whole time," he says.

The next morning, the George Mason players got a group text from an assistant coach setting up an impromptu Zoom call. The players—scattered from New York to California to Alaska playing collegiate summer ball—weren't sure what to make of it. When the meeting started, they caught up and cracked jokes. Then they quieted, and Brown broke the news.

"Honestly, it's the worst thing I've had to do," the coach says.

Camp, the pitching coach, spoke next. He reminded the players their feelings would hit them at different times and in different ways. When it happens, he said, let those emotions out.

Henson, Sang's throwing partner, turned off his camera and cried.

For the rest of the day, the team group chat was filled with memories and photos of Sang. *Love you guys. Sang will always fly high.* Kaiser had missed the Zoom call. He was at the grocery store when the texts started coming through. He thought back to the last few days of the season. Kaiser was a senior, headed home to northern Virginia and life after baseball. "I'll miss you," Sang kept telling him. "I'm going to need to call you for advice."

"This is sort of tough to say," Kaiser says now, his eyes welling with tears. "I don't think I realized how much he impacted my life, and how much I'll miss him."

Teammate Scott Morgan organized a GoFundMe to help the Baek family pay for medical and funeral expenses, and it drew widespread attention, raising more than $50,000. Brown says George Mason plans to make a lasting memorial for Sang, "something that will be here long after all of us have moved on," but no further details have been announced. "We have to move forward, and we will," Brown says, "But Sang will always be with us."

The day of Sang's funeral, the George Mason baseball team bused to Salisbury. Sang's parents had expected a small ceremony, but more than 400 people—friends, coaches, teammates and even some teachers who never had Sang in class—attended. The parents hugged everyone they saw. "I didn't want to let go of them," Henson says. "I couldn't even imagine the pain they're going through."

The ceremony painted a portrait of Sang's beautiful baseball life. A brief biography laid a timeline of Sang's career and ended with the line, "He left us and went to heaven, leaving behind his dream to throw a ball from a major league pitcher's mound." Lefort gave the first eulogy, and Serig the second. Both were also translated into Korean. Behind the podium was a painting of Sang, with his bleached-blond hair, pitching in the championship game.

After the ceremony, walking around the chapel, Henson came across a display of Sang's baseball gloves. Henson saw that one— Sang's favorite—was missing. He wanted to be sure the family had that glove. But when Henson approached the open casket, he noticed two things. Sang was wearing his George Mason baseball jersey. And the glove was in the casket, on Sang's left hand.

ON A WARM WEEKNIGHT IN SALISBURY, the father, mother and sister sit in the living room of their home and laugh and cry as they tell stories about the son whose ashes are in a decorative wooden box across the room. It's been three and a half months since Sang died. A memorial grew along one wall in the living room after the funeral, with trinkets and paintings and photo albums and a Bible and the wooden box, and stayed there all summer.

They tried returning to normal—the father and mother went to work; the sister is back in school—but their lives are locked in stasis. They started to clear out Sang's bedroom but got lost in their grief and gave up. Sang's beloved truck sits under a tree, next to the driveway. The wood bordering the pitcher's mound in the backyard rotted, and the father threw it away.

Sang found fame, like he always said he would, but not in a way any of them wanted. News of his death spread on social media and then to *Sports Illustrated,* the *New York Times* and *People* magazine. Who'd heard of someone dying after Tommy John surgery?

Sunny is now a senior in high school. The girl who didn't speak in the fifth grade is now her school's student government president. She and Sang had made plans to road-trip in Sang's truck later in the summer to visit four colleges Sunny is considering. She never took that trip. Instead, she and a friend painted a toy truck black, glued a baseball glove and bat into the bed of the truck, and added it to the memorial in the living room. It sits on the floor beside a card Sunny gave Sang on his last birthday, Jan. 31, in which she wrote about how they'd grow famous one day and buy their parents a house.

Little things hit Sunny hardest now. She'll be driving and break into tears. She'll eat dinner and remember how much Sang liked that meal. She'll think of an inside joke and pick up her phone to text him. She doesn't know if she'll ever finish Harry Potter. "I know it's not going to be the same anymore," she says.

The father comes home from work each day and parks beside the black bicycle that is leaning against a wall in the garage. His mind is overrun with memories. More than anything, he says, he is thankful for the time he had with Sang. When they lived in Seoul, the father and son went on camping trips together. When Sang's travel-ball trips took them up and down the East Coast, the two of them would share a hotel room and talk as they sat in bed watching TV.

In Korean culture, Seong Han says, fathers and sons rarely tell each other, "I love you." They feel it, but they express it in different ways. So, when Seong Han spoke to close his son's funeral service, he had something he wanted to tell Sang: "It seems too late. However, there's one thing I want to say out loud to my son: Thank you for being born to me, and for having been my son. I love you forever."

Still, the father can't sleep. Only after visiting doctors has he been able to sleep a few hours each night. The mother is struggling, too. She has developed a skin condition, and she's losing hair. They'll have some days when they think about Sang and smile, and others that break them.

"It takes time," Seong Han says.

The mother has been quiet. En Young speaks less English than her husband and their daughter, and she's relying on family friend Hyo Jung Choi to translate the conversation for her. The mother is sitting in an armchair, a blanket pulled over her. She is tired. She says something softly, in Korean.

"I'm consoled by the fact that he is in heaven, yet …"

Choi chokes up, then finishes the sentence.

"I miss him."

The room is silent as everyone wipes their eyes. The mother continues. Fall is a difficult season, she says. Sang should be starting his sophomore year. You learn a lot about a loved one after they die; people tell you things you'd never heard before. "I didn't realize it when he was here," the mother says, "but now I can tell that wherever he went, that place became richer, bigger, happier."

Each morning, the mother gets out of bed and kneels on the living room floor. The Bible sits open in front of her. She holds a framed image of Sang—his high school senior class photo—close to her chest, closes her eyes and prays. She sings a hymn she sang the last time she saw her son, at the funeral home just before his body was cremated.

This morning, the mother says, she held Sang's photo close and sensed something different. "I felt a warmth swelling from my heart," she says. She clutched him tighter, and it was like he was there with her, like he was waiting for that moment to comfort her. The mother rocked back and forth, and tears rolled down her cheeks. For an instant, her sadness lifted. She felt lucky that Sang was her son.

Stephen J. Nesbitt is a national baseball writer for The Athletic. He previously worked for the *Pittsburgh Post-Gazette*, first covering college athletics and Major League Baseball and later as an enterprise writer. He is a graduate of the University of Michigan and lives in New England with his wife, Colby, and their toddler son, Luke.

Why Giannis Antetokounmpo Chose the Path of Most Resistance

ZACH BARON

FROM *GQ* • NOVEMBER 16, 2021

Not long ago, Giannis Antetokounmpo watched his partner, Mariah Riddlesprigger, give birth to their second son, Maverick, and when he saw Maverick he immediately burst into tears. This happened with Antetokounmpo's first son, Liam Charles, too— that Giannis wept. "But I thought maybe it was because he was my first one," he told me. He doesn't think of himself as someone who cries, he said; he's survived too much deprivation, too many provocations, to be reduced to tears by just anything.

We were in the living room of his red brick house in the Milwaukee suburbs, hiding out from the August sun. Mariah was napping in the other room. Liam, big now and curly haired, was wandering around saying hi to everything that moved. Mav was in Giannis's lap. Giannis was trying to explain just what these boys did to him when they arrived.

Giannis and Mariah named Liam in part after Antetokounmpo's father, Charles, who passed in 2017, and so Giannis thought that might have been part of it, too, at the time—that maybe he was crying out of delayed grief. Ever since his dad died, he'd felt an emptiness he didn't know how to fill, he said. Then all of a sudden here was this new being with his father's name. I lost somebody that I loved, Giannis thought, and now I've got somebody back that I love a lot. But his mother told him: Let the memory of your father be the memory of your father. "You cannot fill that void," Giannis realized. He still thinks about Charles every day. When his team, the Milwaukee Bucks, won the NBA Finals in July, one of the first things Giannis did after the buzzer sounded was find a quiet place in a very loud arena to sit and talk to his father: "'Man, we've come a long way. I wish you were here to see this. Please watch me.' You know?" But Liam, Giannis decided, would be his own person, not a replacement for the father Giannis lost.

Then Giannis was in the delivery room again this past summer, marveling at what Mariah had to endure. "Seeing what the body has to go through in order to bring this beautiful, sweet thing into the world, it's insane," he said. Giannis is one of five boys; looking at Mariah, he thought of his mother, who gave birth to her first son in Nigeria and then to four more after she'd emigrated to Greece, doing so without most of the painkillers or other comforts Milwaukee hospitals use to help mothers ease children into the world. In Greece, they were undocumented, citizens of no nation. No one helped them. "Six months before I came to the NBA, I was selling stuff in the street," Giannis told me. "My mom was in the market. I used to go help her. People don't know about this, but I did it." Epidurals? Extended hospital stays? Postpartum doulas? "She definitely didn't have access to any of it," Giannis said. "I'm like, 'Mom, you went through this for all five of us?'"

And then Mav emerged, and to his genuine surprise, Giannis started sobbing again.

BY NOW, MUCH OF HIS STORY IS KNOWN. How he was discovered as a gangly kid running around an Athens playground; how he didn't touch a basketball until he was 13. How he had yet to become even the best player on his second-division Greek team when he was drafted in 2013 by the Milwaukee Bucks, who picked him at 15. All anyone knew about him at the time was that he was tall and super athletic and that he would occasionally do something remarkable, like run from one end of the court to the other in just a few strides, or jump higher than anyone else to block a shot he had no business blocking. Who was this guy? Would he be any good? Well, this is what happened next: Most Improved Player (2017), Defensive Player of the Year (2020), two MVP awards (2019, 2020), and an NBA championship this past July. A journey unfathomable in its sheer improbability, its storybook ending, an ending that may in fact be just the beginning of something even more grand and unlikely. He is already back out there, defending his title. Got handed his championship ring and went right out and scored 32 points in 31 minutes against the Brooklyn Nets in the first game of the season.

Some players seem haloed in greatness from the moment we lay eyes on them. They don't always attain it, but you see it with athletes like LeBron James or Kevin Durant within seconds: They are playing a different, easier game; they are competing more against history, against gravity, against spectral forces in the dark, than they are against the regular guys around them. Guys who are talented but not great. I'd argue that Giannis was one of these guys, first: a curio, an intriguing combination of traits and potential, but no more than that. Even his nickname: The Greek Freak. It was basically, "Wow, this guy does some wild stuff sometimes." He was regarded, in his early NBA days, as capable, not destined. "He looked like a guy who was going to be a project," his longtime teammate Khris Middleton said. Giannis will tell you himself: "What I am today, nobody saw it. You know why nobody saw it? Because I didn't see it. Ask my mom. No. 'I thought you would be an NBA player and have a better life. Not what you are today.'"

What is he today? Something remarkable. Singular. One of one. All summer I'd be walking around, and flashes of the Finals, in which the Bucks beat the Phoenix Suns 4–2, would come back to me, unbidden. These moments are lore now. Giannis's block on Deandre Ayton at the end of Game 4, a feat of athleticism so impossible and otherworldly that it's even *more* confusing in slow motion, how he did it. Even to Giannis himself: "I look at the block—How the fuck did I do this shit?" This is a player who had fallen to the floor two weeks earlier in Game 4 of the Eastern Conference finals with a left-knee injury so gruesome that he told me his knee looked like an elbow afterward. "My leg was the opposite way," Giannis said. "To this day, I feel the effect, the traumatic stress. I still feel it, and I think I'm going to feel it until I die."

Somehow he played in all six games of the Finals anyway. And when he jumped to block Ayton's shot, that was the leg he jumped off. How the fuck is that possible? He was in one place and suddenly he was in a completely different place in about a millisecond.

In the shower, after the next game, he started cramping; his lips turned purple; his hands got white. "I'm naked, I only have my towel," lying on the trainer's table, he remembered. "I ask, 'Can you give me that trash can?' Throw up five times." They gave him an IV—he was so dehydrated it took them 45 minutes to find the vein. Then he went back to the hotel and got a second one. This happened again after Game 6, he said: that he needed an IV. In that game, he scored 50 points, even while there were possessions in the fourth quarter where it looked like he could barely walk up the floor. Went 17 of 19 from the free-throw line when all series he could barely make one of two. As pure an exercise of concentration and will as you could ever, or will ever, watch. Greatness achieved.

So: How does a now 26, formerly stateless kid from Greece become…this? A champion. One of the two or three best players in the league. Some of it, he said, is just luck, genetics. He is 6 feet 11. He's 242 pounds. He moves so gracefully around his own house, even with the leftover limp from his knee injury in last year's playoffs, that you are forced to reevaluate how poorly you've been getting around all these many years on this earth:

Am I walking...wrong? Is there a better way? But the NBA is full of men who are tall and acrobatic. The body, sure, whatever, it's impressive, but if you ask him how all this happened, what he'll say is: "I'm going to work as hard as possible. God gave me that gift."

Even the night his father passed. "I went to the gym," Giannis said. "He was there with me." He said the lesson from his parents was: stay in motion. Never stop. "I try to not feel pain," Giannis said, "because I feel like whenever my parents felt pain, they never showed it."

Stubbornness, persistence, hard work, going to the gym even on the night your father dies—that can get you pretty far. But Giannis, in the past few years, began running up against the limits of hard work, he said. There's a sports psychologist who works with the Bucks, and Giannis talks to him almost every day. They work on coping mechanisms. They work on anxiety. They work on being in the moment. They work on separating the guy who is arguably the best basketball player in the world right now from the guy holding his newborn child trying to knock down the walls between him and his own feelings. One thing the sports psychologist led Giannis to try was: Cry! And not just at the birth of your sons.

"I had to break down the barriers I was talking about and be by myself, cry, and realize, 'I got to fucking help myself,'" Giannis said. "This guy, he's like, 'Sometimes, being persistent and stubborn? Sometimes it fucks you up.'"

HE LOOKED DOWN AT THE SLEEPING BABY he was holding. "You're not going to put the curse words in here, right?"

He can be like this: a little innocent. Seemingly unsure of himself, despite his absolute certainty pertaining to basketball. "Silly," Khris Middleton told me, affectionately. Superstar athletes have long been conditioned to think of themselves as brands, spokespeople for the million- and billion-dollar businesses they front. This is not Giannis. "I don't want to be the face of the league," he said, adamantly. "I want to play great basketball. After that, if I disappear in the night, good. Don't even talk about me, don't even remember me. I don't care."

He called out to Mariah: "Babe, do you want to be the face of the league?"

"No," Mariah said, sleepily.

He loves basketball but is not of basketball. "Let me show you downstairs," he said, suddenly.

He padded down the carpeted stairs in his socks, through his not particularly giant suburban house, which he bought from an old teammate, Mirza Teletović. The door frames were too small for him, and he had to duck under each one. Next door, the ground had been torn up and the foundation laid for a second house for his mother, who currently lives upstairs.

Down in the basement, he has a weight room. Soon he will have a basketball court, too, connected to it. Giannis famously would go to the Bucks practice facility so often, at so many different times of day and night, before and after games, that the team sometimes took action to keep him out so he could rest: "'They had this term, 'lockout,' that you cannot go to the gym, because they know I will go to the gym. Now, see what I did?" He gestured toward the construction outside, toward what would soon be his own facility. "Fuck lockout. Sorry. Oh, my God, I'm cursing. *Eff* lockout. I build a gym right here."

He also has a slew of framed jerseys down in the basement. Some of the jerseys are hung, proudly, on the wall; others are stacked haphazardly on a pool table or near the bar stocked with alcohol that Giannis doesn't drink. Many are his, but curiously, he also has dozens of framed jerseys from other NBA players too. Some are perhaps what you'd expect: the uniforms of greats who've played the game and since retired or passed away. Dominique Wilkins, Dirk Nowitzki, Dwyane Wade, Vince Carter, Kobe Bryant. But many of them—the majority of them—are from his peers: guys he competes against during the regular season and the playoffs.

He's got a framed Blake Griffin Pistons jersey. He's got one from Kevin Durant, and one from Steph Curry. James Harden—"A lot of people think that I have beef with James Harden, which is not true," he said, because if it were, why would his jersey be here? He continued the tour. "This right here is from Luka Dončić, the wonder boy. Anthony Davis. L.A., you know him. Jokić. I love the game! Oh, this is mine from this year. This is from the MVP I won. The All-Star MVP. Bradley Beal. Damian Lillard. Derrick Rose. I love Derrick Rose. LeBron James, man. Look! Look what he wrote for me."

Many of the jerseys are signed, some with brief messages, but this particular one, a LeBron Lakers jersey, had a longer note, and Giannis read it out loud: "To Giannis, a.k.a The Greek Freak. Continue to strive for greatness every single day you wake up, brother. Love everything you represent to this game of hoops, and off the court as well. The limit is not the sky. Go beyond it." LeBron had signed off with the sketch of a crown.

Giannis beheld the inscription proudly: "That's big time, you know?"

He is aware, if distantly, that by the hypermasculine competitive codes of the NBA, you are not supposed to venerate your competitors, let alone collect their jerseys, let alone adoringly read what those competitors write on those jerseys to note-taking reporters. But Giannis has never been good at those codes, and at times he has found freedom in defying them. For instance, he said, "People that talk to the sports psychiatrists and stuff like that, they label us 'soft.' We've seen that in the past, like, 'Oh, man, I'm having anxiety.' 'Man, you're soft. Go deal with that.' That's how it's labeled. That's why it's hard for people to talk to somebody and open up. Even for me, it was extremely tough."

He's convinced that all the really good athletes are secretly in some form of therapy. Some not so secretly. They use a word or a phrase and he knows. The other day, Giannis was watching *Naomi Osaka*, the three-part Netflix docuseries, and was struck by the way the tennis star spoke about the challenges that have come with her success. This happens more and more now—in dealing with himself, he's noticed how many other people are dealing with something. He said he could recognize a kind of struggle in Osaka's eyes, even before she began speaking. "She wasn't happy, she wanted to get away from the game and all that stuff, and it's fucking hard, man," Giannis said. He was talking about her, but he was talking about himself too. "I started doing it when I was 18. When you're that young and you're doing it, people don't understand the amount of pressure because at the end of the day, you don't only have to perform and be the best, you have the big brand that you got to fucking carry on your shoulder. You have your own country, Japan, that you got to carry on your shoulder. Or Greece, in my case. You have all these people that you got to take care of. Sometimes..."

He paused. "I've never said this: I don't want to fuck up."

That fear of fucking up, of not being able to carry the weight and support the people around him, was what drove him for a long time. He said he was just walking around Milwaukee yesterday, remembering what it looked like to him when he first got here. "You're 18," he said. "You have very small experience of life, of being by yourself. I came here, and I was scared. I never felt lonely in my life, and I was scared. I was going back to the hotel at 8:30 p.m. because I was scared. I was by myself."

Scared of what, I asked him.

"Scared of life! I was fucking 18," Giannis said. "I was a kid." Playing a sport that was still new to him with a bunch of grown men. "So, I was already scared of life, now you're putting me on the basketball court? I'm scared of these dudes, for sure. But you know what I knew? I have no fucking choice. I have no option. I can't fucking stop. If I stop everything, my family, I can't help them. I cannot be in a position to help them. So I kept going."

He went between home and the facility, the facility and home. "He lived in the gym," Giannis's longtime agent Alex Saratsis said. "He would sleep at the gym." Before Giannis met Mariah, that was literally all he did.

"I was on a mission," Giannis said. "That's why, seven years later, I had to fucking talk to somebody. Because I had issues now, you know? But there was no stopping me." For eight years he put his head down and chased greatness. Then he won a championship. Now, he said, he was working on all the things greatness cost him. Peace of mind. Life outside of basketball. A family. That kind of thing.

JUST A YEAR AGO, Giannis's contract with the Bucks was slated to end, and he had to decide whether to stay in Milwaukee or leave. We know what happened next, of course. But the way it happened, I think, is instructive, and perhaps suggests something about Giannis and the unique, determined way he sets out to do almost everything in life.

"Everybody was texting me: 'Leave the team,'" he told me—other players, some of whom haven't talked to him since he decided to stay. He understood, he said. "It's human. I will say I want to play with the best players; I wish K.D. was on my team, not against me. I wish LeBron was on my team, not against me. Steph, on my team." And the winters in Milwaukee were cold—"cold as shit," he specified. This would be an opportunity to never see another Milwaukee winter again. To raise his sons in a place where they might see the sun from time to time.

But there was something inside him that just wanted to do it the hard way, he realized. "I chose to stay here even with all the pressure because it's easier to leave. That's the easy thing to do. It's easy to leave."

There is an aversion to easiness with Giannis that can go deep. *Easy* is an epithet when he says it. *Easy*, in Giannis-world, describes almost everything that isn't pain, that isn't suffering, that isn't taking on long odds and trying to beat those odds. He regards the usual perks of being a player in the modern NBA—partying in the better Los Angeles clubs, recording in the better Los Angeles music studios, acting in Hollywood—as, basically, frivolous: "Being in movies? Easy. *Space Jam*, all this? *Easy. Easy.*

I don't want it, though." He is intent on life itself, by which he means the painful stuff of existence, the stuff that neither money nor ability can finesse. Life? "It's hard, life." Or at least, his was. He pointed at his chest: "It molds you to be this guy."

"I think he's never wanted to take an easy way out," Saratsis said. "In every aspect of life. He wants to be challenged."

In the end Giannis decided to stay in Milwaukee because it was difficult. And then, improbably, the Bucks won. "One challenge was to bring a championship here and we did," he told me. "It was very hard, but we did. Very, very hard. I just love challenges. What's the next challenge? The next challenge might not be here." It's not that he doesn't love Milwaukee, he said. But he was always wary of things becoming too easy. "Me and my family chose to stay in this city that we all love and has taken care of us—for now," Giannis said. "In two years, that might change. I'm being totally honest with you. I'm always honest. I love this city. I love this community. I want to help as much as possible."

Did this mean he was thinking about…leaving? I asked his agent.

"I don't think it's, 'I'm thinking about leaving the Bucks,'" Saratsis told me. "But I think he's genuinely like: 'Okay, I have reached the pinnacle. The next challenge is, let's repeat.' But what happens if you do repeat? What's the next challenge? What is that next barrier? When you think about it from a basketball perspective, by the age of 26, this kid has accomplished everything," Saratsis said. "So sometimes you're going to have to manufacture what those challenges are."

ON HIS HOME'S SECOND FLOOR, Giannis keeps a room full of unworn shoes. A literal room, filled to the literal top, in a house with only a normal abundance of rooms. "How many of these shoes do you think I wear?" Giannis asked me, mischievously, and then answered his own question: "I don't wear them."

There's every Jordan known to man here, and shoes that Virgil wrote on. Travis Scott Nikes. Kobes. Giannis is sponsored by Nike, so this isn't surprising, but the fact that he doesn't wear the shoes is a little surprising, and the fact that he is keeping them is more surprising. More surprising still: "I'm going to sell this shit," he said, with a grin. That's why he's devoted an entire room of his own living space to them. Not to wear them but to keep them as an investment.

Mariah's father makes jokes about Giannis. "You know when the birds go in the morning?" Giannis said, quoting the joke. "*'Cheep, cheep'*—cheap. That's who I am." On airplanes, he used to buy coach tickets and would seek out whoever was sitting in the exit row and ask them to switch: "'You're a Bucks fan?' 'Yes.' 'Want two tickets for the game? When? November?'—I'm a great seller, that's what you don't know. I'm a great seller—'Would you trade my seat with you?'"

I said that if Giannis Antetokounmpo approached me to switch seats on a commercial flight, I'd probably be surprised that he wasn't on a private jet.

"Nobody has money for a private jet, man. Hell no, man."

Not even to Greece?

"Why would you spend $150,000 to one-way trip there? That's $300,000. The market makes 6 to 10 percent every year... He's laughing."

(I was laughing.)

"So, you can make, for the rest of your life, with that money you just spent, 24- to 30,000 a year, because that's what the market makes on average. If you take that money and you take it away, that 24- to 30,000 growth every year goes away—correct? So why would I teach my kids that?"

Giannis drives a 2011 GMC truck he bought not long after he got here, or a Mercedes he bought in 2018, or the G-Wagon he got for free. "I don't put my money in my stuff that loses value," he said. Meals, sure. He and Mariah go out and eat well. "But ain't nobody got time for spending money on clothes and time for…what's it called?"

A stylist?

"Fuck—sorry. *Eff* no. Man, let me tell you one thing. This is me. If you try to spend time on how you're going to look to the tunnel, man, you already took away focus from the game. Just put on some stuff and just focus on that 48 minutes. Not how I'm going to look in the tunnel when they show me. Now, if you're talking about one thing I enjoy, I love watches."

Why? Because they increase in value. He named a few, and then asked that I not say which ones. He is trying to give less free promo, now that he's a champion: If you want your product to be mentioned by Giannis, from now on you're going to have to pay. As we talked, he'd be deep into some anecdote and then wonder if he was supposed to promote his businesses, the sponsorships he's already acquired, the investments—like the piece of the Milwaukee Brewers he just bought this week—he's already made. Is he supposed to promote his businesses? How does one do that in an interview? He was unsure. He settled for leaning into my recorder, listing his endorsements, then going back to whatever story he was telling.

A mosquito flew by, and he reached out one giant hand and closed his fingers around it.

"I caught that," he said, showing me.

AFTER HE WON THE NBA FINALS, he went to Chick-fil-A with the Larry O'Brien trophy and the Finals MVP trophy and ordered exactly 50 nuggets—one for every point he scored in the last game of the series. But he's trying not to tell that story anymore, either, until Chick-fil-A pays up. His teammates went to Vegas the night the Bucks won, but he didn't. "They understand," he told me. "They be like, 'Giannis doesn't care about this shit.'" His teammates have been around him enough to know that they don't really know him at all, he said. "If you asked them if they really know me: 'No.' I'm about work, and then I dip. I go back home to enjoy my time with my family, and then I do it again, over and over again. I don't have time to go for dinners and stuff. I don't have time to go and mess around and go out. I don't do that." Middleton said that it took him five years to feel like he knew Giannis even 50 percent—now, after eight, he figures he's up to 60 or even 90. But Giannis, he said, had matured too. "He's grown and realized he's the franchise player," Middleton said. "So he knows he's got to have some kind of chemistry with his teammates."

A few weeks before we met, Giannis flew to Greece and went to the Acropolis with his brothers and walked around with the trophies. And that was the extent of it. He is already done celebrating, he said. "It's over with. The championship is over with. Over with. Now, I'm working. In order for me to get better, I leave this championship bullshit stuff in the past." He is back to playing basketball this fall. Back on the hard path to the hard thing.

But before he put those memories away entirely, I asked him if he could just give me one or two—were there moments, in retrospect, that had stuck with him? That mattered? He thought about it and agreed to share a few: the IVs he got; the long sleepless nights between Game 5 and Game 6; the first frantic minutes of Game 6, when he kept rushing and getting ahead of himself, instead of being in the moment.

But what he wanted me to remember most, he said, was the end.

After the Bucks had won the game, "What happened?" Giannis asked me. "The team, everybody gathered around when they realized we won, and immediately Coach came and grabbed me. Go watch the tape. Coach came and grabbed me and I pushed him out of the way. I went to my family. I hugged my mom, I hugged my brothers, I hugged my wife-to-be, I hugged my son, then I sat down and thought about my dad, right?" They were in Milwaukee; the whole arena was going crazy. So were his teammates. But Giannis found a place to sit again, by himself.

Giannis asked that I pay particular attention to what happened next, because to him what happened next illustrates something essential about him. Some of it has to do with his family: how close they are, how much he depends on them.

And I don't want to put words in his mouth; it was an image he offered, not an explanation. But without speaking for him, I think some of what he wanted me to understand was about the singular loneliness of the path. What "hard" actually means. In the end, greatness is fundamentally isolating. What you have to do to achieve it separates you from everyone else in a way that is difficult to undo.

The image was this: "Everybody was celebrating," he remembered. "They said, 'Giannis, you got to go up there.' I said, 'No, I'm good.'" They told him he might win the MVP, and if he did, he was going to have to go up and get it. He said fine—if I win, let me know. And then he won, so he got up there and he said a few words. He turned to Middleton, whom he'd been playing with since the very beginning, and said, "Khris, we did it." He held the trophy for a moment. And then he walked away again, to be by himself.

"Go and see the picture," he said. "I'm the captain of the team. Go and see the picture when they lift up the trophy. I'm not there."

Zach Baron is *GQ*'s Senior Staff Writer.

Advisory Board

The Year's Best Sports Writing 2022

Paola Boivin is the director of the Cronkite News Phoenix Sports Bureau, a professional newsroom at Arizona State's Walter Cronkite School of Journalism and Mass Communication. She spent most of her career as a sportswriter in Los Angeles and Phoenix and has won numerous awards, including recognition as an APSE Top 10 sports columnist in 2011 and an APSE Top 10 sports feature writer in 2013. She recently completed a four-year term on the College Football Playoff Selection Committee and was just the second woman picked for the group, following Condoleezza Rice. She is a former president of the Association for Women in Sports Media and is a frequent speaker for topics related to sports and the intersection of society. She also listens to way too much '90s hip hop.

Richard Deitsch is the parent of twins, so he is perpetually tired. He currently works for The Athletic, where he writes about sports media and other topics, and also hosts the weekly *Sports Media with Richard Deitsch* podcast. Prior to joining The Athletic, Deitsch worked as a writer and editor for *Sports Illustrated* where he covered seven Olympic Games as well as multiple NCAA championships and U.S. tennis Opens. Now based in Toronto, Deitsch served as one of the co-hosts on Sportsnet's (Canada) *Prime Time Sports*, which aired across the country on the Sportsnet Radio Network and is regarded as the most well-known sports-talk show in Canadian history. He cites Toronto, New York City, Buffalo, Barcelona, and Venice as his favorite cities.

Gregory Lee is the senior assistant managing editor at the *Boston Globe*. He helps in leading recruitment efforts for staffing the *Globe* newsroom. He also serves a role in assisting the *Globe* to build communities around the newsroom's work to attract new readers and strengthen the bonds with the subscribers that the *Globe* has. This is Greg's second stint with the *Globe*, spending eight years from 2004 to 2012 as a senior assistant sports editor; he returned after a two-year stint as senior managing editor of The Athletic DC. He has had previous stops over a career that started in 1993 at the *Times-Picayune* in New Orleans,

The Washington Post, the *Sun-Sentinel* in Fort Lauderdale, and NBA.com at Turner Sports. He is the former president of the National Association of Black Journalists and a 2013 winner of the Missouri Honor Medal. The New Orleans native is married and is an avid New Orleans Saints fan.

Iliana Limón Romero is the *Los Angeles Times* deputy sports editor. The El Paso, Texas, native joined the *Times* in March 2021. She previously was the sports editor at the *Orlando Sentinel* and co-founder of the website Pro Soccer USA. Limón Romero is chair of the Association for Women in Sports Media and co-chair of the National Association Hispanic Journalists Sports Task Force.

Glenn Stout served as series editor for The Best American Sports Writing for its entire 30-year run. He is the editor, author, or ghostwriter of 100 book titles, among them *Red Sox Century*, *Fenway 1912*, *Nine* Months at Ground Zero, and, most recently, *Tiger Girl and the Candy Kid: America's Original Gangster Couple*. His biography of Trudy Ederle, *Young Woman and the Sea*, is soon to be a film starring Daisy Ridley for Disney+. He also works as an editorial consultant on book manuscripts, long features, and book proposals. A graduate of Bard College, before becoming a full-time freelance writer in 1993 he worked construction, sold minor league baseball tickets, was a security guard, and a librarian. He lives in Vermont and is a citizen of the United States and Canada.

Notable Sports Writing of 2021

Sam Borden

The True Story of the Patriots Fan Who Stole the Giants' Super Bowl Rings. ESPN, February 6

Candace Buckner

At a Quiet Senate Hearing, Four U.S. Gymnasts Made Sure the Truth Was Loud and Uncomfortable. The Washington Post, September 15

Frank Bures

Epic Battle to Break the Mississippi Canoe Record. Outside, November 3

Monte Burke

The Lone Star State's Latest Phenom. Garden & Gun, August/September

Scott Burnside

"Can't Mess Up The Plan." The Athletic, July 26

Ryan S. Clark

"I Don't Think We Will Ever Be Healed." The Athletic, April 16

Kelly Cohen

Inside the Mysterious World of Missing Sports Memorabilia. ESPN, May 7

Jeremy Collins

Three Falcons Players Died Off the Field in the Late '80s. Could Their Old Teammates Help Me With My Own Loss? Sports Illustrated, August 18

Michael Croley

One Last Round with My Brother Tim. Esquire, September 30

Karen Crouse

Michelle Wie West Was Ready to Retire. Then She Got Mad. The New York Times, June 3

Rustin Dodd

The Legacy Bowl. The Athletic, February 4

Emily Giambalvo

Simone Biles Said She Got the "Twisties." Gymnasts Immediately Understood. The Washington Post, July 28

Joseph Goodman

College Football During a Pandemic Revealed Heart of America. AL.com, January 10

Henry Grabar

The Woman Who Read Hank Aaron's Hate Mail. Slate, January 22

Paul Gutierrez

Hall of Famer Tom Flores' Impact Goes Beyond Raiders, Across Hispanic Football Community. ESPN, September 29

Joe Hagen

Riding the Waves and Coming of Age. Texas Highways, November

Dan Hajducky

Hall of Fame–Bound Tamika Catchings and Our Conversation that Affirmed Everything. ESPN, May 15

Ashley Harrell

Mexican Traditions Live On in California Through Female Rodeo Performers. National Geographic, September 17

David Guavey Herbert

Inside Baseball's Most Notorious Dad-on-Dad Rivalry. Esquire, May 27

Benjamin Hochman

50 Years Ago, a Boy Met Bob Gibson and Asked for a Shutout. St. Louis Post-Dispatch, August 15

Baxter Holmes

Allegations of Racism and Misogyny within the Phoenix Suns. ESPN, November 4

Lizzie Johnson
They Trusted a Coach with Their Girls and Ivy League Ambitions. Now He's Accused of Sex Abuse. The Washington Post, January 30

Adam Kilgore
Christian McCaffrey and the Plight of the Modern NFL Running Back. The Washington Post, November 30

Mina Kimes
Mets GM Acknowledges Sending Explicit Images. ESPN, January 18

Eddie Kingston
Eddie Kingston Got No Business F***ing Being Here. The Player's Tribune, November 9

Brendan I. Koerner
One Man's Amazing Journey to the Center of the Bowling Ball. Wired, May 27

Jon Krawczynski
Anthony Edwards Throws Down Dunk to Remember in Forgettable Wolves Season. The Athletic, February 20

Aishwarya Kumar and Paula Lavigne
Olympic Runner Emily Infeld's Harrowing Three-Year Ordeal with a Stalker. ESPN, July 30

Tim Kurkjian
Willie Mays at 90. ESPN, May 6

Michael Lee
"We All Thought that He Would Be the One." The Washington Post, November 12

Meg Linehan
"This Guy Has a Pattern": Amid Institutional Failure, Former NWSL Players Accuse Prominent Coach of Sexual Coercion. The Athletic, September 30

Steve Politi
The Predator in Plain Sight. NJ.com, September 27

Alex Prewitt
Bowl Season Is Coming. And There Are Only 36 Pylons Left. *Sports Illustrated,* November 19

Nora Princiotti
The Doinks Are Loud, and They Are Plentiful. The Ringer, October 20

Brendan Quinn
The Iceman and Eastern Michigan. The Athletic, December 14

Daniel Riley
Secrets of the World's Greatest Free Diver. GQ, September 21

Dan Robson
Donald Brashear's Toughest Fight. The Athletic, December 20

Jourdan Rodrigue
Rams Legend Torry Holt Has Shaped Communities Since Childhood. The Athletic, December 24

Alex Schiffer
Full-Court Diplomacy. The Athletic, December 20

Mike Sielski
Philly's Fairmount Park League Is Fading. So Is a Piece of the City's Black Baseball History. Philadelphia Inquirer, July 21

Michael Silver
Appreciating a Legend, John Madden. Ballysports.com, December 28

Bre'ana Singleton
The Flyest AAU Team. The Athletic, October 15

Marc Spears
Randy Livingston No Longer Hides His Story of Gambling Addiction. The Undefeated, November 9

Jesse Washington
David Fizdale Seeks a Deeper Purpose as He Prepares to Return to NBA Coaching. The Undefeated, June 24

Josh Weinfuss
A Different Diana Taurasi. ESPN, July 26

Jon Wertheim
Forty Years Later, One Horse's Run at the 1981 Triple Crown Is a Story of Failed Promise, Shattered Lives and, in Certain Eyes, Something Deeply Sinister. Sports Illustrated, April 27

Dan Wiederer
Steve "Mongo" McMichael Is Suddenly in a Vicious Fight Against ALS. Chicago Tribune, April 23

Mike Wilson
He Just Wanted to Play Catch. The New York Times, January 15

Jason Wolf
"He Had No Memories of It Whatsoever": How Chuck Crist's Family Discovered He Had CTE. Buffalo News, July 11

Clinton Yates
Williamsport, Pennsylvania: Home to History and Hardball. The Undefeated, August 29

Wufei Yu and Will Ford
171 Runners Started This Ultramarathon. Runner's World, October 15